HIT BY A TON OF BRICKS

Dr. John Vawter

General Editor

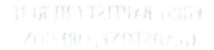

Hit by a Ton of Bricks:
You're Not Alone When Your Child's on Drugs

Editor: Angie Peters, Anne Wooten
Graphic Designer: Jerome Nelson

Published by FamilyLife
Dennis Rainey, President
5800 Ranch Drive
Little Rock, Arkansas 72223
(501) 223-8663
1-800-FL-TODAY
www.familylife.com
A division of Campus Crusade for Christ

DEDICATION

To Stephanie

Your mistakes, hard work, willingness to share your story in order to help others and your belief in God, have made everything we do in You're Not Alone possible. I am proud to be your father.

To George Butzow

My dear friend, you carried me during tough times and your wisdom is scattered throughout the ministry of You're Not Alone. George, you are in heaven…but your influence here is strong.

Contents

SECTION 1
Living with the Pain of Having an Addicted Child

SECTION 2
Persevering When Your Child is Addicted

SECTION 3
Keeping Your Marriage Healthy When Your Kids Aren't

SECTION 4
"Not My Kid"

SECTION 5
Understanding Your Child, the Addict

SECTION 6
Listening to the Recovering Addicts

SECTION 7
Hoping the Best for the Future

ADDENDUM #1
The Path to Parental Health:

ADDENDUM #2

Resource Directory
Services for Parents

ACKNOWLEDGEMENTS

To all our conference speakers and book contributors—Gene and Norma Bourland, Pat Boris, Dr. Ray Burwick, John and Deb Casey, Al Ells, Bill and Linda Faulkner, Mark Halverson, Bill and Margaret Hansell, Dr. Kim and Lynda Hodge, Evan Hodge, Greg and Rita Iverson, Jim Smoke, Todd Smoke, Noy Sparks, Stephanie Vawter, Zach Whaley and Dr. Terry Zuehlke

To special friends who gave strength and encouragement—David Harowitz, Michael Fike, Curt Phillips

To special friends who have helped us get where we are because of their wisdom, insight and vision—Dick Damrow, Tom Anthony, Bethany Community Church Elders, Willis and Beth Creighton, Dr. Steve Nicholson, Lynnda Speer, The Murdock Charitable Trust, Dr. Jim Wetherbe and those donors who have believed in what we are doing

To the whole gang at FamilyLife who saw the vision and need for the book and encouraged us to do it…and then made it happen. And, to Gina Stavros and Bebe Winterberg for all their work on getting the book ready

To all those who have helped us along the way since that awful phone call came. You know who you are. You are appreciated.

Foreword

It Feels Like a Ton of Bricks
By John Vawter

The call started out ominously, "Mom and Dad, are you sitting down?" We weren't, but our 23-year-old son Michael continued.

"Stephanie is using heroin."

The shock of learning that our daughter, who was 25, was using drugs took us to an emotional place that was beyond description. We were devastated, depressed, fearful for her life, guilt-stricken, and filled with questions about our parenting skills. How could such a thing happen? Our wonderful daughter had fallen into the world of drug abuse without our knowing it. What signals had we missed? How could we have been so blind? How had she been so successful in lying to us?

Despite the involuntary shutting down of our emotions, my wife Susan and I knew we had to spring into action. We lived in Phoenix; our daughter lived in Denver, where she had been attending college and working. At first we could not locate her. But after making several calls, we learned that she was in Juarez, Mexico. Was she alive? Was she in prison? God seemed so remote.

This day of pain was my first Sunday as pastor at Bethany Community Church. I had recently resigned as president of Phoenix Seminary to return to pastoral ministry. So, we were not new to the area but we were new to the church.

Through a lot of detective work, we determined that the next day, Stephanie would be returning to her home in Denver. We flew to Denver Monday, made arrangements for her to be admitted to a detox center, and waited by driving around until we saw her car in the alley around 12:30 Tuesday morning. When she returned home, we walked in unannounced and said, "We know you have been using heroin. We want you to come to get help."

Her response was conditional: "Okay," she said. "But I will not go cold turkey, because I have tried to quit ten times and thought I was going to die each time." We learned later that she had cried out to God many times for help. Her purse was full of cards with Bible verses related to God's protection and deliverance.

She allowed us to take her to detox at a facility in Denver immediately. By Thursday she was declared ready for treatment. She chose to come to Phoenix to the very hospital where my brother, Dr. Michael Vawter, had been chief of staff of cardiology before moving his practice to another city. When we went with Stephanie to check in, a number of people asked us if she was related to him. At first, it embarrassed us to have acquaintances and friends find out that our daughter needed treatment for drug abuse. But we soon got over it, because we realized that our daughter's treatment and sobriety were far more important than any negative thoughts people might have about her or us. Indeed, we learned that if people could not be constructive and helpful, we did not need them in our lives. We needed encouragement, not discouragement.

> *We realized that our daughter's treatment and sobriety were far more important than any negative thoughts people might have about her or us. Indeed, we learned that if people could not be constructive and helpful, we did not need them in our lives. We needed encouragement, not discouragement.*

The morning after Stephanie checked into the hospital, with desolate feelings of depression, fear and loneliness, Susan and I went to a Nar-Anon meeting, a support group for people whose loved ones use drugs. As we made our way to our seats, I was thinking, "What in the world am I doing here? I am a pastor. I don't need help." But I did need help. As I listened to others in the group share their stories, I realized these people were all committed to getting or staying healthy, to supporting one another and to helping each participant learn that the addict is responsible for his or her own sobriety.

Thankfully, our daughter has now been clean and sober for five years. She is working, has returned to college and is attending Alcoholics Anonymous meetings regularly. She has learned that sobriety for her happens one day at a time; it requires a daily walk of faith.

For Susan and me, recovering addicts in the church overwhelmed us with love and support. Their care and ministry have helped us understand that keeping a family member's drug abuse a secret is only a way to deny its reality. When we deny that reality, then we cannot let wise and experienced people help us. That's a harmful reaction, because we do need help; having a family member abuse drugs is not something that we can endure and conquer alone.

So we do not hide the fact that our daughter is a recovering addict. We have learned much through this experience, including the fact that we are not to blame for Stephanie's mistakes. As she says, "You taught me the right way. I made the wrong decisions."

We Are Not Alone–You Are Not Alone

Susan and I, as a couple in the ministry who has had a child involved in drug abuse, are not alone. In fact, according to a study the "You're Not Alone" ministry commissioned by the Barna Group, 17% of pastors in the United States have kids who have abused or are abusing drugs/alcohol. Unfortunately, only 25% go for help. The statistics for parents not in ministry are even higher.

Because of those startling numbers and because of Paul's words in 2 Corinthians 1:4 where he says, "God comforts us in our afflictions that we may comfort others in theirs," Susan and I started the ministry of "You're Not Alone." It's designed for pastors, missionaries, Christian workers and their spouses whose kids abuse drugs/alcohol. (We do not delineate between drugs and alcohol. They are both deadly. They are both "controlling" substances.) The ministry presents conferences throughout the United States; operates the web site, www.notalone.org, as a source of help and encouragement for pastors; commissions studies on these issues; and offers a speakers' bureau for organizations seeking speakers on this topic.

Dennis Rainey, Executive Director of FamilyLife Ministries, a Division of Campus Crusade for Christ, after interviewing me on the "FamilyLife Today" radio program, challenged me to write a book for any parent whose kids are abusing drugs/alcohol. As I considered his challenge, I realized the book was already written. The contributors included my wife, some of the speakers at each our conferences throughout the past three years, and me. We call the book *Hit by a Ton of Bricks* because that's how most parents describe the news that a son or daughter is abusing drugs or alcohol.

Our speakers—and therefore the contributors to this book—include parents of children who have abused drugs, the abusers themselves, and counselors whose ministries and professions focus on helping families through the dark trauma of substance abuse.

The parents share stories that have been chiseled out on the anvil of the pain and despair of having a child abusing drugs/alcohol. Articulate and authoritative, they communicate in realistic tones about their anguish ... and about how God has worked and is working in the lives of their children and their own lives.

The drug and alcohol abusers relate some of the reasons they started using drugs to begin with. They describe the confusion and helplessness they felt as they descended into the frightening world of substance abuse. With honesty and openness, they recount the details of their experiences, pointing out along the way what worked and what didn't so that others might benefit from their experience.

The professionals and counselors offer, in down-to-earth terms, specific suggestions to help parents understand some of the whys and hows of their situation. And they give practical guidance for navigating around the spiritual and emotional wreckage created by the drug abuse of a family member.

As you read each chapter, you will make many discoveries. For example, you may be surprised to find that drug abuse is not for "bad" families; it happens to the best of families. You may find comfort in learning that most of the kids who abuse drugs and/or alcohol do not blame their parents for their abuse. They admit it was their choice to start using. And you will learn the important lesson that when this "ton of bricks" crashes through the ceiling and shakes the foundation of your home, both your child and you need to get help and advice from someone more knowledgeable and experienced than you.

We do need others.

As we say in the "You're Not Alone" ministry, *You're not alone.*

John Vawter

Rev. Dr. John Vawter

SECTION 1

Living with the Pain of Having an Addicted Child

When we discover our kids are abusing drugs and/or alcohol, we all have similar reactions: guilt, anger, denial, and a pain so intense that it has no name. Another common reaction is for fathers of addicts to want to physically harm those who have sold drugs to their children. In this section, parents share how they dealt with the news that their kids had become addicted. While the personalities and circumstances of each parent differ, their responses bear many similarities: "God, where are you?" "What did I do wrong?" "Will my child survive?"

The content of the first three chapters doesn't—can't—soften the blow of the impact of drug or alcohol abuse on a family. Drugs bring havoc. They upset our routines and disrupt the natural rhythm of our lives. But, as the following stories illustrate, in the midst of the chaos and pain, God does show Himself to be real.

Chapter 1

Keeping Your Head above Water:
Surviving the Turbulence of Drug Abuse in the Family

By Gene & Norma Bourland

One Christian parent recently shared his experience with us:

> I'll never forget our first meeting with [a support group]. After a short
> indoctrination, we had a chance to tell the group the story of our son.
> His grades, as a sophomore in high school, dropped from A's and B's in
> September to F's and incompletes in January. We told of how he was
> expelled from school; of how his use of pot expanded to include LSD and
> who knows what else; of how he stole from us; of his verbal abuse; of his
> living in and out of our home. As we told the tale, there was neither a
> single expression of shock, nor a single raised eyebrow. If we hesitated a
> bit, the group filled in the blanks for us. There was no condemnation,
> only empathy. These folks were going through it, too.

The unique experiences you've had with your child who has used drugs or alcohol
could, we're sure, could "fill in the blanks" for us. It is our hope and prayer that sharing our story will fill in some blanks for you as well.

Our son Steven chose to taste what he believed were the enjoyable delights of alcohol and drugs when he was 15 years old. He was a freshman in high school when he
began using marijuana and alcohol. Soon he expanded his drug profile to include
cocaine, crack and probably whatever else he could find to buy.

After graduating from high school, he failed several times to get further education
and a job; he broke the law and got caught a few times; he unsuccessfully attempted

a six-week in-house drug treatment and halfway house; and then he left home without telling us where he was going. For the next two years, we did not know where he was or whether he was alive. Finally, thankfully, Steven contacted us. He told us that his girlfriend Cindy, whom he had met on the road, was pregnant and that they were headed back to Minnesota, where we were living at the time.

Steven and Cindy came home in December of 1991 in a beat-up Chevrolet station wagon with their few worn-out belongings. They had not been home long before Steven was arrested for having previously broken the law. After serving time in jail and paying fines, he was released. But even after the birth of his son, Stevie, he continued to struggle with his use of drugs and alcohol. He was unable to keep a job. His anger became explosive.

Steven, now 30, lives in Virginia with his wife, Cindy, and his seven-year-old son, Stevie. To our knowledge, he has been clean and sober since then, and his police record is now nearly clear.

During the turbulent years since discovering he was abusing drugs and alcohol, Norma and I have experienced a full range of emotions. Our hopes and dreams have gone from the heights of seeing clearly who God is and what He wants us to do ... to the depths of despairing that anything would ever change. We have felt at times as if we were thrown out of a raft into a raging river; we have done everything we could to just keep our heads above water. We have found many different ways to survive. We hope that sharing some of these with you will be helpful.

Norma's Story

I thought maybe I would start with maybe a joke or a funny story that I could drum up from our past, but as I looked over the last 15 years, I couldn't find anything to laugh at. Drug abuse, addiction, alcoholism—these do not sketch a funny picture. They are all serious problems with the potential to destroy life and faith.

> *I shamed him with my tears and pleaded with him. I became very angry and I became very tired.*

In the early days of Steven's drug abuse, I just thought he was having difficulty adjusting to high school and to being around others who didn't have Christian values. I prayed a lot and talked to him often about setting a good example for his friends and being a good influence on them. I thought for sure that God would use Steven's rebellious moments, broken curfews and drinking parties to teach our son some good life lessons.

Slowly, after time went by, I became confused and frustrated as I tried to make sense of things by preaching great passionate sermons, some of my very best, to him. I punished him with endless groundings, sometimes for a month at a time. I became desperate. I shamed him with my tears and pleaded with him. I became very angry and I became very tired.

Turning Point

Four years later, when Steven was 19, marked a turning point for me, a time when I began to regain a bit of clarity. This happened when we finally accepted the fact that Steven was using drugs and abusing alcohol. At this point, we were able to get the help that we really needed to address the problem rather than all the symptomatic behaviors.

The year following Steven's graduation, we sent him to a private prep school in Maine with great hopes that he was going to get all straightened out. But when he returned to our home in Boston at Christmas, he was in very bad shape. He had been using cocaine heavily. He was very depressed. Right away we were able to get him into an outpatient treatment center for teens there in Boston. Meanwhile, during this same period, Gene decided to take a new position in a church in Minnesota and we were preparing to move. This move promised a new beginning for all of us, but it was also difficult--especially for our daughter, who was just beginning her junior year in high school.

Shortly after settling into our new home in Minneapolis, we discovered that Steven's drug use had escalated greatly. After finding crack cocaine and paraphernalia in our car, we admitted him into a six-week residential treatment program in Minneapolis.

One of the requirements of Steven's program was that the whole family had to participate in a weeklong session. This required us to be at the facility every day to attend drug education classes, seminars, and workshops, and to sit through emotionally painful group sessions.

Fostering Friendships

During this same time, our new church family was trying to welcome the new pastor and his family into their fellowship. I had repeatedly declined invitations to a monthly Newcomers' Brunch. But finally, after the third invitation, I decided that I couldn't say "no" again.

The morning of the event, I pushed myself to get ready and then drove to the beautiful suburban home of the hostess. I sat outside in my car in front of the house, not wanting to go in, feeling ashamed of having our son in drug treatment and of our family being in turmoil. Finally, I got out of the car and went into the house. The hostesses were friendly and warm, and I started to relax.

But as I sat down with a small group of women of different ages, I heard to my horror the hostess saying, "Norma, why don't we begin with you? Tell us a little bit about yourself and your family, then we will go around the circle and share."

I thought I was going to die. I took a deep breath, smiled as big as I could, and said, "Well, my husband is your new pastor of counseling. We have four children. Our oldest son, Peter, is a sophomore at Westmont College; our second son, Steven, is in drug treatment at St. Mary's in Minneapolis; our daughter is a junior in high school; and our youngest son, David, will be in seventh grade in junior high."

I then turned quickly to the woman on my right, hoping that she would just continue with her introduction and that nobody had really heard what I had just said. She picked up the thread of conversation quite well and we continued to take turns introducing ourselves around the circle. To tell the truth, I couldn't have remembered any of those women's names; I hardly heard a thing until it was the turn of the woman on my left.

This woman looked right at me and said, "Hi, my name is Carol. I, too, have four children, and my second son was in drug treatment at St. Mary's, also."

I felt like I had been kicked in my spiritual gut.

Then I didn't hear another word. I was thinking, "Here is a woman who is smiling, well groomed and all put together. She is behaving normally and she has been through what I'm going through, and she is still alive. She is functioning!" All of a sudden, I was touched deeply with hope. In fact, somehow Job 23:10 started to run through my mind: "But he knows the way that I take; when he has tested me, I will come forth as gold" [NIV]. I hoped I would "come forth as gold" after my trials with my son, as Carol appeared to have done.

This woman became a friend to me in a very desperate moment. One of the ways I cope with anything in life, as Gene knows well, is that I talk about it. I talk it through, I talk it through thoroughly, then I talk about it again, and then I talk about it again. My new friendship with Carol enabled me to begin talking with others about my situation. I began to talk to everyone I could about Steven. I seemed to need reassurance. I needed new friends to confide in as well as long-time friends to listen to me and tell me that they remembered what a good mom I was and what a sweet child Steven had been. I wanted my friends to remember what a great family we had. I needed to be reassured that the past as I remembered it really had happened, that it had been real. I guess I was hanging onto some pride. My friends were really patient with me.

From Assurance to Anger

Slowly the assurance I gained from looking at the past turned to anger, especially when I heard Christian friends saying things like, "I don't know where my kids would be today if I hadn't prayed for them." To me, statements like these implied that I hadn't prayed hard enough, that I hadn't prayed "good" enough, that I hadn't said the right things.

I became angry when I realized that God hadn't protected our kids. I stopped reading Christian books and magazines, avoided group prayer meetings, and turned off Christian music and radio. Even the thought of going into a Christian bookstore upset my stomach. I felt like I had been kicked in my spiritual gut.

Our family life began to feel like a mockery to me. I screamed inside when I would see images of the public's view of a drug addict as being a "loser" or a "scum bag," and when I would hear the declaration by so many in our society that drug addicts should be "put away" for life. I wanted everyone to know that one of those "losers" was my son, whom I had nurtured every night with stories and songs of "Jesus loves you. This I know." I was furious. Things had not turned out like I thought God had promised they would.

From Anger to Al-Anon

My long-time friend, Susan Vawter, listened to me vent my anger, and my new friend from the Newcomers' Brunch took me to Al-Anon, where I listened to words that expressed my hostility coming from others' mouths. Going to Al-Anon was really painful for me. I left each meeting saying I would not go there again. They talked a lot about "letting go" and I just didn't understand what that meant. I didn't know what it looked like. I didn't like sharing my personal story to strangers who would only give me their first names.

But something compelled me to keep going back. Each time I went, I repeated the Serenity Prayer,: "Lord, give me the grace to accept the things I cannot change, the courage to change the things I can, and the wisdom to know the difference."

I listened to others. I read the "Twelve Steps for One Day at a Time." I began to realize the decisions my kids make are not mine. They do things for their own reasons just like I do things for my own reasons. Even though our decisions affect each other, we are not the source of one another's happiness or peace of mind. I cannot change them or control their choices and some days I have to work very hard not to allow their degree of well being to affect my happiness. My well-being has to be my choice every day. This understanding releases me from being enmeshed in Steven's choices.

> *I wanted everyone to know that one of those "losers" was my son, whom I had nurtured every night with stories and songs of "Jesus loves you. This I know."*

From Al-Anon to a Peaceful Perspective

One day in a training workshop, the speaker walked up to the podium without any introduction and said, "He is God. And I am not." He is God. And I am not. I heard nothing else after that as those words sank deep into my heart and freed me. I gave God back His job of saving my children. I took back my job of being mom, of loving my kids the best way I could, and of being available to them.

Slowly I began to understand that "letting go" doesn't change the circumstances, it simply frees me from feeling as if I should fix things or control the situation. "Letting go" allows me to experience peace in the midst of chaos.

A Unique Birthday Party

During the two years that Steven was on the run, I felt depressed most of the time. I forced myself to get up each morning. I cried every time I talked about Steven. I cried every time I tried to pray. I cried when I heard beautiful music in church. I cried a lot. One of my journal entries during this time said, "Each day I wake feeling the urgent need to do something and then I realize there is nothing I can do. The emptiness just has to be."

I gave God back His job of saving my children.

Steven had been gone almost a year without a word and his birthday was coming up. I sat in my bedroom chair (that was my safe place to go) and begged God to prompt Steven to call, as I had done several times before.

On August 12, his birthday, he did call. There were a lot of quiet moments during that call. He said that he was in Florida, and that he had been thinking about his childhood and how good it had been. He thanked his father and me, and he said that he didn't want us to think that we had been bad parents.

We were amazed. We were so glad. This reassured us that God was at work in our son's life. After we hung up, I started baking his favorite cake, and I called some friends to have a little party—without Steven, of course.

About a week later, on September 14, I had a vivid dream in which Steven was bound in chains and surrounded by all of us who had been at his party. It was dark and scary, and then a light came on. Then someone said, "He's free." Beautiful peace and light and soft music followed, and suddenly I realized I was awake and saying, "Steven is free." God, through this strange dream, assured me that He was in charge.

A few days later, we received a letter from an old friend in Indiana who said that he had begun praying for Steven on August 29. He had prayed for seven days. His prayers had been that Steven would remember his youth and his home, that he would repent and call us. When the seven days of prayer had ended, our friend had decided to pray seven more days, even fasting for a couple of those days. He told us he had finished praying on September 14, the same day I had had the dream. God used this friend to encourage us just when we needed encouragement.

Spiritual Serenity

Slowly the anger has quieted. I sit still often in the presence of God. I let Him hold me. Sometimes I squirm like a two-year old, but He doesn't let go. He reminds me from the words in Psalm 103:13-14 that He looks upon me with compassion as a Father looks on His child because He knows of what I am made. As an answer to the "Serenity Prayer" I've often uttered throughout the years, I do find courage, the courage I need to change the things in my life I can change; I find grace, the grace to accept the things I cannot change; and I find wisdom, the wisdom to know the difference ...and to let God be God.

Gene's Story

I coped with our experiences in a much different way than Norma. Some of the differences between our approaches have been due to the distinctive way males and females operate; some have been the result of my own temperament and the way God has wired me; and some have been the result of our upbringing and responses to life's experiences.

My primary method of handling our situation has been and still is perseverance. I don't give up. I keep going. I believe that for those who believe in Jesus, it's always too soon to quit.

My coping skills have been highly affected by my emotional attachments and by my glaring need to have people like me. It has been difficult to get in touch with the feelings that God created in me because the words of my mom have sometimes colored my somewhat naïve and often superficial approach to life: "Smile. Everything is okay."

"It's Just a Phase"

Many times, I have dealt with what was going on with our son by thinking it was normal. Steven was simply going through teenage rebellion and testing a parent's love, I would reason. I had been through it, too: drinking in high school, sneaking around, breaking rules. It was just a part of growing up that we simply needed to ride out. I had gotten sick and tired of my own life and I had come back to the Lord, so naturally Steven would, too, wouldn't he? This "phase" would be temporary; certainly Steven would eventually come to his senses. Besides, Steven was an excellent athlete. He was caring and sensitive. He had grown up around many good Christian role models. He would come out of it. God would not fail us. God had changed my life and He would not give up on Steven.

Anger and Despair

As time rolled on and nothing changed, I realized that there was little we could do until Steven became willing to get help. I began to deal with my hurt by becoming angry. I got angry with Steven for lying over and over. I got angry with him for breaking the law and for breaking our rules. I often got mad at Norma for demanding that I DO something to get involved and tell Steven what he needed to do.

My desperately wanting, needing, Steven to change led to extreme disappointment

Friendships: Vital Connections

When Steven and Cindy were living in Minneapolis, we watched the roller coaster lifestyle affect their young son's life. Stevie was about three years old. Steven was not working. They had been evicted from their house. They were not keeping in touch with us. We were in the process of moving again. I was concerned about not staying connected to our grandson. I finally discovered where they were and arrived at their apartment building just minutes after Steven had been taken away in a squad car. Little Stevie had withdrawn into his own little play world and Cindy was hysterical. We took our grandson home with us and we ended up keeping him for two months.

A year and a half later, when they were living in Virginia, we learned that Steven had been in jail again. He was not working and once again he and Cindy had been evicted from their home. Cindy asked if I would come and get Stevie and take care of him again until they could get things sorted out.

I went to Virginia and it turned out wonderfully that an old friend of ours lived 45 minutes from Steve and Cindy's place and she was willing to let me stay with her. She even drove me over to pick up little Stevie. He was thin and bewildered, and all of his little mismatched clothes were packed in a garbage bag. Steven had disappeared because he didn't want to see me. I could not have coped with the sadness of this situation had my friend not been with me. Stevie ended up staying with us this time for three months.

As I review this story and many others like it, I realize that my friends were available when I needed them. Friends listened to me. Friends took me to Al-Anon. Friends gave us legal advice. Friends helped us pay fines and treatment fees. Most importantly, friends prayed for us.

and often despair. I would spend extended time in prayer. Sometimes I would just drive out to a deserted park and drink a bottle of beer.

Ministry Matters

I also had a church to pastor, a sermon to prepare, and services to lead. I needed to give leadership and counsel to a church that was undergoing struggles. So I would often avoid Steven, Norma and my family by over-indulging in the ministry and the needs of others.

Support System

One source of comfort in the raging river of our ordeal was occasionally hearing the stories of other families who were going through similar situations. These families helped us realize that we were not alone. God was there by His grace, and He placed people in our lives to help us make sense out of a journey that was stretching our faith to the limit.

Family Conflict, Family Pain

We were desperate at times to do something, to fix the problem, instead of really seeing Steven as a person. We tried everything to give him a second chance, a new start, over and over. Getting Steven drug treatment, arranging counseling for him, having him tested for drugs, changing his schools, sending him to work in construction for a summer with a friend in Florida, moving him into his own apartment—all of our efforts and ideas proved futile. We were making his choices for him, which was an inadequate way to cope, since Steven had decided not to change. He was making his own choices and we didn't have to like them or agree with him.

A Great and Gracious God

We all keep our heads above water in a raging current in different ways. God knows just how He made us and matches His abundant grace to fit the shape of our own needs.

Rebellion is real. Steven's choice to assert his own identity and deal with his internal conflicts by turning to drugs need not have come as a surprise. The Bible clearly teaches that sin is ravenous and parasitic, and that it feeds on the good. Thankfully, though, the Bible also teaches us that God's grace--seen in the hope-filled death of Christ on the cross--is greater than sin.

I am thankful that I trust God's goodness. It seems to me there are no quick answers or short pragmatic procedures to fix the problem. Because the problem is not a machine, but a person who needs understanding and the experience of God's amazing grace. Besides, what is so bad about suffering pain in a sinful world when there is the healing freshness of the Good News of Jesus Christ? C. S. Lewis said, in the wonderful movie *Shadowlands*, "Pain is God's megaphone to get the attention of a needy world." My Abba Father, who knows what is good for me, used pain to get my attention. I know it helped me understand myself better. In a group session with the other parents of kids who were going through drug treatment, the group facilitator asked me as she went around the circle how I was doing. I replied I was really sorry for the pain that Steven was going through. Her hard-hitting reply woke me up in a helpful way. "What about your pain?" I knew then that I was focusing on the wrong pain and that I hadn't dealt with some of my own.

All Things Work Together for Good

In spite of all the pain and difficulty we've been through with our son and his situation, we've seen that God has been faithful to show us, just as He promises, that good things can come from even the worst of situations. Here are a few of the blessings I've experienced:

- The excruciating pain of having a child addicted to alcohol and drugs has made my heart softer and more compassionate for others. It has been probably the best preparation that I could have had in order to be able to listen to and minister to others as pastor of counseling.

- Our experience has challenged my own response to God's Holy Spirit prompting me to love others when I receive nothing in return except pain.

- I have a great grandson, whom I love and really enjoy.

- I saw God's wonderful healing love and freeing grace in my son's life through this experience, as well as the personal growth of our daughter-in-law, Cindy.

Healing Hearts

While Norma and I were in Michigan for our oldest son Peter's wedding, Steven, Cindy, and Stevie had driven out from Virginia to be a part of the wedding. We were staying at the same hotel. Norma and I were at breakfast when Steven came into the room and gently asked to join us. I was not prepared for what he said. He said to us, "I know that I have misused and lost my youth and my teenage years and I know the pain that I have caused you together as my parents. I just want to ask you to forgive me." Neither Norma nor I had thought we would ever hear those healing words.

The healing continues in the process of one who has dug a very deep hole and one who needs to see the clearness of God's grace in order to get out. I am discovering that prayer is not a magical lamp that I rub and get three wishes from God, but it is an intimate conversation—yelling out my dependence on Him. God is good and pur-

A Letter From Our Son

Dear Mom and Dad,

   I want to say I'm sorry for the way I acted today and tonight. I don't know what happened. It is hard to keep a positive attitude about all of the hours, the restrictions, the consequences when inside I'm so frustrated and mad with myself.

   It feels like I have thousands of things to do and it feels like I'm not doing any of them. I feel like my senior year is really beat. I feel like a total failure in everything…the whole deal and then the whole scene at school. I feel like I got nothing out of all of my attempts at soccer, not even the league's most valuable player, let alone any kind of honors from a high school. And then I know I won't get into colleges and I haven't heard from any of them.

   Dad and you and I are always arguing. You don't trust me. I know. I feel like I'm so angry inside that I can blow up so easily. I'm sorry that I do it to you and Dad, but I'm frustrated. I feel like when I leave the house and I'm alone I really should make the most of it because I know I'll have to be home soon. I want to do well this term. I want to get my community hours out of the way quickly. I want to pay off my bills. I want to get this thing out of the way. I'm really sorry about being such a letdown always. Sometimes I don't know what goes through my mind. I hate being told when and what to do and I guess I shouldn't. I'll try to do better. I promise.

poses good in our lives in and through our pain. Jesus' Good News is for broken lives, for those who have no one else to put them back together again.

Romans 8:31-39 probably best sums up so much of what has been my confidence during this time:

What, then, shall we say in response to this? If God is for us, who can be against us? He who did not spare his own Son, but gave him up for us all--how will he not also, along with him, graciously give us all things? Who will bring any charge against those whom God has chosen? It is God who justifies. Who is he that condemns? Christ Jesus, who died-- more than that, who was raised to life-- is at the right hand of God and is also interceding for us. Who shall separate us from the love of Christ? Shall trouble or hardship or persecution or famine or nakedness or danger or sword [—or addiction]? As it is written: 'For your sake we face death all day long; we are considered as sheep to be slaughtered.' No, in all these things we are more than conquerors through him who loved us. For I am convinced that neither death nor life, neither angels nor demons, neither the present nor the future, nor any powers, neither height nor depth, nor anything else in all creation, [—not even chemical addition—] will be able to separate us from the love of God that is in Christ Jesus our Lord (NIV, with notes from author).

Chapter 2

Carrying On When Your Heart Is Broken

By Dr. Kim and Lynda Hodge

God has used the most agonizing of experiences—discovering that our 11-year-old son was using drugs--to teach us His important truths. While we are far from experts on the subject of substance abuse, we have found that our story—which has spanned 12 years--has been common to many others who have found themselves in similar situations. So we would like to share our story with you in the hope that it will offer you encouragement. Second Corinthians 1:4 says that we receive God's comfort so that we can share it with others. We pray that you will be comforted with the kind of peace that God has given us.

Ten Steps from Ignorant Oblivion to Rejoicing and Thanksgiving

As we sought to organize our thoughts on the subject of how to carry on with a broken heart, we realized that each of us has gone through 10 stages since discovering that the younger of our two sons was using drugs. Both of us experienced these stages at different times over a period of years. It seems, however, that they appeared in approximately the order we will share with you. You may recognize some of these stages in your own experience.

1. Ignorant Oblivion

Kim: We thought we were wonderful parents. It seemed that we had all of the right pieces to be good parents, anyway. We believed in Jesus Christ; we were convinced that God had given us the two sons that He wanted us to have.

We were in ministry and felt called to ministry; and so it seemed to us that being in the ministry should have been a protective shield that would make it possible for us to have kids that would do exactly what we wanted them to do. We had watched other families struggle. There were families who had children with severe problems and we cared about them and we even prayed for them. But that was not us.

Our first son was a good student, a talented musician and an excellent athlete. So we assumed that our second son would be the same. However, soon after our younger son started the sixth grade in the middle school, it began to seem as if an alien inhabited his body. We noticed a change in his attitude and temperament that was so pronounced that we felt we did not know him any more. It was as though he became a total stranger from that moment on.

2. Suspicion

Lynda: We thought Evan was using drugs but neither of us wanted to believe it. He was young, but we just figured that he would have more sense. We could not believe this was happening in our home.

However, we soon were led into suspicion. One of the first clues was his use of incense in his room. I hated that smell. I detested it. When I would complain, he would say, "I will just change to a different brand, get a different smell." I would say, "I don't care what brand you get, I don't like it. Why do you insist on burning that stuff?" He would always give me convincing, logical answers such as "I just like the smell of it," or "all my friends like it too," so I would just let it slide.

Later, when we would ask him about drug paraphernalia that we found in his pockets, in his schoolbooks or in his room, he would use the same kinds of convincing, logical excuses. So we would believe him. We trusted him and we had seen no reason up through the fifth grade not to do so. Soon, however, that trust factor eroded. Doubts began to creep in when we saw some of the following signs:

- changes in his behavior
- redness, haziness, and a glaze in his eyes
- a lack of interest in things he had previously loved to do
- sullenness
- frequent talk about and threats of suicide
- anger and tremendous rage

3. Denial

Kim: Even with all of these signals, I was not willing to believe that our son was using drugs. I immediately denied the possibility.

Lynda and I have very different temperaments. Lynda is much more discerning than I am. I am slower to accept something, slower to deal with an issue; I want to give it some time. She would see these red flags and say, "I think we have a problem." I would answer, "I don't think we have a problem." I continued to live in denial.

Lynda: I realized that we had a problem, and that this situation was beyond our control. I saw that I had two choices: 1) I could choose to cover up Evan's drug use, try to catch him and protect him; or 2) I could choose to put myself in God's hands and have Him handle our situation His way. I chose to put it into God's hands. He started working on me right away. I thought He ought to be working on Evan, but He didn't. I kept asking the Lord, "Why don't you ask Evan to keep making right choices? You keep pestering me."

He started by dealing with my pride. That pride wanted to cover up the situation and to keep making excuses for Evan's behavior. But the Lord helped me realize that our son was making these choices on his own. We were not doing anything to cause him to make these choices; we were not forcing him to do this.

In order to keep on going, I had to make another choice. Not only could Evan's behavior have disastrous effects on our marriage and on Evan himself; it could also be devastating to the ministry God had given Kim as a pastor. The Lord and I got into lots of deep discussions about this issue and I decided with God's prompting to give Him my pride and our reputation. I gave Him Kim's ministry. Actually, it was not Kim's ministry. It was the ministry into which God had placed Kim.

"Lord, if You want to allow Evan's behavior to destroy himself and destroy us as a family and the pastorate that you have given Kim, then that is Your decision," I prayed. "That's Your responsibility. Lord, I want to ask You to keep

> *I gave Him Kim's ministry.*

> *My constant prayer continued to be, "Lord, get me out of the way. Keep me out of the way. Help me to be the person you want me to be so that I do not give Evan any cause to make the choices he is making."*

me out of the way so you can keep working on Evan." My constant prayer continued to be, "Lord, get me out of the way. Keep me out of the way. Help me to be the person you want me to be so that I do not give Evan any cause to make the choices he is making."

The opportunity to put that prayer into practice came soon enough when a police officer called and told me he had Evan in custody. He told me to report to the police station. At that moment—I can still remember it—I felt like a huge boulder had hit me. I could hardly breathe. When I came to my senses, I said, "Lord, I am to keep out of the way. I think this is a father-son event." I promptly went out to the study to tell Kim the news.

Kim: When she found me in my study and told me of the phone call, I was absolutely overwhelmed. For the first few moments I didn't have the strength to get up out of my chair because the last thing I had expected was a call from the police.

4. Confusion and Questioning.

Kim: Questions flooded into my mind: "Why?" "Why us?" "Why now?" "Why would you even allow this kind of thing, Lord? Isn't there a verse--Proverbs 22:6--that says: 'Train up a child in the way he should go and when he is old he won't depart from it?' Lord, what happened to that verse? What happened to that truth?" On the ride to the police station, my questions continued. "What did I do wrong?" "What did we do wrong?" "Was I too busy for Evan?" "Could I have spent more time discipling my son?" "Could I have done a better job of disciplining my son?" "Was I a good example?" Not one of those questions seemed to have an answer. I picked up Evan at the police department and brought him home, where Lynda met us at the front door.

Lynda: Evan looked very hard; yet, when I looked into his eyes, I saw that he was very embarrassed. I said, "Evan, your Dad and I love you. We don't love what you're doing, but we love you as a person. I want you to know that we will never get in the way of your experiencing the full weight of the consequences of your choices. However, I want you to understand that your Dad and I will always stand beside you; we will never turn our backs on you." Then I put my arms around him, hugged him hard, and looked at his face, where I saw a tear trailing down his cheek. He said, "Thanks, Mom," then went to his room and closed the door. Kim told me that he had said the same thing to Evan on the way home from the police station.

5. Anger and Frustration

Kim: Over the next days, my anger and frustration grew. The anger was not even directed clearly. Sometimes I was furious with Evan. How could he do this to us? How could he do this to himself? I was often mad at the world. It just did not seem fair that we had to try to bring up a kid in a world that is so evil, a world that has so many opportunities for sin. I was upset with the kids he hung around with because I knew that they must have had a tremendous impression on him. And I was also irritated that Evan was more interested in what his friends thought about him than what we thought about him.

I also have to admit, although it was extremely hard, that I was angry with God for allowing this to happen to us. I don't remember having felt that way before.

This was a very heavy time for both Lynda and me. Our differences in temperament showed up in a variety of ways. For instance, when I struggled with anger and frustration, she did not seem to be struggling the same way as I did. My response to our situation was very different from hers.

Lynda: I have always tended to be strong-willed, determined and more rigidly disciplined than Kim. This strength has helped in many ways but in other ways it hasn't been so good. For example, Kim asked me not to deal with the discipline of Evan, but to just concentrate on loving our son and having fun with him and his friends. Kim did not want me to have to carry the weight of being the disciplinarian; he would assume that role.

At that point, I had to go to the Lord in His Word for direction. In Ephesians 5:22, Paul says we wives are supposed to be obedient to our husbands. However, I found it difficult to be obedient when I knew that Kim was not right. When I did not feel Kim was dealing with the drug issue as strongly as he should, it really did go against my authoritarian grain and the way that I had been brought up.

But the Lord was precious. He tenderly taught me that I was to obey that Scripture, especially in this situation, and honor Kim's directive. When I finally let go and submitted to my husband, I found that it really freed me up not to blame Kim for everything that wasn't working out correctly with his plan in taking over with Evan.

I did continue to believe that Kim was too easygoing, and that fact brought me countless feelings of frustration. But Kim did tell me that when my frustration level would get too high, I should not take it out on Evan; I was to come to talk to him. I can still see Kim sitting on the bed in our room, patiently listening to my ranting. He never criticized me; he was always very gracious because he knew I had to get it out of my system. I know those confrontations were very painful for him and left him sagging because he also felt at a miserable loss as to what to do for or with Evan. I found that releasing my feelings on Kim not only gave me a sense of freedom from the heaviness of it all; but it also freed me from carrying the blame for what didn't appear to be working. I could go back into my life and do what Kim asked me to do: have fun with Evan and love him.

6. Discouragement

Kim: This whole process with Evan literally broke my heart. I think I moved into discouragement first, although I know Lynda experienced the same problem a little bit later. This intense discouragement eventually led me into depression. That dark frame of mind seeped into every part of my life and affected every aspect of my ministry.

I finally concluded I could not continue in the pastorate. A number of times, I was reminded of Christ's question in Matthew 16:26, "What good will it be for a man if he gains the whole world, yet forfeits his soul?" (NIV). Then I paraphrased it, "What good will it be for a man to gain the whole world and lose his son?" What good was ministry if I was a pastor and I could help other people but I could not do anything for my own son? I concluded there was no answer but to quit. I was disqualified, and there was no one to turn to. However, Lynda was struggling in another way.

Lynda: To keep on going, I knew I had to spend a lot of time with the Lord and study His Word. I had learned early in our marriage that Kim could not always be there for me. This was certainly true during this time. I learned that no human being can be there for you and ease that gut-level heart and soul-wrenching pain within. So I was with the Lord a lot. In fact, I was intensely focused on Him. When I was in His Word, I came across a verse I had known for a long time.

First Thessalonians 5:16-18: "Be joyful always; pray continually; give thanks in all circumstances, for this is God's will for you in Christ Jesus" (NIV).

"Lord, how in the world can I be thankful?" I asked after reading this. "What's there to be thankful for?"

The Lord is so gentle and so kind, and through His Spirit it was just like He was asking, "Why can't you be thankful?"

"What do you mean, why can't I be thankful? I don't like what You are doing, Lord. How in the world can I be thankful, when You are allowing our son to be on drugs! And another thing, God, I trusted You. You let me down. How do you expect me to be thankful for that?

"Lord, You are simply a Person I cannot trust; You are unworthy of my trust."

Heart to Heart

I said to 13-year old Evan one day--this was in a calmer moment, "I think that I am going to have to stop being a pastor."

He sat up straight and said, "Why would you do that, Dad?"

I said, "Evan, what you're doing right now appears to me to be disqualifying me for ministry."

He said, "Who told you that you were disqualified?"

I said, "The Scripture says very clearly that if a father can't take care of or control his own children, then he has no right to think that he can care for the church." Then Evan got angry--not with me, but with anyone who could tell me I couldn't be a pastor.

"Dad, you can't stop being a pastor," he said. "That's what you are supposed to do. You're supposed to keep doing what you are doing." I said, "Evan, I know right now I am putting tremendous pressure on you. If I leave the ministry, I'm not going to say I left the ministry because of you, but I have to tell you that I don't have the confidence anymore that God is going to want me in the ministry because of your actions."

Evan was frustrated and angry about the thought of my leaving the ministry; but at this point in his experience, he was still not ready to make the necessary changes.

I was absolutely shocked when those words came out of my mouth.

I realized that I thought for years that I had trusted Him; but I had only trusted Him in situations over which I had control. This situation, however, was way beyond my control. I felt that I could not trust God because I didn't feel He was trustworthy. Anyone who would do something like this to me for my "good" definitely wasn't trustworthy

I don't know how long I struggled with this matter, but finally, one soul-wrenching day, I verbalized a prayer once again. But this time I said, "God, I truly believe You are worthy of my trust and You definitely know what You are doing. I want to thank You, Lord, for this very struggle, which has led me to really evaluate my level of trust in You."

The moment these words came out of my mouth, something wonderful took place in my spirit. God knew I really meant what I said. Philippians 4:6-7 sums it up: "Do not be anxious about anything, but in everything, by prayer and petition, with thanksgiving, present your requests to God. And the peace of God, which transcends all understanding, will guard your hearts and your minds in Christ Jesus" (NIV). Something wonderful took place in my spirit. God's peace was settling down into my heart and He was guarding me and taking control of the situation.

7. Dependence on God

Kim: Moving from discouragement and depression to dependence on God may have been the longest part of the process. Two issues converged in my life at the same time to propel me toward dependence on God. First, I got a new job and then, I lost my voice.

We had decided that rather than leaving the ministry, we could change ministries or move somewhere else to get Evan out of Southern California, which to us seemed to be more evil than any other place on the planet. Then a wonderful ministry opportunity opened up in Eugene, Oregon. So we interviewed for the position of senior pastor. The next day, the church voted to invite us to become their new pastor, and we began to plan for our move. But I suddenly and literally lost my voice. I could not speak at all. A visit to the doctor revealed medical problems with my vocal chords, which required surgery. Now, I had resigned from one church, accepted an invitation to be pastor at another, and I was a preacher who couldn't talk. Think about that for a moment. It was a tough position to be in, especially since Evan was still in the midst of his struggles, with no solution in sight.

When I came to that point, I said, "Lord, I have two choices. I can either finally trust You, which I have been rebelling against doing with this situation with Evan, or I can just give up on life altogether."

I don't believe that I had ever seriously considered suicide before. I had thought of quitting, but never of suicide. Yet at that moment, my options seemed clear: Trust God or give up on living. I concluded that the only thing left for me to do was to trust the Lord. I know that must sound foolish for someone who has believed and taught this all his life.

I got down before the Lord and said, "Father, I can't talk and I don't know if I'll ever have my voice back; our son is using drugs and we're not sure we will ever get him back. But I choose and am determined to trust You."

8. Patient Waiting/Endurance

Lynda: Through the 12 years of struggle, Kim and I learned many God-given lessons. Today they have become a natural part of our lives. Here are some of the things God has taught us:

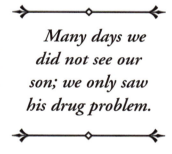

Many days we did not see our son; we only saw his drug problem.

- We learned to practice the unconditional love shown to us by the Lord Himself. Many times we had to call upon the Holy Spirit to direct this unconditional love through us to Evan as a person, especially when it was so hard to get past the continual problems and heartache he was giving us. Many days we did not see our son; we only saw his drug problem. But when the drug problem got in the way of our loving our child, the Holy Spirit always came through for us; He did exactly what we would allow Him to do. When Evan developed a relationship with a girl who later became his wife against our better judgment, we practiced extending this unconditional love to her as well.

- I learned how important it was to get out of the way so the Lord could work both in Evan and in Kim. Doing that took a weight off my shoulders by allowing me not to have to be so fixated on them. Kim and I never expected Evan to even get to his 20th birthday. We thought he would be dead. But I found that by getting out of God's way, I was able to get out of the center of the fire, and stand back as if I was on the outside looking in. Being on the outside felt much more comfortable when we knew God was in control.

- I learned that I needed to let the Lord know daily that I could fully trust Him. I realized He was sovereign, and even though I didn't know where He was going in all of this or where we were headed, I knew that He knew. That brought such comfort and peace to my soul that I was able to keep on going. At times I felt that I was alone, but I wasn't alone. I had the Lord with me because my guys were certainly bouncing up and down on this sea of constant uncertainty.

- We learned to recognize and appreciate that God was sending along angels to minister to us in the form of godly men and women. When we moved to Eugene, two retired men--one who worked with the high school department and one who worked with nursing home ministries--took Evan under their wings. They each took him out to lunch, and they would call to tell him they were praying for him. All this time, Evan was doing drugs. Our son had a very tender heart; he loved these men and he was just amazed that they loved him.

- We learned that God was also sending along mighty powerful prayer warriors for our family. These pray-ers did not criticize us; they just prayed. This was a tremendous gift.

Kim: During this long waiting period and time of endurance, God was working energetically in my heart. I was not only coming to the point of choosing to trust Him, but I was also coming to the point of spending a lot more personal time talking with Him, studying His Word, and trying to determine what He wanted me to do. I knew He didn't want me to quit ministry now. I knew He didn't want me to be a depressed pastor, so I was convinced that He would provide an answer to our situation.

One day I was reading in 2 Corinthians 10 about the battle we are all a part of as believers in Jesus Christ. I also read about the obstacles that Satan wants to build in our lives to keep us from knowing God and becoming all that He wants us to be. A little phrase in verse 5 grabbed my attention: "… we take captive every thought to make it obedient to Christ" (NIV). I have one of those minds that races most of the time. I might have eight thoughts working at once, and of those thoughts, seven might be negative and only one is worthwhile. Through this verse, God taught me that I could, by His grace, take my thoughts "captive." So, over the next few months, I developed a pattern that helped exercise that truth:

- I would ask His Spirit to teach me and allow His Words to enlighten me so I could recognize offensive thoughts such as worry, anger, or frustration.

- I would "capture" those offensive thoughts that had no right to linger in my mind for the next hour or two as they often had done previously.

- And then I would refuse those negative thoughts. I don't know if you have ever tried to refuse thoughts like these, but the harder you try not to think about something, the more the thought seems to get a grip on you.

- So, I realized I could refuse destructive thoughts if I would replace them with those that were beneficial. I could stop thinking about one thing only if I started thinking about something else.

Over and over, I would capture those negative thoughts and by God's grace bring them into obedience to Him. This practice has literally revolutionized the way that I think. This kept me afloat on the very turbulent seas of struggle with Evan.

9. The Breakthrough

Lynda: We don't know what put it all together for Evan. As I said before, he married a girl that we did not approve of. We believed they were both too young and unstable for marriage. They were both using drugs and weren't thinking clearly. During their wedding and many days afterward, I just wept. Our hearts were very grieved. Yet the Spirit continued to give us unconditional love for both of them. The marriage lasted two horrible, rocky years. Just a few weeks before his wife walked out on him for the last time, God got hold of Evan and brought him to his knees. The experience was so dramatic that Evan came right over from his house to ours to tell me about it.

"Mom, you're not going to believe this and you may think I am nuts, but the Holy Spirit literally pushed me out of the chair and down on my knees," he said. "I cried like a baby before the Lord, asking his forgiveness. Mom, I know He has forgiven me."

Evan came into my arms and both of us just wept like babies as I said, "I know the power of the Holy Spirit. I have been praying for years to give God the freedom to do whatever it took to break you and He has done that today. Our prayers are answered."

After his marriage ended, Evan moved back home. While he was living with us, he and I would have long discussions that stretched into the early morning hours. One night we were talking about some deep issues when I said to him, "I have three questions I would like to ask you, but I've kept them hidden in my heart for years."

He said, "Go ahead Mom, ask me."

"Did your dad and I spend so much time in ministry that you felt you were cheated or did not have quality time with us? I really need to know that."

Evan responded, "No, I felt that you and Dad were always there for me whenever I needed you."

Then I asked, "Did you ever feel that we did not love you enough?" He answered, "No, I knew you and Dad loved me, no matter what I did. I was always assured of your love."

My third question was: "Why in the world did you choose to make these bad decisions; why did you choose to do drugs?"

I can still see the smile on his face because he recognized my frustration. He said, "Mom, you and Dad did everything right. I did what I did because of my own self-focus and self-centeredness. I thought that what I did would not make any difference to or affect anyone else, but I can see now that kind of thinking was incorrect."

10. Rejoicing and Thanksgiving

Lynda: I recently asked Evan, "If you could dream, what would you like to be doing today?"

He answered, "Just exactly what I am doing, Mom. God is so good and I don't deserve it."

I have had to keep reassuring and reminding Evan that God's grace is not something we earn. It stems from His unconditional love for us. We need to accept it and give Him all the thanks and praise.

Kim: As we look back today at God's work, we are absolutely convinced that His hand was in all of this. His desire was to shape us and mold us. His plan wasn't to remove us from ministry but to prepare us for the ministry that He had for us.

Lynda and I sat down recently and considered what we have learned from this experience. We discovered five critical lessons:

1. **No matter how out of control circumstances seem, God is still in control.** I know you've heard that before. I have preached that before. But today I am absolutely convinced of it. He remains faithful even when the situation appears hopeless. It seemed at times during our ordeal that even God had lost control, but we are confident today that He never did.

2. **God in His great wisdom and love has used these extreme difficulties to shape us for His glory.**

   I know you believe Romans 8:28, which says, "… God works for the good of those who love him, who have been called according to His purpose" (NIV). But often we do not go on to verse 29, which describes His eternal plan. It says that He is sovereign and is working to conform us to the "likeness of His Son." God uses even the most difficult of circumstances, such as the struggle with a wayward child, to conform and shape us as we trust Him in the situation.

3. **God's Word is a tremendous source of encouragement in the midst of our struggle.**

   Again and again, we found His Word to be exactly what we needed. Now it has become the pattern in both of our lives to say, "God, if You have given us Your revelation, it has to have an answer for each of our needs." God has been renewing our thinking and shaping our actions as well through His Word.

4. **We recognize that each of us is still a work in progress.**

   Evan is at a great place in his life right now, but God is still shaping him and He is still working on us. That shaping continues. Ephesians 2:10 says that we are God's workmanship, or God's poem. Our lives are still poems in the process of being perfected, and I am thankful for that.

5. **Our struggles have made our hearts tender toward others.**

   I have a lot less criticism in my heart for poor parenting or what appears to be poor parenting. I have a lot less criticism in my heart for people who have kids who refuse to do what they ought to do. It used to be easy for me to say: "If those parents would have just done this, or that." But I'm deeply concerned for them because I understand that sometimes the situation with a child is completely out of a parent's control. Fewer pat answers come out of my mouth for people in the middle of challenges like this; I am more patient. The relationship between Lynda and me has deepened greatly through the struggle.

Whatever stage you may be experiencing in your struggle right now, however broken you may be in your heart, I am convinced that God truly is working all things together for your good and for His glory.

Open Doors

Our home had always had an open-door policy. I grew up in that kind of a home, and we continued the tradition with our kids. We always said our boys should feel free to bring their friends over any time, all hours of the night and day. We wanted them to feel that they could do things at home with their friends whatever they would like to do. As a result, Evan thought he could just bring his drug friends home. I did want to close the door and lock it at that point, but I recognized that we couldn't do that. We had to continue living our lives as we always had.

I also recognized that visiting our home might be the first time that many of these kids would ever have an opportunity to see the love of Christ. I remember coming home from work and finding these really strange-looking guys with their heads in our refrigerator digging out whatever food they could eat.

One day in particular, Evan brought home 11 of his friends because he had been telling them that I knew how to cut hair and could do it any way they would want. So I said, "Okay, I'll do that," and they thought that was really cool. It was really quite a day. It took me over three hours to cut and style their hair. Some of them wanted weird, way-out styles, but I cut as directed. At the end of those fun-filled hours, I had about a three-foot area piled high with hair. Evan's friends talked about that for a long time. They said to him, "My mom would never do that. My mom wouldn't even let us bring our friends to the house."

Chapter 3

When Parenting is Painful, God is Faithful

By Noy Sparks

"I'm sorry to have to make this call. But I have it on good report or I wouldn't call you. I haven't caught Mark, but I understand he's using marijuana."

I'll never forget the day I came home from the office to these words during a phone call from the assistant headmaster at the Christian school that our son attended.

"I have been careful to do all that I can to make sure that what I'm telling you is fact," he said. "I really wouldn't alarm you or make the call if I didn't believe this was the case."

***

The news shattered me. The idea that my son, Mark, who was 16 and a junior in high school, could possibly have used drugs was the furthest thing from my mind. We had a good family. I never in my wildest imagination thought we would go down this road.

I was enraged.

I let Mark know in no uncertain terms that this would not happen ever, ever again. I gave him strict boundaries which, as I look back, I realize I did in an effort to control the situation. In retrospect, I don't know how I could have handled the news any differently. I was just grasping for a solution.

After that, things seemed to be okay for a few months. At the end of the school year, he and I went to Africa on a short mission trip. I thought it would be good for him to be with me helping others. We had a great time. When we came back from the trip, Mark completed his senior year and graduated from high school.

After graduation, there were a couple of nights he didn't come home. Those instances were pretty traumatic for us, but we thought things had settled down.

The September following graduation, Mark told us he didn't want to go to college. I wanted him to go, but I didn't push the issue. He said he just wanted to get a job and work a little bit first; I told him that would be okay.

Soon after that, on the Thursday he was to go for a job interview at a pharmacy, I went to the office as usual. When I came home at noon for lunch, his truck was gone so I assumed he had spent his first day at work. But when I went in the house and happened to go by his room, I noticed that it seemed different. I walked into the room and was shocked to find that almost all of his clothes were gone. He left a note indicating that he had moved out.

I immediately called his older brother, who lived in Jacksonville, Florida at the time.

"Listen, I got this note," I said. "Mark is gone. He may be on his way to your place just to get away. Do me a favor. If he gets there will you disable his truck? Take off the distributor cap. Do whatever you can so that I can get up there to him."

My older son said, "Dad, I can't do that."

"What do you mean, you can't do that?"

"That's not right. Mark is 18 years old. I don't agree with what he's done but I can't disable his truck."

Right after that he said the strangest thing.

"Dad, where are your guns?"

I had been brought up in Texas and had hunted with my father since I could walk. Naturally, I've had guns for many years. I put down the phone and checked to find all of my guns were gone—my handgun, my rifle and my shotgun.

I went back to the phone and said, "The guns are gone."

My son replied, "I'll disable his truck."

Waiting, Worrying, and Praying

Mark didn't go to Jacksonville. We didn't know where he was. Needless to say we were shattered; we were broken. By the next day, Friday, we still hadn't heard a word from him so I called a good friend, Jack, who is a private investigator and former policeman. He told me that since the truck was registered in my name, I could call the authorities and have Mark stopped.

"They'll stop him but you have to be willing to do two things," Jack said. "Number one, you've got to be willing to press charges. If you don't press charges, they're not going to get involved. Number two, you've got to tell them that he has weapons in the truck."

I didn't think I could do that.

"If they pull him over and he turns the wrong way in the cab then they shoot him," I said.

"You've got to do that if you want them to stop him," Jack said.

I can't really communicate all that happened during the next couple of days. One day led to the next. Sunday came. I didn't know how I was going to preach, but God got me through it. At the end of the message, I shared with my church family that my son had left. Spontaneously, all the men in the church got up from their seats, came down the aisles, and gathered around me at the front. They put their hands on me and prayed for me.

On Monday, I told the Lord, "If I don't hear something tomorrow I'm going to have to call the authorities." We had searched through Mark's room and called his friends for clues about where he might be. We discovered that Mark had taken his passport and had talked to a few friends about going to Mexico.

"A few days in Mexico with these guns and we may never see him again," I thought.

He wasn't "streetwise." Sensitive and bright, he had been editor of his high school yearbook. He was an exceptionally gifted young man, but he was gone. We found out that he had left town with a girl he had just met three weeks earlier.

On Tuesday morning, I decided that if I didn't hear anything by the end of the day, I would call the police. At about 2:30 in the afternoon, I received a call from the Pueblo, Colorado Sheriff's Department.

"Are you Mark Sparks' father?"

"Yes."

"We've got your son. He's in a pawnshop. He hasn't done anything wrong. He's 18; he's of age, but he's trying to sell some guns. We just want to know are these his guns or are they your guns?"

"They're my guns."

"We'll take them away if you'd like us to."

"Please do that."

"Okay, but he's not done anything wrong."

"Let me talk to him."

"We will let you talk to him if he wants to talk, but we can't make him. Again, we're not holding him. He hasn't done anything wrong."

"If he'll talk with me, let me talk with him."

The officer told me to go down to my local police department, so someone from there could confirm with the Pueblo department that the guns were mine.

"We'll take him to the station," the officer said. "If he'll talk, we'll do that."

I said, "Good."

I did talk to our son. Before I could ask whether he was okay, when he first heard my voice, he said, "Dad, I love you."

I felt a strong wave of emotions. "Are you okay, Son?"

"I'm okay."

"Son, what are you doing?"

"Dad, we want to get married."

FIRST BAPTIST CHURCH
GLADSTONE, OREGON

I thought things were insane enough as it was and then he was telling me he wanted to marry a girl whose name we didn't even know.

"Why don't you come home and we'll talk about it?"

"Dad, don't make me come home."

"I can't make you come home, but I would appreciate it if you would," I said. "I'll tell you what. I'll put the truck in your name. I won't keep you; I won't hold you. Just come home and see your mother." I was grasping for straws. "Face your mother and at least tell her—in person--what you want to do."

"Dad, please, please don't make me come home."

"Okay. If you will just stay there, I'll go get your mom at work and we'll call you back."

I rushed to picked up Lynda and we returned to the police station. We called him back. He maintained that was what he and the girl wanted to do.

"Okay," I said. "But first, I want to say a couple of things. Number one: If you're going to get married, that's your business, but realize that you are stuck with whomever you marry. You better make sure you know what you're doing. Number two: Do you have any money?"

"I have $35," Mark said. "That's why I'm trying to sell the guns."

"I'm going to wire you $300."

"Thank you, Dad."

He told me that he and his girlfriend were going to San Francisco, and I said I imagined that $300 would be enough to pay for the trip out there and to live on until he could get a job.

Long-Distance Parenting

About four days later, Mark called us. He never had left Colorado, and he remained there for three months.

Mark would call us periodically. I would think that to be a good father, I needed to tell him that he was sinning and that God would deal with him. In fact, I did tell him that a couple times. But then I realized that if I told him something he already knew every time he called, pretty soon he wouldn't call us at all. I would be destroying the already fragile lines of communication between us. So after that, when he called, I would want to say something serious, but I would hold my tongue and listen to him talk about how beautiful the mountains were in Colorado. Or we would talk about the Dallas Cowboys. I tried to make conversation just to keep the door open. God, in His ways, did just that.

In and Out of Home

Four months later, Mark called and said, "Would you mind if I moved back home?"

I said, "Please do." Then I added, "But understand, Mark, that if you come back home there will be some boundaries. You're not going to use drugs. You're not going to use alcohol."

He said, "I know that." So he came back home.

For the next year, things were up and down. When I would find out he was using drugs, I would make him leave. I'd see him open the door to his room and pack his stuff. He'd come out, stand in the front door, and say, "I love you guys, but I'm gonna have to leave."

I'd say, "I don't want you to leave, but you cannot stay and do what you're doing." And he would leave.

He wouldn't have anywhere to go. Sometimes he would live in his truck or with a friend. Then he would come back home and say, "I know what the boundaries are. May I come home?"

I would say, "This is your home. You're welcome; but again, we're not going to enable you. You cannot use drugs."

I can't say how many times this happened, and the pattern continued for several months. Then one day after he had come home again, Mark said, he would like to go to college. He attended Liberty University for 11 months before I got a call from the dean of men.

"Pastor Sparks, I hate to say this but we found marijuana in your son's room. He's going to have to leave the school. We ought to call the authorities but we're not going to do it. But we can't have this on campus." Mark left the university and came back home.

Deeper into Drugs

Mark was home for a few months and then he moved out again. This routine continued for a while. At one point, he moved back home, got a job, and was doing pretty well. Then he met a girl who introduced him to heroin. I don't blame her because she didn't make him use heroin, but she's the one who introduced him to that drug.

Mark was arrested a few months later for grand theft and he received a sentence of three years probation. While he was on probation, he was arrested for possession of marijuana and sentenced to 18 months in a state rehabilitation residential facility. He stayed there for eight months, then left without permission. He was arrested again, and he is still in jail as of this writing.

The state prosecutor wanted to give Mark the minimum sentence of a year and a half in the state penitentiary. Thankfully, the judge said, "I don't think he's going to get drug help there. I'm going to keep him in the county jail for a year."

Even More Reasons to Despair

I'd like to say that we've handled this ordeal with great, unshakeable faith. But the fact is we have not. We have been riding a spiritual and emotional roller coaster. We have felt the shock, the denial and the guilt: "What have we done wrong?" We have

> ### Public Pain
> The day after Mark was arrested, before I could get out of bed that morning, a friend of mine called and said, "Pastor, have you seen the morning paper?"
> I said, "No."
> He said, "Your son's picture is on the front page of the inside section of the newspaper. His picture is there along with some girl telling about his arrest."
> There was great humiliation and great embarrassment.

felt confused, angry, and fearful.

I remember praying right before he was arrested for grand theft. I was lying in bed but couldn't sleep.

"Lord, I don't know what Mark's up to, but I ask You to please, please, Father, do not let him get involved in the legal system. I may not know what I'm asking, but I think, Father, that I would rather see him dead than in jail. So I beg You, don't let that happen."

Within three weeks, Mark was arrested for grand theft. I'll never forget the day the police came and handcuffed my son in front of the parsonage, put him in the patrol car and drove off.

That event left us disillusioned, hopeless, depressed, profoundly sad, and grieving. Legal fees, rehab, and counseling expenses devastated our finances, and socially we have felt humiliation and embarrassment.

God's Power for Perseverance

Spiritually, I experienced times when I didn't want to read the Bible. So I didn't. My prayers were often mechanical and repetitious. Many times, I didn't know what to pray. I had prayed a million times. I didn't know how to word my prayers differently. I just didn't know what to do.

But God, through His tremendous grace and power, enabled us to persevere through the spiritual, social and emotional darkness of this time. Here are some of the ways He has done that:

- To begin with, by His grace God has given me a good relationship with Lynda. We've been able to communicate. That has been a lifesaver. That is not to say that we haven't had some heated differences. On the contrary, we have not always agreed on everything. But through it all, we've been able to communicate and stay together.

- He has also allowed us to complement one another during the rough spots. For example, when one of us has been in low spirits, the other one usually has been more optimistic. God has been great in that regard.

- He also has given us seasons of reprieve during which everything seemed to be going well.

- He has provided us with good legal counsel in an attorney who happened to be a believer. Our attorney has been an immense help and encouragement, and has even prayed with us.

- He has given me a wonderfully supportive church. About a year before I resigned as pastor of my church to go back to school, the church gave me a three-month paid sabbatical. Our denomination doesn't usually offer sabbaticals and I had not asked for one. This was providential. We've always been up front with our church. After our initial discovery of Mark's marijuana use when he had been in high school, I told the deacon board what had happened. "If you want me to resign, I'll resign," I said. "If I can't take care of my own household, how can I take care of a church of God?" They said, "You've been here for a long time. We've known your children since they were small. We know how you raised them. We don't think that 1 Timothy 3 would apply in this situation." The church's support and love have been a tremendous blessing.

Lessons Learned

In looking back over events of these years, I realize that I might have been a bit rigid as a father. Now I see elements of legalism and self-righteousness in some of the ways I parented, but obviously I didn't see them at the time. We ran a pretty tight ship at the house. Now we look back and think we might have loosened up in some areas.

Our experience with Mark's drug abuse and its consequences has relaxed that rigidity in a lot of ways. God also has given both of us an element of compassion. For example, I used to sit in my office sometimes and counsel parents about their children. I wouldn't say it, but I would think, "Why don't you get control of your own children?" Now, I don't see it that way at all.

In addition, God has taught us about choosing our battles. My son loves to smoke. He shaves his head. His nose is pierced, and he has a marijuana emblem tattooed on his leg. But after all we have gone through, I have realized that I don't need to fight with him over the issue of whether or not he should smoke, how he wears his hair, whether his nose is pierced or whether he needs a tattoo.

Be Anxious for Nothing

When my son left for Colorado, a woman in our church called and said she had been praying for my family. She shared Philippians 4: 6-7: "Don't be anxious about anything, but in everything, by prayer and petition, with thanksgiving, present your requests to God. And the peace of God, which transcends all understanding, will guard your hearts and your minds in Christ Jesus" (NIV).

As I thought about that verse, "Don't be anxious for anything," I did all that I could to find some loophole around it. But I realized that this one passage has been an anchor for me over the years. I take comfort in remembering that God said those words. I guess He really does mean that I'm not supposed to worry.

Fighting off Fears with Prayer

Mark called us two nights ago. A guy in his cellblock had been severely beaten. Another inmate had beaten and beaten him. Mark said after the attack, the young man had gone into the shower. When he came back out, the guy who had beat him up said, "I'm not finished," and he beat him some more.

They had to take him out of the cellblock and put him into isolation for his own protection. Mark is probably the smallest guy in the cellblock. Fear and a lot of other emotions came over me. And I'm thinking, "God, You've protected him this long. Please, I beg You to continue to protect him."

Part of me wants to admit that any physical harm that comes to him in jail would simply be the consequences of my son's actions. But the legitimate consequences do not take away the concern and compassion that I have for my own flesh and blood.

Shaky Optimism; Unshakable Faith

What does the future hold? I don't have a clue. Mark sometimes calls from jail and says he has been thinking of us. He says to his mother, "Mom, I want you to know you've got your son back." I am both skeptical and hopeful about his recovery.

I may not know what the future holds, but I do know that God holds the future. I know that's a cliché, but it is true. God is doing something. I thank Him for what He is doing in my life and in the lives of my wife and children. I confidently hold the hope that when we've made it through the pain, we will be able to look back and see His hand at work for our good and His glory.

SECTION 2

Persevering When Your Child is Addicted

Living a "normal" life when one of your kids is abusing drugs and/or alcohol is difficult. The whole ordeal sucks energy from your personal life, your marriage and your relationships with your other kids. The child engaged in substance abuse can quickly become the focus of the entire family.

After we realize that our kids are abusing drugs and/or alcohol, it's difficult to regain our balance. The ordeal can genuinely test our faith and all that we have believed and practiced for years. In the next two chapters, two couples share with honesty and in great detail the stories of how they managed to keep their faith during the troubled times sparked by their children's drug abuse.

Chapter 4

Sudden Impact: Keeping Faith When Things Go Wrong

By Bill and Margaret Hansell

I have at my home a piece of metal that almost took from me the most important, precious, and valuable person in my life. The concave steel bar only weighs a couple of pounds. A hole is drilled in the middle. The dimensions are approximately 2" wide, by 13" long, and 1/4" thick. I believe it is a leaf from a truck or trailer spring.

On June 15, 2001, my wife, Margaret, was driving our Ford Taurus westbound on Interstate 84, traveling at the rate of at least 65-mph. About 40 miles east of Portland, the hunk of metal came crashing through the windshield. Margaret says it seemed to have just come out of the sky. We have no idea where it really came from, but it hit the car hood with such force that it gouged an opening in the upper part of the hood. The car's hood looked as if a big can opener had been used on it. The bar crashed through the windshield, creating a blizzard of glass shards and slamming into my wife's upper chest. Its end pushed against her seat belt, the only protection she had.

If that chunk of metal had hit her an inch or so higher, she would have been killed, or at the very least, incapacitated. Either scenario would have resulted in a serious car wreck. Who knows how many other lives might have been lost had that happened!

Miraculously, Margaret ended up with only a bruise--and enough of the windshield left intact for her to manage to limp the car into town. Obviously, we are very thankful that God spared her life.

As we travel the highway of life, many events come crashing through our windshields in much the same way as this metal slammed into our car.

1. They certainly are not planned.
2. They can cause a lot of pain and damage.
3. Often we do not know why or where they originated.
4. We do not know why they happen to us.

For example, on Saint Patrick's Day in March 2000, something came crashing through "my windshield," as Margaret and I sat in a doctor's office.

"Cancer cells have been found in your prostate" were the urologist's words to me. Like Margaret in the car, I had no choice but to deal with this event of dramatic proportions.

And in the spring and early summer of 1992, another ugly item came hurling into our lives. The object that made the impact was called by various names, including substance abuse, addiction, alcoholism, and drugs. But the individual whom it hit the hardest had one name: Bill.

A Family of Faith

Let me digress here for a moment to tell you a bit about my background. I was raised on a farm north of the little town of Athena, Oregon, about 220 miles east of Portland.

Margaret, who is from Portland, and I met at the University of Oregon. We both became Christians through the ministry of Campus Crusade for Christ, and were active in this ministry on campus. We were married during spring break of our senior year. After graduating from the University of Oregon in the spring of 1967, we joined the staff of Campus Crusade for Christ. We were on staff for the next 12 years, at Berkeley, Sacramento, and the last five years in Sydney, Australia, where I served as the national Campus Director. Besides our son Bill, we have five daughters. One is married, and she and her husband have given us our two grandchildren.

We returned from Australia in 1979 and moved to the Athena area to raise our six children in a rural environment and to be near my side of their extended family. I worked on the family farm through 1982. That year I ran for County Commissioner, was elected, and took office in 1983. Presently I am in my 19th year, the third year of my fifth term.

Shocking News

Alcohol has never been a part of our lives. Margaret and I have never had any alcohol in our home—no beer, no wine, no liquor of any form. So when we learned that our son had a drinking problem, we were shocked and surprised. The concept was totally foreign to what we had done and taught in our home.

We learned of Bill's use of alcohol while he was a 21-year-old student at Willamette University in Salem, Oregon. In the fall of 1992, he went through a month-long treatment program, where he was diagnosed as an alcoholic/addict. That means he has multiple addictions or at least addictive behavior. He remained clean for about nine months and then began using again for the next eight years.

Solace in the Shepherd's Psalm

One of the questions I asked after we learned of his problem was, "Lord, how did we get here? What happened? We were driving along seeking to serve and glorify You in all we do, and this came suddenly crashing through the windshield, changing our lives dramatically."

Being a farm boy, the 23rd Psalm—The Shepherd's Psalm--has been of great help to me.

The fourth verse of that Psalm is very helpful:

"Even though I walk through the valley of the shadow of death, I will fear no evil, for You are with me" (NIV).

Three aspects of this verse ministered to me as we were in the "Valley of the Shadow of Drugs":

1. **The words "walk" and "through" have important meaning.** We travel through the valley. It is not a box canyon. We do not go there to stay. We are passing through to greener pastures, and God has a plan for us. Sometimes traveling takes longer than other times, but we are always moving through the valley.

2. **Fear doesn't need to control.** "I will fear no evil." There is a fear of what sin can and will do to a person, especially the sin of substance abuse. People die from it every day. I do not know of anyone who wants his or her child to die such a death. That fear is real. But at the same time we do not need to live in fear. We can fear no evil, because the Lord is with us.

3. **I am not alone.** Just like the name of the ministry, "You're Not Alone," I am not alone in the valley. The promise is "You are with me." The Lord is in the valley with me. He never abandons or leaves me to face the issues by myself.

Seeking Answers

I had two important questions I needed to answer as I was in this valley.

1. Is there a reason I am in this valley?

My answer before, which remains the same today, is "yes." I did not choose to be in this valley; in fact, someone else's poor choices caused my family and me to be in the valley. But God is still sovereign, and He loves me. This is not the only valley I have ever been through, nor will it be the last. I am being refined and that sometimes is a painful process. But it is His way to lead me to greener pastures, to make it to higher ground in my walk of faith.

I can also say that when the Lord has taken me through those valleys of life, I am a better person with a stronger faith. These have been tremendous times of growth, maturity, and learning to trust. I wish I had never entered this valley, but I am trusting God while I am in it. I look forward to the time when I will exit it! But the real issue, I believe, is how should I travel through this valley? Will I trust in my Shepherd?

2. How do I relate to my son?

I have always desired to maintain a relationship of love with Bill. I believe I have been successful. I have tried to be honest with him in love. And I have realized the person he has become was not the person God intended him to be. I did not accept his choices, though I knew he had the right to make them. Bill is a free moral agent, and I cannot make his decisions for him. But you know what? I would not make them for him, even if I could. Bill, not me, needs to make them.

Two years ago, when I was speaking at a conference in Phoenix, I concluded my remarks with a new concept I had just learned and was putting into practice. It had to do with prayer for our prodigal son. For many years my prayer had been, "Lord, whatever it takes." I prayed this because I did not know what it was that would get Bill's attention. Whatever it would be, I wanted the Lord to do it.

Then some dear Christian friends whose youngest son had been deep in addiction, but who was now clean and sober and serving the Lord, shared with me what they had done. They had begun to take their son to the Lord in prayer for healing.

The Gospels record several instances of parents asking Jesus to heal their children:

- Matthew 15: 21-28
- Matthew 9:18-26
- Matthew 17:14-19
- Mark 8:24-30
- Luke 9:40-56
- John 4:46-54

In some events, the child was too sick to come, and the parent brought Jesus to the child. But in every case, the child had a serious problem and needed healing, and it was the parent who saw the need and took the initiative to seek healing from Jesus. We never read of children ever asking their parents to take them to Jesus. In each case, the child was healed. It seems it was really the faith of the parents, and not of the children, which caused Christ to heal.

So I began in the spring of 1999 to take my son to the Lord each day in prayer for healing—spiritually, physically, mentally, and in every other way. As I concluded the talk I presented at the conference about this topic, I prayed, "And I believe some day our son Bill, his mother, and I will pass through this valley together."

I was finished. There was nothing else to share. We were in the valley, trusting the Lord.

The Prodigal Returns

Our granddaughter, Rachel, was born to our daughter, Susanna, and her husband, Paul, on September 1, 2001. Margaret flew down to Sacramento to be with Susanna at the baby's birth. I drove down later to meet the little one and then bring Grandma home.

When we returned home, having driven most of the day and night and arriving at 3 a.m., our answering machine had recorded a series of messages from our son. He said he wanted to talk with me. On the last message, he left a phone number where we could reach him.

As far as we knew, Bill was in Sun Valley, Idaho, still feeding his habits and working to be able to afford them. He had been there off and on for a couple of years.

When I called him a few hours later, I discovered he was staying at a Motel 6 in Twin Falls, Idaho. In a halting voice, he said he had recommitted his life to the Lord, and wanted to know where he might go to get some spiritual grounding. My first question to him was, "Are you in any kind of trouble?" (I was wary of the "foxhole conversion" syndrome that involves turning to Christ in a time of trouble, then forgetting about the Lord when the trouble subsides.) He assured me he was not.

Because I needed to leave for work, I did not have much time to talk, and I suggested he come on home. He was reluctant until I reminded him that when the prodigal son had decided to make some changes, he had gone home. Bill said he would be home in the late afternoon. I told him we would "kill the fatted calf." That is, Mom would serve roast beef, one of his favorite dinners.

As I drove to work, I started to feel a cautious hope. "I have been praying for this kid's healing every day for nearly 15 months," I thought. Yet I wasn't confident enough to shout from the rooftops. Bill had experienced a couple of spiritual renewals in the past, but his addiction had always pulled him back.

On my 18-mile drive home from work, for some reason my thoughts turned to my son's long hair. It was not a major issue, but Bill wore long hair, which I thought was pretty ratty. It was his way of identifying with his lifestyle. What, if anything, would he do with his hair? I knew I would not make it an issue, but still I wondered.

When I arrived home, as Bill came up the basement stairs, I saw that his long hair was gone. He had found a hairdresser in Boise on his way home and had his locks shorn. He looked great to his old-fashioned Dad.

A Convicted Heart

After dinner, we sat down and asked Bill what had happened. He related that over the last week, he had grown more repulsed with what he was doing, and with what he was becoming. He knew he had to get out of Sun Valley. He had loaded his meager belongings in his car and had driven to Twin Falls. While there in this restless state, he had tried to figure out just what it was he wanted to be. What kept coming to his mind was to be a godly man, and he knew he was not. Not even close.

He had watched a movie on TV that had some real family values, and it had touched his heart. He knew that was what he wanted.

Bill then said, "Dad, I know you are not supposed to do this, but I went to the nightstand and pulled out the Gideon Bible and randomly opened it. I turned to Exodus 30."

Compelling Scripture

As he started to read it, he realized it had to do with the tabernacle and priestly duties. These were not everyday devotional Scripture readings. So he had decided to read something else. But then Bill said, "No, I am 30 years old, and I am going to read the 30th chapter."

What the Holy Spirit did in the next few minutes in that motel room probably violates most of what is taught in seminary classes about how to study the Bible. Through reading Exodus 30, Bill became convicted of his life choices, and he took action.

One of the commands in this chapter to the priests was the prohibition of burning false incense. Bill remembered reading in a "druggie" publication about someone's assertion that the priests really had been burning marijuana, which caused them to hallucinate, see visions, and hear voices. "No false incense." Bill said this was how God had spoken to him about his drug usage.

Exodus 30 also gives instructions regarding the libations, or drink offerings. Somehow the Holy Spirit used these passages to convict Bill about his drinking.

The chapter also mentioned the smoke from the altar; our son felt God was using those words to talk to him about his smoking.

Once he finishing reading Exodus 30, Bill got up, flushed his drugs down the toilet, poured out his booze, crumpled up his cigarettes, and threw them in the trashcan. He had then recommitted his life to the Lord and started trying to reach me by phone.

A Convincing Conversion

My one question to Bill after he shared this with us was how this experience differed from some of the other spiritual renewals he had previously had. His reply was concise and clear. "I have never been repulsed by what I was doing before." I believe that true repentance took place when Bill turned from his sin to his Lord.

"We Have Our Son Back!"

Life for Bill is still one day at a time, and he has had to deal with some issues, such as the desire every so often to take a drink. But he is walking with the Lord and living in a Christian community in Eugene, Oregon. He attends the University of Oregon and works with troubled youth—a job he has stayed with longer than any other job he has had in the past 10 years.

As Margaret stated after a recent conversation with Bill, "We have our son back!" We lived in the "Valley of the Shadow of Drugs" for around a decade. At this point we have exited the valley because of some of the choices our son has made.

As I conclude, I want to talk about some of the elements of my coping strategy while I was in this valley.

- I prayed. Our Shepherd desires for us to come to Him in prayer. I took my loved one to the Lord for healing. I put aside any personal agendas such as: "Lord, you do this in this way at this time" and "Lord, make this happen or cause this to take place." Rather, we parents presented our child to God for healing. He was sick and needed the touch of the Great Physician. Taking our son to the Lord in prayer for healing every day for 15 months was the best investment in his life, I believe, I could have ever made.

- I nurtured and protected important relationships. I worked at maintaining a healthy father/son relationship. I kept the lines of communication open. God gave our children to us and us to them. I am not talking about enabling or condoning or encouraging their behavior. I am saying we must love them and care for them. We need to be careful not to drive them away. That way, when they need someone to turn to for help, they will know where to go. This certainly was true in our son's case.

  In addition, I did not forget my relationship with Margaret. We worked to maintain our marriage and grow in it. Under no circumstances did we allow Bill's bad choices to divide our relationship. We remembered our commitment to each other—"for better or for worse."

  One last relationship we focused on was our other children. Our son had five younger sisters, in whose lives we continued to invest, to love, and to provide. Sometimes, during the tough times, they needed us even more than Bill did.

- I refused to let fear rule our lives. If we live in fear, it will absolutely take over our lives. In the valley, which is a scary place, we need to trust and walk with the Lord. The Shepherd's Psalm states, "I will fear no evil." Why? "For You are with me." I am the first to admit this is easier said than done at times. But we have to cast all our fears upon Christ. If we don't, we will find it very difficult to cope in that valley.

- I kept moving. We walk through the valley. We need to keep living our lives. We cannot let these bad situations rob us of the joy of living.

- I trusted God. I knew that my Savior was with me in this valley. He had promised me that, and I believed Him. His heart broke for our son even more than ours did. I did not understand why the piece of metal in the form of substance abuse had come crashing through the windshield of our lives, but I was willing to trust Him.

- I tried not to blame others for our problems. After the bar came through the my wife's car window, I never asked God, "Why? Why our car? Why my wife?" In the same way, during Bill's situation, I learned not to spend very much time trying to find the answer to most questions that begin with "why" or "what." "Why me, Lord?" "Why did it happen to us?" "What did we do wrong?" "What should we have done differently?" Bill was always very forthright with us. He told us he chose to do what he did. He was responsible for his actions and choices.

God is still in control, even when addiction comes crashing into our lives. Because I did not play the blame game, I had real peace and could focus on the Lord.

Margaret's Story

Unlike my husband, I did ask "Why?" I asked "Why?" because I had watched our son grow up. He had been a charming, precocious little towhead. All through grade school and high school, he had excelled in everything, it seemed, that he had chosen to do. He could have done with his life anything he wanted. Yet, for some reason he chose to get involved with using substances that brought disharmony to his life and to our lives, too. So, I did ask those questions of "Why?" "Why would he do that?" and "Why, Lord, after the years that we gave to You, why would You allow it?"

Letting Go of the Wheel

One evening I took a walk out in the country and lamented to God, asking Him those questions. He revealed to me that my distress wasn't about trying to find out why Bill had chosen to use drugs, but it was because I had no control over what was happening.

God urged me to trust Him, to have faith in Him, and to believe that He could bring something good out of the situation. "Let go" is basically what He was telling me. I learned that there was not anything that I could do.

I guess being a mother with six children had turned me into quite a controller. In order to get anything done during our day-to-day lives, I had to maintain control over every decision, every activity. So, I wanted to control our son's life, too.

The message came so clearly: Was I willing to trust God in this situation? Did I really believe God was in control and could bring something good out of it? That night, He began to give me the faith to trust Him for that. I did continue to try at different times to grab hold of the wheel, and then I would have to learn to let it go again.

From Fear to Faith

Part of what made it difficult for me to let go of control was fear, because my brother had died of a drug overdose. As our son began to mature, I had started seeing in him characteristics similar to those of my brother. Although they had hardly known one another, my brother had been very charming, personable, persuasive and, at times irrational, traits I watched develop in Bill as he grew up. If we believe that what is going on in our child's life is far worse than what is really happening, we react to that fear rather than to reality. That's what I was doing.

God is still in control, even when addiction comes crashing into our lives.

Thankfully, God took away some of that from my life. He began to give me the confidence to trust Him and believe He would bring something good out of Bill's life. So, it was so exciting to me to hear Bill come to us that evening, eat dinner with us, and map out what he believed to be God's direction for his life. As he spoke with us, Bill listed a number of things that he felt God wanted him to do. He thought God wanted him to be in a place where he could be discipled, where he could continue his education, and where he could also support himself. He shared many desires and plans based on what God had revealed to him, and over time we have watched those things come about. As Billy has had the desire to carry out those plans step by step, it has been exciting to see God's faithfulness to all of us.

We get excited about those steps Bill has taken because many times he was not able to take any. He would get a job and then leave it. He didn't have the motivation to "hang in there."

As a mother, there are certain things I think he should be doing. Yet, God has shown me that these are not my issues. I have to give God the freedom work in Bill's life and make sure I don't get in His way. This is not an easy lesson to learn; I am sure it is one I will have to learn over and over, even in the rest of my children's lives.

A Father's Wisdom

I believe God gave my husband real wisdom. For example, when we first found out that Billy had a drug problem, he decided to use our extensive mailing list from our missionary days with Campus Crusade for Christ to share what had happened with our son. At the time, I didn't think this was a good idea, but people call us even today because they remember that letter. As their children have faced the same types of problems, they have felt free to call us and talk to us. God has used that as an open door for us to be able to minister to many different people.

Honesty and openness were traits that God has been able to use. We need to be open to how God wants to use each of our lives, because each one of us is unique. Even in our son's life, we can begin to see how God is taking what has happened in his life and is giving him a desire to work with autistic children. He really believes he can understand them because of his drug addiction past and what his drug abuse did in his mind. So, I guess we can have hopeful hearts in spite of what all of us are going through. God does not waste any opportunity. He wants our faith and trust. I have found contentment in wanting, seeking and submitting to God's will more than my own.

Chapter 5

One Day at a Time

By John and Susan Vawter

In the world of addiction, we often hear the phrase, "One day at a time," for the addict to stay clean and sober. We tend to think this applies only to the addict, but it applies to those who are parents of the addict, too.

Why is it so hard to live one day at a time? The pain and fear that we've lived with in regard to our daughter, Stephanie, and our son, Michael, are probably the worst we've ever experienced. We are going to share some of the reasons for that pain and fear and describe some ways we have each learned to face our situation one day at a time.

Susan's Journey

Both of our children received Christ when they were around five or six years old. Those years of mothering young children were delightful. We didn't see the first signs of rebellion in our daughter until she entered early adolescence. The rebellion marked the beginning of some very tough times and, of course, it opened the door to the more serious problem of drug use.

A Mother's Fears and Feelings

Both of our children walked away from their relationships with Christ in their teen years. Their rebellion, their denial of their faith, and their use of drugs hurt me deeply because, to me, they signaled our kids' refusal of all that we had tried to teach them about their actions and their faith. Of course, I couldn't help but take that rejection personally to some degree, so that caused part of my pain.

We feared for our children's eternal salvation, that they might never come back to Christ and walk with Him. To intensify our worries, we realized that the teen years and early 20's are the years when young people normally make decisions about education, career, and marriage—decisions that chart the course for the rest of their lives. I was afraid they might make bad decisions, ones that would have lifelong implications.

I felt great sadness as I looked at both of our children and tried to imagine what they must have been going through. I sensed that they were experiencing a complete lack of peace in their lives. As children, they must have been touched or felt touched by God's love and grace. Now they obviously were at a point where they no longer felt that love and grace. Recognizing this brought me such compassion for them as they experienced this separation from God.

Important Lessons

So then, how have I coped with these sorts of fears, hurt, and pain? How do I live one day at a time, learn to put this pain and worry and fear in God's hands, and live victoriously?

1. **I have learned to face the reality that the decisions my children make are their choices, not mine.** God gives all of us a free will. In Ruth Bell Graham's book, *The Prodigals and Those Who Love Them*, she relates an episode when a guest at their table, a pastor, was sharing about his own son and his son's rebellion:

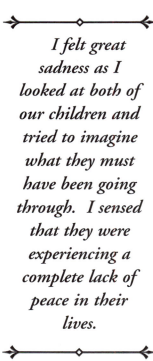

I felt great sadness as I looked at both of our children and tried to imagine what they must have been going through. I sensed that they were experiencing a complete lack of peace in their lives.

"Dad, I'm not at all sure I can follow you any longer in your simple Christian faith," stated the clergyman's son when he returned from the university for holidays with a fledgling scholar's assured arrogance.

The father's black eyes skewered his son, who was lost, as C. S. Lewis put it, "in the invincible ignorance of his intellect." "Son," the father said, "That is your freedom, your terrible freedom." [1]

The decisions my children make are not ones I would make, but I can't force them to change their minds. Only God can affect what is happening in their lives and affect their decisions.

2. **I have relied on comfort from Scripture.** Scripture has given me hope and helped me get through many tough days. I often put passages of Scripture that have been very meaningful to me on cards. I take the cards with me and meditate on the verses when I take walks in the morning to look at my day and talk things over with the Lord. Here are a few passages that have been especially helpful:

1. Ruth Bell Graham, Prodigals and Those Who Love Them (Colorado Springs, CO: Focus on the Family, 1991) p. XVII.

- **Luke 15:** The parable of the prodigal son. As you may remember, the prodigal son takes money his father gives him, goes off to a far country, squanders it all, "hits bottom," and recognizes that his lifestyle just will not work. He heads back home to try to throw himself on his father's mercy, but as he nears home, we learn that the father has been watching and waiting for his son. When the father sees his son approaching from afar, he runs to him, embraces him, and with forgiveness and compassion brings him back into the home and the family. This passage always gave me hope about the terrible choices our kids were making.

- **Psalm 103:11-13:** "For as high as the heavens are above the earth, so great is his loving kindness to those who fear him. As far as the east is from the west, so far has he removed our transgressions from us. As a father has compassion on his children, so the Lord has compassion on those who fear him" (NIV). This Scripture gives me great comfort by pointing out that in God's compassion, He reaches out in forgiveness and acceptance not only to me, but also to my son and daughter. One example of God's compassion in our lives is when He reached out to our daughter in the midst of the time she was using drugs. She told us during her time of recovery that often before she was about to shoot up, she would think of her two late grandparents, John's dad, Harry, and my mom, whom she called Nana. Stephanie said she would think, "I wonder if Nana and Grandpa Harry are sad in heaven as they see me doing this?" God was making Himself known to her in reaching out to her and reminding her of the love that she had known.

- **Jeremiah 29:11:** "For I know the plans that I have for you, declares the Lord, plans to prosper you and not to harm you, plans to give you hope and a future" (NIV). Hopelessness is a great deterrent to the practice of living one day at a time. But this verse reminds me that there is hope. When our son told us that he had been smoking pot for a year, we came home very depressed, sad, and shocked at the news. We called Dr. Terry Zuehlke, a friend and a counselor who knows our son and us well. As we were relating these circumstances, I shared with him my hopelessness and fear. Terry said, "You know, Susan, if you look at these circumstances, you are going to be hopeless. But if you can focus on God, then you can see that there is hope." And so this passage reminds me that I can focus on Him; that is where my hope comes from.

- **Proverbs 21:1:** "The king's heart is in the hand of the Lord; he directs it like a watercourse wherever he pleases" (NIV). I loved Ruth Bell Graham's explanation of this verse in *The Prodigals and Those Who Love Them*. She says, "And how does God deal with the stubborn will, especially when that will is the object of loving concern, even desperate prayer? I found encouragement in Matthew Henry's commentary on Proverbs 21:1. Henry writes: 'God can change men's minds, can turn them from that which they seem intent upon, as the husbandman by canals and gutters turns the water through his grounds which does not alter the nature of the water nor put any force upon it any more than God's providence does upon the native freedom of man's will but directs the coarse of it to serve his own purpose'" (Graham, p. 135). These words were such an encouragement to me because I know God won't violate our will; yet I know He can use the circumstances of life to draw my children to Himself. He can bring them to the bottom of whatever issues they are dealing with and then, hopefully, they will to turn to Him.

3. **I have drawn support and strength from others.** We cannot go it alone, knowing we have others to share with and help us along the way. I've been so privileged to have my husband, John, to walk through this time with, to share with, and to depend on, even though we have not always agreed. Also helpful have been trusted friends and groups such as Nar-Anon, as well as the members of my neighborhood Bible study group. I knew I could relate my feelings with this group of women who have prayed with me and for me for about six years.

4. **I have understood that God is a God of love, forgiveness, and strength, and He does have a plan.** He will bring His glory out of these things. Part of his plan for bringing me through this experience, I believe, has been to provide me with more compassion and understanding. I'm not as quick to give advice to other people anymore; rather, I want to hear what they are going through and come alongside to offer my empathy and support.

As you can probably see from the thoughts I've shared, getting to the point at which I can live one day at a time didn't have to do with specific strategies for coping with drug addiction or recovery. Rather, I reached that milestone by learning more and more about God's love, compassion, forgiveness and strength. Those aspects of His character—and the realization that He not only loves me but He reaches out with love to my addicted children as well--have given me the ability to trust Him and to get through each day. One day at a time.

John's Story

"Everything that does not come from faith is sin" (Romans 14:23, NIV).

"Without faith it is impossible to please God" (Hebrews 11:6, NIV).

The Bible instructs us to live lives of faith. But when our children abuse or become addicted to drugs or alcohol and are ruining their lives, it is difficult to live by faith. It can be difficult to trust God. Fear can consume us. Concern for our children can cripple us. Life can look bleak; the future can look bleak. The future, indeed, may be bleak. It may not turn out well. We parents can feel hypocritical at worst or at least inconsistent, because of our weakened faith.

Ruth Bell Graham's book, *The Prodigals and Those Who Love Them,* deals with historic prodigals who through history turned from God and yet were brought back to Him. However, in the book, Mrs. Graham also intersperses those historical accounts with her own writings, poems, prayers, passages of Scripture, and writings of other people that were meaningful to her. She knows what she's talking about because she and Billy Graham had two sons who were prodigals who are now walking with Christ and serving God. In one excerpt from her book called, "What Makes the Trials Easier?" she makes four brief points:

- It helps when I know who is in control and God is in control.
- It helps when I know He is sovereign.
- It helps when I know I'm not alone in my suffering.
- And Thankfully, God walks with us through this hard time.

We have been taught that "the joy of the Lord is my strength" (Nehemiah 8:10) and we believe that Jesus was telling the truth when He said that the peace He gives is better than the peace the world gives (John 14:27). Yet, with drugs and alcohol in our families, we may not be experiencing that peace. We may be thinking the relationship with God is not all that it was cracked up to be.

So, when pain and fear sidetrack us, how do we get back on the road of trusting God for the future of our children? This is a fundamental question in our recovery and maturity as parents of addicts who abuse drugs or alcohol. I certainly want to be candid in stating that I have not arrived in this area. But, I can explain the journey that I have been on since July 7, 1997, my 30th anniversary of being married to my wife, Susan, and my first Sunday as pastor of Bethany Community Church in Tempe, Arizona, when we discovered our daughter Stephanie was addicted to heroin.

Drug Abuse: A Family Stressor

Pat Boris, a pediatric nurse practitioner who has researched stress in parents of substance abusing adolescents, pointed out in her masters' thesis that more stress is in the home of families with children who abuse drugs or alcohol than there is in homes where none of the children do so. (See Pat Boris' chapter in this book, page 181). In the former, Boris says, "extreme turbulence" often is present. She says irritability, secrecy, lying, skipping school, poor grades and arrest may accompany such substance

No Quick Fixes

I get a fair number of calls and emails from parents whose kids are abusing drugs. I see the same reaction in them that I had. They want the "Jesus pill" to make this all go away quickly. I hear their frustration when I tell them it can be a long process and they have to take it one day at a time. If we are honest, we recognize that faith does not come naturally. The flesh wars against the Spirit. Godly life and responses do not come naturally. So, why would faith and living one day at a time come naturally? Maybe that is why Jesus told us to have no concern for tomorrow.

abuse. This behavior debilitates family relationships.

Sometimes, just as in the life of Job, our critics and friends alike "encourage" us by judging us and assuming the drug issue in our families is a direct result of bad parenting on our part. All of this stress requires adjustment in our families. Boris says these adjustments are difficult to make "when the equilibrium is tipped and a crisis results." I know from personal experience that when the equilibrium is tipped, it is hard to make sense out of today and trust God for today; it is even harder to trust Him for tomorrow.

Boris says resilience and positive behavior allow the parents to recover and maintain the integrity of the family. This requires flexibility, because parenting an addictive or abusive child is far more stressful than parenting a non-addictive child. This is all very confusing, time consuming, energy draining and frightening. In the midst of all this turmoil, we are to live one day at a time and live by faith. Thanks a lot, God!

It's Not That Easy

Having faith and living one day at a time have been difficult for me. I am an A-type personality. I love to fix situations. I am a good controller. My kids using drugs was the one thing I could not control. I feared for the future of my kids--and I still do.

The "one day at a time" principle both bothers me and helps me. It bothers me because it forces me to realize I am doing something wrong. I am focusing on the problem. I am losing my way. I am getting emotional. On the other hand and in a more productive light, the "one day at a time" principle forces me to rethink where God is in all of my pain over my children's use of drugs and where He is relative to working in their lives.

In some of our darkest days when Stephanie was an adolescent, I was encouraged with Paul's words in Colossians, "Christ in you, the hope of glory" (Colossians 1:27, NIV). I realized that my only hope for heaven is my faith in what God says in the Bible. It then dawned on me that I could work backwards from that eternal truth. "Christ in you, the hope of glory" to "Christ in you, the hope for today" to "Christ in you, the hope for Stephanie." This helped me begin to take my focus off my pain and put it back where it belongs, on Christ, Who is our hope.

However, I am afraid that as a minister and teacher of God's Word, I sometimes make things too simple. My sermons and my teachings sometimes make it sound as though living by faith is as easy as swallowing a "Jesus pill." I forget that Paul says in Philippians 2:12, "Work out your salvation with fear and trembling." Faith is to be nurtured, and it grows over time.

Focusing Through the Lens of Honesty

I have found that for my ability to trust God to grow, I have to be honest. I have to be honest to say, "God, I am scared today. God, I am angry today. God, this is not a good day." That honesty, when I can achieve it, allows me to focus on four things:

- The situation
- My fear
- God
- His ability to work

Such honesty means there can be no Christian platitudes or "Christianese." It has to be downright candor.

This honesty allows me to ask God to work today in my children's lives. This honesty allows me to acknowledge that there is nothing I can do today to help my children except to turn them over to the care and love of God, Who loves them more than I do.

I also find that when I can and do give God my fears today, the future does not look so bleak because I am focusing on today and what God can do today. The future and my fears for it do not seem to be so big because I am allowing God to minister to me today. Moreover, instead of being held captive by my fear for tomorrow, I am asking God to work today. And, when I see Him working today I can thank Him for the good, step-by-step benefits and improvements I see.

Four-Point Attack

In her research, Pat Boris tells us that our kids' abuse or addiction can attack or affect us in four areas: physically, emotionally, socially and spiritually. I have found that identifying those can help me as a parent. Stephanie was in Mexico when Susan and I first learned she was on heroin. My first reaction, after catching my breath, was fear, absolute fear. "Terror" might be an even better word. We were fortunate because she returned to her Denver home and was in detox and then in treatment within 30 hours of our getting the news. But, a year later, almost to the day, our son told us he was smoking marijuana. Again, that emotion of fear arose and persisted because he did not think he needed help.

Of the four areas Boris names--physical, emotional, social and spiritual--I was and am affected by three. **Emotionally**, I went into my new ministry as the pastor of a church with 2000 in attendance with a low-grade fear always about me. It never left. **Socially**, I withdrew. I did not want to talk about drugs in my family. I did not mind talking openly with close friends, but I did not care to talk to others. I was always on guard against the person who would pry, want details, assume I was a bad parent or want to give advice. **Spiritually**, I just felt as though I was running on half my cylinders. Fear was a stronger motivation than my faith.

Godly Counsel of Friends

In the providence of God, He brought a veteran of detachment and living one day at a time into my life. I had formed a prayer team of three men at the church who prayed for me every week. One hammered me, and I mean hammered me, with the fact that I was not responding but reacting to the drug situation in my family. He forced me to see that drugs had become the center of my life. That sounds strange, because I am not the drug addict. We usually perceive the addicts as the ones who have drugs at the center of their lives. My friend helped me see that I was not trusting God. I had become drug-focused rather than God-focused. Circumstance-focused rather than God-focused. In fact, I was not helping the situation; I was probably hurting it.

My friend helped me realize that I needed to let my kids accept responsibility for their actions. I needed to let Michael stumble and tumble, if need be. I needed to allow God to work in his and Stephanie's lives and I needed to let God work in my

Fear was a stronger motivation than my faith.

life. My friend was honest, however. In the midst of his no-nonsense approach, he told me things that I knew and had taught others, but that I did not know how to apply to the painful issues surrounding drug abuse.

For example, he reminded me that faith and trust in God are step-by-step developments. How am I doing today? What can I do today to help my kids? What should I ask God to do today? Slowly the blinders on my eyes began to come off. What my friend saw so clearly, I began to see with ever-sharpening focus.

I now see more clearly much of the time. I am learning to be honest today about where my kids are and where I am emotionally, socially and spiritually. Is there anything I can do today to help them? Is there anything I can do today to turn the situation over to God and ask Him to work in my kids' lives? I am learning to ask these questions daily.

A Healthy Principle

Living one day at a time really is the equivalent of recognizing temptation. Paul tells us to flee temptation. But to know what temptation is, I need to know God's standard for what is right. For example, His standard is to trust Him, and not worry.

Learning the "one day at a time" principle has not been easy for me. It has taken lots of work and honesty. When our children's drug use hit our family, I tended to look at the next 30 years and assume the worst. What if Stephanie relapsed? What if her drug dealer called her? What if our son did not quit smoking marijuana? What if his wife got tired of him? What if he could not get a job? The "what ifs" are similar to looking at the Grand Canyon. You cannot jump across. But you can start down one step at a time, get to the bottom, rest and then start up the other side one step at a time. Additionally, all the way you have to be drinking water and hydrating yourself or there will be internal effects you do not even recognize until you are dehydrated, exhausted and unable to go on.

To follow the analogy, I first thought I could jump over the canyon and do my kids' work for them. When I realized I could not, I started the step-by-step, day-by-day process of learning to live one day at a time. One day at a time is necessary because our kids' addiction may be short-term or long-term. Only God knows.

Milestones to Celebrate

I would never suggest that what has happened and is happening in our family is the norm. How God worked in our family may not be the way He will work with your

Day by Day

About a year or so after she left treatment, Stephanie told us about a man who said one night at an Alcoholics Anonymous meeting, "I am going to drink tomorrow."

I did not get his meaning. Stephanie explained, "He is tempted to drink today. He is not ignoring the temptation. He made a commitment this morning not to drink today. So, he is putting it off until tomorrow."

You probably understand it, but I did not.

So, I asked, "And, what will he do tomorrow?" She answered, "He will put it off again. He lives one day at a time. He does not ignore temptation. He keeps his daily commitments."

family. It may be coincidental. But, nevertheless, I am watching our daughter move farther and farther away from heroin. She celebrates 58 months of sobriety today and tells us she thinks less and less about heroin. Michael told us that he has not smoked marijuana since his son was born three years ago.

So, I am learning in brand new ways that God can work in my kids' lives without me and that He wants me to focus on Him, on His ability to work. He wants me to focus on Him today. He wants me to be honest with Him today. He wants me to remember that it is the Holy Spirit who works in my kids, conforming them to the image of Christ one step and one day at a time. It is not easy, but it is worth the journey. I am doing better today than I did yesterday and I hope to do better tomorrow than I am doing today.

SECTION 3

Keeping Your Marriage Healthy When Your Kids Aren't

As parents, we don't expect our kids to use and abuse drugs and alcohol. However, it does happen—to the best of families. Kids can be deceptive enough that some are actually hooked before we know they are using. Discovering our kids are abusing indeed hits our homes like a "ton of bricks." We lose our balance; we move like zombies.

The use of drugs and/or alcohol by our children tests even the strongest of marriages. There is no school we can attend whose entire mission involves preparing us for the day our kids start using drugs. Often our marriages suffer—many times because of our differing temperaments and individual reactions to the problem. In the following two chapters, two married couples discuss how their kids' use and abuse of drugs tore at the fabric of their marriages and how they struggled to maintain marital health in spite of the conflicts.

Chapter 6

Four Principles for a Strong Marriage

By Bill and Brenda Faulkner

Basic principles for success apply to every growing marriage. If we practice those principles, our marriages will remain strong whatever life struggles may come. Our marriages won't be perfect, but they will be sturdy enough to withstand the strong winds of adversity that will blow into our lives. If we aren't working at our marriage in the first place, then the winds more than likely will knock us over.

We would like to share four principles that we have learned about making our marriage work. We'll relate how those principles have specifically applied to some of the storms that blew into our lives, particularly when the "storm" of the news of our son Scott's drug abuse raged against our home.

Establishing a Covenant Relationship

First of all, we entered into a covenant relationship when we got married 39 years ago. This wasn't a contractual agreement or a social convenience. It was a covenant, or binding agreement, that we made to each other and to God. We are in it to the end. Our marriage vows went something like this, "I, Brenda/Bill take you Bill/Brenda, to be my lawful wedded husband/wife. I promise to honor you, to cherish you, to respect you, for better or worse, in sickness and health, for richer or poorer, 'til death do us part."

We have never used the word "divorce" as an option. We renewed our wedding vows 25 years into our marriage, and found what a deeper meaning those promises took on after being enriched by the time and experiences we have shared through the years. We had experienced better and worse, riches and poverty, sickness and health. We discovered that we really were committed to each other!

> *We have never used the word "divorce" as an option.*

So how has our covenant relationship carried us through the storms of our lives, especially when we began to deal with our son, Scott, who chose to use drugs and abuse his own life? It has simply meant that we are a team ("us," not "me"); the two of us have become one. In fact, even Scott recognized this. He wrote in a letter that he knew that we were "tight." He knew that he was not going to come between us. We are not each other's enemy. We do not attack each other. We do not blame each other. We work through things together, not individually. In the wedding ceremony that Bill performs, he says, "In marriage, joys are doubled, and sorrows are halved." That is true as we realize that we are totally committed to this relationship as one.

Nurturing a Deep, Intimate Love

We have a deep love for each other. It is a caring, intimate love, a love that cares about the other's welfare, a love that sacrifices when necessary, a love that forgives and does not hold grudges, a love that is patient and kind, a love that comes from our Heavenly Father. We didn't start out at that level. We had some emotional baggage when we began our marriage.

> "I was extremely jealous," says Brenda. "And Bill had a serious temper. I dealt with a need to control and Bill did not know how to deal with any conflict."

We were both very selfish young people. But we didn't have to stay in those places. We grew emotionally, physically, mentally and spiritually.

Our love is strong and active, not just mushy and passionate. We realize we must guard this love by not allowing anything to come in to hurt it. When we were faced with the news that Scott was abusing drugs, we had to realize that we were both hurting. Hurt people hurt people. To get through the circumstances without jeopardizing our love for one another, we focused on the reality of God's sufficiency and trusted His promise to work all things together for good to those who love Him and who are called according to His purposes (Romans 8:28). We have kept our relationship a priority in the midst of a circumstance that has had the potential to tear us apart. We have been careful not to become consumed by the problem and neglect ourselves. We have tried to keep fun in our lives and not feel guilty for enjoying life. Our child has made his own choices, and his choices haven't been ours.

> **We have tried to keep fun in our lives and not feel guilty for enjoying life.**

Keeping Open Lines of Communication

We have learned how to communicate on a deeper level than "Hi, how was your day?" We sit down face to face and talk about our days, listen to each other, enter the other's world and be genuinely interested in what the other is interested in. We have found out how to allow each other to express emotions and not to shut them down. Emotions are God-given. We all have emotional needs such as acceptance, encouragement, comfort, security, and respect. Being able to meet the emotional needs of another means that we must esteem others better than ourselves. To have our emotional needs validated is an incredible feeling, knowing that what we feel is valid, not stupid or insignificant.

As we have learned to share on an emotional level, it has opened up the deepest of relationships, one that is completely trusting and safe. When confronted with our son's drug abuse, we found our communication to be vital as never before. We realized that it is important to talk together about the situation and not to let feelings pile up. Some days, we may be overcome with sadness or fear or anger. But we allow each other the freedom to share his or her feelings without fear of being put down or having to hear 10 steps to correction.

> "Exhortation is my spiritual gift and I am quick to give those steps, even when they are not wanted," says Bill. "It was during these years of great stress that our communication with our Heavenly Father grew."

Philippians 4:6-7 says, "Be anxious for nothing, but in everything by prayer and supplication with thanksgiving let your requests be made known to God. And the peace of God which surpasses all comprehension, will guard your hearts and minds in Christ Jesus" (NASB).

We spent time intense in prayer, knowing that only through Him were we going to survive this. We prayed together, interceding on behalf of our son, asking for wisdom and direction, and asking for the peace and for energy to continue.

Celebrating Differences

We have learned through the years to celebrate our differences. Different is not wrong, it is just different!

> "Brenda and I are almost total opposites," says Bill. "I love the outdoors. Brenda loves indoors. I love sports. Brenda loves shopping. I love long country drives. Brenda loves being home. I do not need much space. Brenda needs lots of space."

Our differences have stretched us as people and made us better individuals. Realizing that we are very distinct in personalities, we understand that we respond to the difficult situation of having a child abuse drugs or alcohol in different ways.

Other couples may react differently, but it's important to recognize that both husband and wife are hurting, and both want the same outcome: the child's healing and wholeness.

> "I am a fixer," says Brenda. "I want to make everything better—now. I get frustrated when I can't control things. I was always thinking of what we might 'do' to bring this pain to an end. One might call it manipulation. But Bill is more patient and longsuffering. He has a great ability to watch and wait. One might call it faith. I wanted to call it passive, non-confrontational behavior."

Encouragement for Couples in Turmoil

- Admit your pain to others. Admit that you need others to help you through the struggles of life. Don't be in denial. People will really appreciate your transparency. They will feel comfortable to come to you with their own hurt and struggle.
- Don't isolate yourselves. People who love you will only want to be there to help and to pray for you.
- Educate yourself on the issues (drugs, manic depression, alcohol, etc.). Go to support groups and conferences. You will gain so much insight and understanding and be more equipped to deal with your situation. You will be encouraged as you share with others going through the same things.
- Focus on the goodness of God and not the badness of the situation. Satan wants to destroy your child, your marriage and your ministry. He wants you to feel unworthy and hopeless and to make your life ineffective. But He does not win! God will be faithful to lift your head, to empower you to persevere and to accomplish what concerns you! Remain steadfast and stand firm. You are an overcomer in this life!

Remain steadfast and stand firm. You are an overcomer in this life!

Chapter 7

Preserving Your Marriage when Times are Tough

By John and Susan Vawter

God uses many experiences to help prepare us for what lies ahead. In 1988, the son of a very good friend in the church I pastored in Minneapolis committed suicide. Later, his father, Reuel Nygaard, wrote the book *From Triumph to Tragedy*. Since then, Reuel has become a much sought-after speaker on the subject of suicide.

When Reuel asked me to read an early manuscript of the book, I noticed that Mary, his wife, was not mentioned one time. I asked Reuel about this and he answered, "Each of us grieves in our own way. Mary is not a public person and only speaks at Survivor of Suicide support group meetings. She affirms my being public about suicide, as long as I do not mention her."

Thus, when the devastating news of drugs hit our family, I was crushed. But, Susan and I learned from our friends Reuel and Mary that two parents who love each other have the right to grieve and deal with that grief in entirely different ways. Susan and I have tried (notice the words "have tried") to practice that principle. This also means that we have the right to find answers to our pain and grief in different ways.

—John Vawter

***

John's Turn

Alcoholism has been a part of my family for as long as I can remember. On my mother's side, I lost two uncles to alcohol. I remember as a little boy hearing one alcoholic uncle saying of another alcoholic uncle, "If we had given him beer we probably could have kept him alive." As a little boy, I did not understand the "d.t's" – the tremors alcoholics get when their bodies do not have the alcohol that they desperately need-- and the body's unquenchable craving for alcohol once addiction sets in, but I knew my uncle had them. On my father's side, I had an uncle who died as a "hopeless alcoholic". Because of these experiences and my parents' example of total abstinence from alcohol, it never held any allure for me. I simply was not interested, even in college where I lived in a fraternity where drinking was a huge part of that subculture.

As parents, Susan and I modeled total abstinence. We discussed the risks of using alcohol and drugs with both our children from the time they were little kids. We also prayed diligently that they would stay away from alcohol and drugs. I thought recounting the deaths of my uncles, the example Susan and I set as total abstainers, the anti-drug/alcohol training they received at school, plus our diligent prayers would be sufficient. Unfortunately, they were not.

Different Approaches

By nature and temperament, I am much more impatient and impetuous than Susan. The sermon title "Why Pray When You Can Worry?" seems to be my theme song. Susan is much more apt to pray and think positive thoughts than I am. So, we have been learning the lessons of encouraging each other to keep hope during the tough days.

For me, this means not judging Susan or assuming she does not care when her equilibrium on the future of our kids seems to be one of balance and mine is not. For Susan, this means accepting the fact that I will have more mood swings, and more ups and downs than she. I need to talk things through more than she does, and I will be slower in applying faith in God than she is.

Susan and I are the best of friends. We have worked hard at our marriage. We do not take each other for granted. However, we have found that drugs and addiction have tested our love as well as our ability to minister to and encourage each other. I am not happy about drugs in my family, but through the chaos created by their impact on our home, I have been thankful for the results of my relationship with God and Susan. Our circumstances have enabled me to understand her more clearly, to be more sensitive to her pain and her fears, and to hold onto her more tightly as we ask God to work in the lives of our daughter, son, daughter-in-law and grandchildren.

Growth in our relationship has meant that I must give Susan the freedom to get advice, wisdom and encouragement from others. I cannot feel threatened when she looks beyond me for those things.

Additionally, I have watched with clearer focus how Susan has manifested her faith in God, expressed her love for me and been patient to help me through my times of discouragement and despair over the issues of drugs in our family.

Susan's Turn

In Stephanie's early adolescence, she went through a time of rebellion and hostility, which really tested us. Her pain and anger were probably the seeds that led her to drug use later. The difficult time of that rebellion helped prepare us to go through the dark valley of addiction later.

Support From Others: Essential Ingredient

One thing we learned during the pain of Stephanie's turbulent adolescence was that we could not handle or solve this issue alone. John and I needed each other. We needed trusted friends and counselors to talk to and on whom we could lean. And, we needed the Lord.

Reaching Out to Friends

One Christmas, in those early days of adolescent conflict, we had just learned that Stephanie had been experimenting with marijuana with a friend in the church. We were devastated. I was going about preparing for Christmas without much joy. After delivering some packages to Toys for Tots, the attendant wished me a Merry Christmas with sincerity and thanks. This simple kindness broke me up. I could hardly drive for tears streaming down my face. I knew that I needed to talk to someone. I headed to the home of my trusted friend Sherry. Sherry was a friend from church and Stephanie's piano teacher. As we sat on her white love seat in her den, I poured out my fears and pain for our daughter. So many tears were shed that we lovingly refer to that sofa as the "soggy white couch." Having a few trusted friends like Sherry got me through many sad times during Stephanie's adolescent days.

Relying on Bible Study Groups, Professionals and Support Groups

My neighborhood Bible study was also a source of comfort and prayer support when we later found out about Stephanie's heroin addiction. Also, we have gotten very good counsel from a number of counselors and psychologists. There were times when we needed their expertise to get through certain phases of our troubles.

Another source of support during the early days of Stephanie's recovery was going to Nar-Anon meetings. That first Saturday at 11 a.m., John and I walked into a room full of strangers thinking, "What are we doing here?" But, every week, I learned something from what other parents of addicts said or shared. I realized I was not going crazy; my pain and fear were common to other parents. I found there were ways to get through this time of trial and pain.

One example of a lesson I learned at Nar-Anon was that it is easy to build up expectations for your child, only to have those expectations and hopes dashed. I might dream and pray that a Christian friend would come into my child's life to influence her or, I might hope she would get involved in a good church that would straighten her out. These are not bad things for which to pray, but I saw that these were my plans to fix the situation.

At one Nar-Anon meeting, I heard that "false hope is self-centered," or what I want for my child, while "real hope is God-centered," or my seeking God's will for my child. The Nar-Anon *Blue Book*, a book of wisdom and principles for parents of addicts, says, "Take no thought for the future actions of others. Neither expect them to get better or worse as time goes on, for in such expectations you are really trying to create. This is God's job, not yours; when man tries to create another life, he makes only monsters. Love alone can create. Love and let be. If I am willing to stand aside and let God's will be done, I free myself from personal anxiety and a mistaken sense of responsibility."[1]

Responding to One Another

John and I are very fortunate to have each other to lean on and to share with. Fortunately, when one of us is really low, the other seems to be able to lift the needy one's spirits.

It is important for me as a more reserved person to keep on sharing my feelings with John whether the feelings are good or bad. If I do not honestly talk about what is going on inside, I can become isolated from John. John often picks me up with his wise perspective and good counsel. For example, I often use an illustration from one of his sermons as a reminder to give my child to God. The illustration is of giving God our burdens with our hands outstretched and our palms turned down not up. With our palms down, we cannot grab back what we have given to God.

Resting on God's Strength, Power, and Promises

A daily time of looking to God for comfort and hope has been my spiritual lifeline. There were some days when all I could do was read a Psalm and let the cries of the Psalmist be my prayer to the Lord. Or, in the darkness of the circumstances, I might only be able to claim that the Holy Spirit would intercede for me, not knowing how to pray. A few passages of Scripture became anchors for my faith. Jeremiah 29:11 continues to give me hope. It says, "For I know the plans that I have for you, declares the Lord, plans to prosper you and not to harm you, plans to give you hope and a future" (NIV).

At one time, I was particularly discouraged and felt there was no light at the end of the tunnel. John and I happened to be talking on the phone to our counselor friend. As I told our friend about how hopeless I felt, he said, "Susan, that sense of hopelessness you feel means that you are looking at the circumstances. You are looking at what you might do to fix it and at what you should have done or what you can do in the future. If you start looking at God and what He can do and how He can work in the

---

1. Palos Verdes Peninsula, CA: Naranon Family Group, 1971, p. 10-11

situation, then there is hope." Thus, Jeremiah 29:11 helps me keep my focus on the Lord.

Another verse that has been a frequent comfort is Isaiah 40:11: "He tends his flock like a shepherd: he gathers the lambs in his arms and carries them close to his heart; he gently leads those that have young" (NIV). I found this promise at a time when I was feeling discouraged for our children, but I was also going through some personal soul searching. I began by praying that God, the Shepherd, would gather my "lambs" into His arms of protection and give me, as the mother ewe, His rest. Soon I was seeing my need to be held in His arms and to hear His heartbeat of compassion and tenderness.

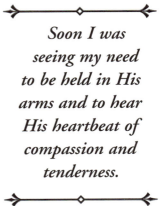

Soon I was seeing my need to be held in His arms and to hear His heartbeat of compassion and tenderness.

This whole process of "recovery" is not only for our children but also for me as their parent, too. I have been stretched and tested through this painful time. I am thankful for having gone through it because it has brought me to a new place of trust and love for the Lord.

John's Turn

I think the Scriptures serve not only as God's love letter for us and to us, but also as our standard by which to judge ourselves. For example, Jesus said in the upper room before He went out to be arrested, "My peace I give you. I do not give to you as the world gives" (John 14:27, NIV). He also said, "Do not let your hearts be troubled" (John 14:1, NIV). That is the Biblical standard: peace and an untroubled heart. I know the standard. I can understand it; I can visualize it. The reality: I simply do not experience it all the time. Indeed, I probably do not experience it much of the time. However, I know the standard. It is there before me. I ask God to build it into my life. It allows me to be honest with myself, with Susan and with God when I am not experiencing the "peace that passes all understanding."

Let me comment on those three:

✳ **With myself**—to admit that I am not as close to Christ or as reliant on Christ as I should be and I need to press on toward that goal.

✳ **With God**—to admit this need to God helps me realize that I need Christ as desperately today as I did when I invited Him into my life as a sophomore in college. As Paul says in Colossians 2:6, "As you received Christ Jesus as Lord, continue to live in Him…" (NIV). I need the same impetus for Christ today and what He can do in my life as I did when I met Him in 1964. I was desperate for Him then, and I need to be desperate for Him now. I need Him, period.

✳ **With Susan**—The Bible is truth; God is truth. It is only when we deny the truth that we remain stagnant. "It is what we keep in the dark that keeps us sick," Zach Whaley has said at a "You're Not Alone" conference. Thus, when I can be brave enough to be honest with Susan that I am not experiencing God's peace, that I am fearful for our kids' future, and that I am angry, then she is able to minister to me. She is able to turn my attention back to Christ. God uses her to recreate hope in me, and step by step we get a little stronger in keeping hope during the tough days.

SECTION 4

"Not My Kid"

Defeating Denial that Your Child is Using Drugs

Parents never want to think their children are using drugs. When our children are born, we have the highest expectations for them. As my daughter said when I told her I felt stupid that she could use heroin for 11/2 years before I found out, "Dad, you can not be a successful addict unless you are a great liar. My ability to deceive is better than your ability to discern."

But when some of their actions begin not to make sense, we do not want to think our kids are using drugs. This is the beginning stage of denial. Denial keeps us in the dark and it keeps us from getting well. We must admit the truth before we can get ourselves healthy and, hopefully, get our kids healthy. The three chapters in this section deals with the temptation we all have to remain in denial instead of acknowledging the truth about our kids abusing drugs and/or alcohol. Once we accept the truth, we can move toward detaching from the addicts and trusting God for their future.

Chapter 8

The Demons of Denial

By Alfred H. Ells

One of the pains of having a child who is drug-addicted or lost or in any kind of difficulty directly relates to how much of yourself you put into that child. How many hopes, dreams and expectations do you have for that child? When I listen to others' stories about their children, I realize that each child is a gift from God. We make huge investments in our children and, therefore, when something goes wrong, we feel an awful lot of anguish.

Subtle Clues

Having a son was one of the greatest things that God could have ever done for me. I come from a family of six boys and two girls. Much of my early life involved sports. My son was always athletic. In fact, he received a scholarship to run cross-country in college. This gave his mother and me high hopes for his future. But he wasn't in college very long before he quit the cross-country team, saying the coach was biased against the guys' team and liked the girls' better. After that, he decided to get a job. It took him a long time to get a job. Once he did, it wasn't long before he lost it. This started a pattern: He would work a little, and then he'd lose the job. Then it would take him a while to get another job.

We started becoming more aware of how irresponsible he was acting and how he frequently would put off doing routine, simple tasks. I kept thinking he was just a little lost right then. Going from college to full-time employment was a difficult transition for him.

My wife, who is very good about tracking details about the comings and goings in our household, began to notice that our son was staying up all night, sleeping all day, and then missing work. She kept telling me that he was not doing what he ought to do, and saying that it greatly bothered her. I would make excuses for him. So, there was a growing tension in the family.

Weak Work Ethic

One of the most important values in my family is "work." I believe that if you don't work, that's a problem. However, my son was having a hard time holding onto jobs. During one period, he either wouldn't come home at night at all, or if he did come home, he would stay up all night. Weeks went by and he still didn't have a job. Finally, I told him, "If you don't get a job, you will have to leave the house." Now, even to say that caused me pain. This was the son I had comforted as a baby, gone hunting with, and enjoyed immensely. But I finally realized that I needed to set boundaries and expectations, and stick to them.

The Crisis

After I told him he needed to get a job, he began getting up and leaving early in the mornings and then coming home in the evenings. But something was wrong. One morning as I was praying, I sensed that something was horribly wrong. I didn't understand it. I finished praying, got my briefcase and left the house. As I was driving down the road, I had an inner sense that he hadn't gone to work at all that day. I felt that he hadn't been going to work lately at all--that he didn't really have a job, but rather was getting up in the morning, leaving, then hiding. So, I drove around the block and went to the backside of a house where one of his friends lived. His Jeep was parked right by the back fence. He had gotten up, put on his work clothes, grabbed his toolbox, hopped into his Jeep, drove around the corner, gone into his friend's house, and fallen asleep. He didn't have a job.

I knocked on the door, went into the house, woke him up, and said, "Son, that's it. You must leave our house." I had come to the end of my rope. I knew I had to tell him to leave. I told him that as long as he was going to be irresponsible, he couldn't live with us. I told him he could come home on Sundays for dinner, and I asked him to let us know how he was doing.

I still didn't realize that he was doing drugs.

The Bad News

He left. We didn't see him again for a long time. We kept getting reports that people had seen him wearing cut-offs, barefoot, and with pockmarks on his face; we heard that he was running with a crowd that was heavy into drugs. For nine months, he really turned himself over to his drug abuse, doing crystal meth and marijuana. We later learned that he had been doing marijuana for years and crystal meth for many months before we kicked him out of our house.

Missing the Signals

What astounds me about all of this is that I am still catching little remembrances and pieces of thought and wondering why I didn't catch on sooner to what was going on. To me, I kicked him out of the house for being irresponsible, for not working, and for lying. It somehow never crossed my mind that my son was doing drugs, and that he had been addicted for a long time.

Another thing that astonishes me is that I had worked as a clinical director of a drug and rehabilitation program for three and a half years. I had lectured on alcohol and drug abuse. I had lectured on denial and how addiction worked. And, yet, in my home, I failed to really understand what was going on.

The Hard Days

When I kicked my son out of the house, it broke my heart. Susan says it brought her great relief, because it stopped some of the insanity that was resulting from his erratic behavior. I wonder if that is the bind we parents of kids who use drugs are caught in: We need something to stop the craziness, but at the same time our hearts are breaking from taking action to stop it.

There is no good answer either way. Even though we were relieved from the distress caused by having a son who abused drugs living in our home, we also felt great worry and pain. "Where is he? What is he doing? Is he running the streets?" We didn't know where he lived, and we didn't hear from him for months and months. He wasn't home at Thanksgiving or even at Christmas, which was one of the loneliest we had ever spent. My wife and I have three other children. The five of us would get together and wonder, "Where is he?" "Where is our son?" "Where is our brother?" The memory of that time still causes pain. Those were hard days.

Characteristics of Denial

Here is a description of denial:

Something isn't right, but you can't figure it out. You may have a vague idea what the problem is or see the symptoms clearly. Others may even be pointing it out to you in very specific terms. You care deeply about the person who seems hopelessly entangled in refusing what you know is reality. You usually interpret his or her rejection of truth as stubbornness, stupidity, rebellion or insanity. (Often we thought he was acting up just against us. He was punishing us. It felt that way.) You're upset, angry and confused. You think, "What's the matter with him/her?" You take his/her refusal to change personally as a rejection of your clear vision and willingness to help. No matter what you do, you can't fix the problem. Nothing you say seems to fit and he doesn't seem to hear or change. You just want the problem to go away--the person to straighten up.

When you are thinking those thoughts, that is denial. Denial, by Webster's definition, is "a disowning or disavowal of reality." Denial is "not letting yourself know what

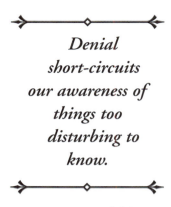

*Denial
short-circuits
our awareness of
things too
disturbing to
know.*

reality is; lying to yourself."

Something in me didn't want to know that my son had a drug problem. This was the one whom I had loved and for whom I had sacrificed! I didn't want to hear that he had a drug problem. Susan was less into denial than I; she somehow saw the situation more clearly than I. (That is one thing that I have noticed about denial: Some people in some situations seem more susceptible to practicing denial than others. Some of these differences are based on differing personalities, and some of them have to do with family dynamics.) Denial short-circuits our awareness of things too disturbing to know.

Why Do We Deny?

Back in 1969, Elisabeth Kubler-Ross, in her book, *On Death and Dying,* was the first author who on a large scale published information about the death process and the stages people go through when they suffer loss. She talked about denial being the first stage of anticipated loss. Her original definition has been refined as follows: Denial is the normal, natural instinctive response to trauma, loss or shock, a conscious or unconscious defense that all of us use to avoid, reduce or prevent anxiety when we are threatened.

To think that my son was on drugs was threatening and painful. The concept diminished my dreams, hopes, and expectations for him. Denial screens out devastating information and prevents us from becoming overloaded. Denial helps keep us from becoming emotionally overloaded. It has a dampening effect; it helps us to slowly absorb news of great impact.

My wife's mom passed away recently at age 79. You would think that since she was that age, we would have expected her passing to be soon. In truth, we didn't anticipate it to happen that quickly at all. Her death came so unexpectedly that for the first three or four days after she died, I kept saying, "I can't believe it." Have you ever had something happen like that where you just couldn't believe it? That's denial. That's that mechanism in us that dampens the dreaded experience, that prevents us from fully accepting it, that stops us from fully embracing it, that keeps us from saying, "Yes, it's true." We all have some of that "I can't believe it" in us.

What Do We Deny?
• How bad the problem is

We don't want to know all the details because they are just too painful. I'm not just talking about the first moment when we find out that our child is abusing drugs. I'm referring to the whole experience of knowing that someone we love is living with pain, addiction, loss, or grief. All along the way we don't want to know. I didn't want the pain. I had many pressures going on in my life at that time; facing my son's drug abuse was just one more painful pressure that I did not need.

- **That we have feelings of pain, guilt, anger, and fear**

    So many times we tell ourselves, "I don't want to go there. It's too painful. I don't want to think about it." Or we say, "I don't want to feel guilty." We deny that we have feelings of pain, guilt, anger, and fear so we don't have to deal with those emotions. I was so scared for my son when I knew he was living on the streets. People do all kinds of insane things in that environment, especially when they're using crystal meth. They freak out when they get wired, and they sometimes do horrible things like shoot people. They live in a subculture with other people who are just as mentally ill. Knowing this places parents whose kids are on drugs and on the streets in a painful place. So we worry and fear, but we don't often admit the truth to ourselves or to others.

- **That our children made these decisions**

    Something inside of us wants to deny our children decided willfully to abuse drugs or alcohol. But that is a reality: He or she decided to use or abuse chemical substances the first time and then many other times after that until the abuse became so powerful that it controlled his or her life. I didn't decide to abuse drugs, my son did. Yet, something deep inside of me as a parent wanted to protect my son too much from the consequences of his decision and therefore to take the responsibility for his drug abuse.

- **That only our kids can truly cure their drug or alcohol problem**

    That is a reality that we want to deny. You know why? Because most of us are "fixers." We believe that if we can't "fix" our kids, then something must not be working inside of us. We especially want to solve the problem when we care about our kids more than they care about themselves. And we especially want to repair their brokenness when we see our own imperfections and failures as parents. But since we didn't cause it, we can't fix it!

- **That parents sometimes contribute to the problem**

    Contributing to the problem differs from causing the problem. We didn't cause our sons and daughters to use or abuse drugs. That was their choice. However, since there is no such thing as a perfect parent, we have contributed. Sometimes our contribution is very small. And it's mainly present in how we react to their addiction; we may give too much blame and shame and not enough honest, loving help. Other times, our own weaknesses cause pain in them that they then choose to medicate with drugs and/or alcohol. It is always good to take the beams out of our own eyes before we take the specks out of the eyes of others. Doing so helps us help our children the right way.

- **That others (especially siblings) know the issues**

  Our other children knew what was going on with our son long before we did. At the time, however, Sue and I were deeply involved in our ministry. The time and attention we had to give the ministry detracted from the time we gave our children. As a result, we were not as connected to them as we needed to be. The kids didn't want to burden us anymore. The connection was not there for the honesty needed. Others also saw the signs we were missing.

My Contribution

When you are fighting many battles and you are trying just to survive, somebody pays the price. My son's battle with drugs came when I was fighting another large battle, one that even ended up on the front page of the newspapers. That battle took so much concentration and energy that I missed things. I didn't have that extra energy required to hear, see or know better. My days of difficulty caused me to neglect my family and therefore be in denial about what was truly going on in my son's life.

What To Do With Denial

1. **Talk about what is happening.**

   The more we share with trusted confidants, the more things "click." Silence is not golden. It's destructive. Find a safe friend or counselor and share both thoughts and feelings. Talk with these people even and especially when it's painful or full of conflict.

2. **Admit to and face your shame.**

   I felt embarrassed to have a son who abused drugs. Shame is the enemy and we are only as sick as our secrets and shame.

   > ❧ Guilt says we did something wrong.
   > ❧ Shame says we are what's wrong (defective).

   Shame makes us hide, not face reality, and lie to ourselves and to others. Remember what happened to Adam and Even in the Garden of Eden? They tried to hide from God when they realized they had sinned. Remember: courage and confession are answers to shame.

3. Mourn, but not as others who have no hope!

To truly mourn means to bare the anguish of your soul in words to God over what is wrong, what you've lost, and what your child is doing. Sometimes this mourning includes tears. I cried a lot. When my son left the house, every single day in my prayer time, I mourned and grieved for my son. I prayed and prayed and prayed. I prayed my heart's anguish. I prayed every thought I had. I shared all of my pain. I reminded God of all the promises that He had stored up for my son's life. I asked God to help me find him, to drag him home, to do anything.

From Tears of Anguish to Tears of Joy

As I mentioned earlier, my son drove a black Jeep. Every time I would see a black Jeep, I would feel the pain. Then I would pray and mourn. One day when I was praying for him, I prayed until all of a sudden the burden lifted. One month later, he showed up on a Sunday night with tears in his eyes, saying he had quit using drugs a month earlier and wanted to come home. I attribute that to the goodness of God. Not all drug abusers come home. I am very grateful that my son did.

Matthew 5:4 says, "Blessed are those who mourn for they will be comforted" (NIV). I believe that one of the best things we can do is to cry and cry out to God. There is a difference between crying to ourselves and crying to Him. When you cry, cry out to the Lord. Do not mourn your pain by yourself. I believe that He hears and He answers. He brought my son home. He will comfort you (2 Corinthians 1:4), He will guide you (Psalm 32:8), and He will hear you (Job 22:27).

> *When you cry, cry out to the Lord. Do not mourn your pain by yourself.*

My son is working now. He is still not where we want him to be, but I tell you, he is a lot better off than where he was this time five long years ago. I am less in denial about who he is and about what he and I both need than I have ever been before, and I take comfort in knowing that "Those who sow in tears will reap with songs of joy!" (Psalm 126:5, NIV).

Chapter 9

Defeating Denial: Facing the Truth of Your Child's Addiction

By Zach Whaley

Denial is very powerful. I'm going to talk about the purpose of denial, the many faces of denial, what we deny, and the results of denial. Then I will share seven ideas for defeating denial.

Purpose of Denial

Denial in chemical dependency and codependency is a defense mechanism that protects us from painful realities and consequences. Many authors and professionals view addictive denial as the first stage of the grief process described by Elisabeth Kubler-Ross in her book, *On Death and Dying.*

I have become increasingly uncomfortable with that view after reviewing my 30 years of living with addictions, followed by almost 30 years of working professionally in the field of addictions. I believe that for the chemically dependent person, denial is not the first step of the grief process. Rather, denial is a childish and selfish manipulation to get out of trouble. In grief, there is a loss and then denial. In addiction, there is denial and then loss.

Denial is Deceptive

Denial is dishonest. It's lying. And dishonesty is a sin. So when we try to sugarcoat addictive denial by calling it the first step in the grief process, "we deceive ourselves and the truth is not in us," as the Apostle John tells us in 1 John 1:18. Children try lying as soon as they learn to talk. Lying is in our genes. The Bible says the human heart is deceitful in every way. Deceiving others and ourselves comes naturally. Addicts don't start lying when they get addicted. They start lying about chemical use when they start experimenting with chemical use, before they get addicted. At this time it's still fun and games, hanging out and getting high. They are unaware of the impact on themselves and their loved ones. They have not at this point experienced the loss associated with their chemical use. So this denial is not part of the grief process. They do it to manipulate those who might interfere with their getting what they want when they want it. They refine lying into a complex constellation of skills that we call denial.

Losing Control

The main feature of addiction is loss of control. When this loss occurs, the addicts simply use their already refined dishonesty skills to deny that they have lost control of behavior that is becoming more and more self-destructive. This denial is the first step in the grief process, but the first step in the recovery process is honesty. This is honesty shown by admitting that they are powerless and their lives have become unmanageable. Denial serves a dual purpose: one that is internal or personal and the other that is external or social.

- *Internally*, denial helps the addicts maintain the illusion of control. They convince themselves they can quit anytime that they want. They believe that they can control the frequency and the amount, but they can't do it consistently. Denial also helps them avoid the reality of self-destruction.
- *Externally*, social denial is still used to manipulate anyone seen as a threat to continued use. They convince themselves that their needs are more important than the needs of those around them. This self-concern then justifies whatever it takes to get the next fix. Whoever is a threat to their continued use becomes an enemy to be defeated or a non-person to be used. I heard an alcoholic say once, "When people hurt me I am deeply hurt; but when I hurt them, I say, 'Oh well. They'll get over it.'" That was his attitude when he was drinking. He was now a sober alcoholic talking, telling his story.

Co-Dependent Denial

Co-dependent denial is similar. The motivation may be different but the process is the same. Wanting to help the addict motivates some co-dependent people. They mistakenly believe that denial helps. Others may be motivated by self-preservation— the need to protect their status, job or their role esteem. They believe that denial will work. For some, the motivation is to avoid the unpleasantness of the truth. They believe that if they deny it, they won't have to deal with it.

Many, especially Christians, confuse confrontation with judgment and condemnation, which of course the Bible tells us not to do. So they avoid confrontation through denial. They have the mistaken belief that denial is grace. And some codependents are simply unaware of what's going on, because they are so focused on themselves that they don't have a strong enough connection to sufficiently be involved in the addict's life to notice the signs. Or, they're just ignorant of the signs of abuse. For most codependents, denial is the first stage of the grief process.

The Many Faces of Denial

Whatever the motivation, the process is the same. Here are some methods of denial that I've seen used by addicts and co-addicts alike.

Lying. Lying is a deliberate attempt to deceive someone by knowingly making a statement that is not true. Many people don't believe a loved one can deceive them. They think they know this person or people in general so well that they can tell whenever a lie is being presented. But for many people, especially in an addictive system, and I emphasize system, lying becomes a way of life. They lie even when they don't need to. You might say, "Well, nobody ever needs to lie." From the addicts' perspective, they need to lie to get out of trouble or to protect themselves. The truth is simply not in them.

When Denial Helps

The grief process starts with denial. There's bargaining, guilt, anger, sadness and finally acceptance and moving on with life. Denial is the first stage and I believe it's a gift of God. The same thing happens with a physical injury.

I was parachuting with a fellow once. When we picked up our chutes in the drop zone and were walking to the meeting point he said, "Zach, my leg is clicking."

I said, "What do you mean it's clicking?"

He said, "Every time I take a step it goes click, click."

We continued to walk about 100 yards. He began saying, "Zach, my leg's starting to hurt."

So I said, "You better sit down here. Let's get an ambulance."

He had a broken leg but the body denied the pain. I believe that's a gift of God to enable us to get out of whatever the situation is that hurt us. Like people in an automobile accident, they're able to maybe crawl away and they don't feel the pain until later. This is helpful denial. In the grief process, denial is usually the briefest of the various stages. However, many codependent people get stuck in denial for years. They don't progress through the grief process to get to the point of acceptance.

Simply Denying.   Simple denial is pretending that something does not exist and pretending not to notice.

- Mom is passed out drunk on the living room floor and nobody is talking about it. Others in the home just act as if she isn't there.
- A 15-year-old comes home with bloodshot eyes and smelling of marijuana and nobody acknowledges noticing.
- A 13-year-old seldom shows up for meals and nobody asks why.

Minimizing and Maximizing.   This is making the bad look good and the good look better. In *minimizing*, we acknowledge the possibility of a problem but not the severity of the problem.

- "Oh, it's not that bad yet."
- "I didn't drink that much."
- "I'm not doing it that often."
- "I didn't like working there anyway."
- "Doesn't everybody try it out? It's no big deal."

In *maximizing*, we exaggerate the importance of a good things like bragging about winning $500 on the slot machines but not mentioning that we put in $600.

- "I know he is experimenting with some drugs but he doesn't dress like those druggers and he gets decent grades."

Blaming.   Blaming is recognizing the problem and maybe even the severity of the problem but blaming someone or something else for the problem.

- "You made me do that."
- "I had to do that because of this."

For the co-dependent, this could include blaming himself for the addict's problem or for the addict's behavior. Co-dependents are good at blaming themselves and taking responsibility for other people's actions.

Excusing.   When we excuse, we offer excuses, explanations, alibis or justifications to make our own or someone else's behavior acceptable. We make comments like:

- "You have to understand. I'm having a bad day."
- "I really didn't have a choice. I had to do that because of what my boss was doing."
- "Wouldn't anybody do this in this circumstance?"

In reality, it doesn't make any difference whether the whole planet is doing it. If it's wrong, it's wrong. If it's self-destructive, it's self-destructive. But excusing is used to deny there's a problem.

Generalizing. This is dealing with problems on a general level, which helps the person avoid personal and emotional awareness. Generalizing makes it acceptable and avoids ownership or helps someone else avoid ownership of the problem. One that I see a lot in counseling is using "you" instead of "I" when talking about yourself.

I'll ask: "What was it like when you walked in and found out that you were laid off?" And the person I'm counseling will answer: "You know, when you face something like that, you really get upset and you begin to wonder about the…." It would be much better for them to say, "When I face something like that, I get upset and I begin to have these kinds of thoughts." This person, then, is taking ownership of it. The person who is saying "you" is saying, "Everybody would think that" and they're not taking ownership of it. I call that generalizing.

Dodging. Dodging is changing the subject to avoid discussing the problem. Someone says, "Mary is surely acting peculiar." We respond, "Yeah, and you know her brother is doing very well on the football team. He plays linebacker and they expect to have an undefeated season." What happened to Mary? The dodging person changed the subject. Dodging is not dealing with that issue by changing the subject.

Attacking. Attacking is becoming angry when the problem is mentioned. That's a form of denial because it pushes people away. Anger is used to warn people not to discuss this problem. Anger threatens some kind of retaliation if the problem is addressed. It pushes people away so they don't get close enough to talk about real issues of the problem.

- "I'd rather be stoned than be uptight like you."

Sideswiping. This is the hit and run. It's addressing the problem indirectly as a sideswipe. It's not a head-on collision. It is similar to saying something general to no one in particular but loud enough so the people in the room hear it, particularly the one you want to hear it. It's kind of a sideswipe and it goes something like this:

- "Gee, this article says that ecstasy is very damaging to the brain. Anyone who risks damaging his brain must be really stupid."

That's sideswiping. That's making a comment not directly to the other person that you want to hear it. That way, you don't have to take ownership of your statement. You don't have to get into a discussion but you make your point.

Spiritualizing. Spiritualizing is using the phrase, "God is in control," to avoid responsibility for taking some kind of action. This is not the same as letting go in order to let God really be in control. This is saying, "God is in control," as a way of dismissing the problem and not having to deal with it.

What We Deny

Behavior. We deny the things that we or others do.

- "He did it tonight but I think it will be the last time."
- "I did it tonight but I think it's the last time. It is not a big deal."

Emotions. We deny our feelings. When someone confronts our anger, we minimize it.

- "No I'm not angry, just a little upset!" we say through gritted teeth.
- "Wouldn't anybody be upset?" We say, as if that then justifies being upset.
- "Oh, the darn pollution is sure aggravating my allergies." We say when someone catches us with tears in our eyes.

Sometimes we totally deny our feelings by numbing ourselves in some way. This is part of addiction. We deny ourselves the rich experience of emotions. We deny others the opportunity to get close to us by not sharing our emotions with them. And to protect our own emotions, we often deny other people's emotions.

A couple of weeks ago, I picked up one of my wife's devotional books for women. I forget what the subject of the first story was, but I don't think I'll ever forget how it ended. A friend came to the author and said, "I feel totally abandoned by God." And the response to her friend was: "That's not true. God never leaves us, never forsakes us." Do you hear what happened? The author totally ignored the friend's feelings and devalued them. Of course, we know God hasn't abandoned the friend. But she was expressing a feeling, a feeling of alienation from God. She probably needed to talk about that, but the author cut her off. We protect our own emotions by denying other people's emotions, too.

Intellect. God gave us brains with which to think and to solve problems, yet we deny our intellect by avoiding the truth that we need to solve problems. We sometimes vegetate in some way, maybe in front of a television so we don't have to think. Instead of taking "captive every thought to make it obedient to Christ" (2 Corinthians 10:5, NIV), we let our brains obsess about things that we can't do anything about, while we ignore the things that we can do something about. We deny our intellect as though we don't even have one.

Will. We deny that we have choices, thereby denying responsibility for our choices.

- We deny our intentions saying, "But I didn't mean to hurt you with that remark."
- Or we say, "Just kidding," after making a cutting remark or a remark that hurts.

Having claimed we have best of intentions, we then insist that we be judged on our intentions, not our behavior.

Body. We deny our body proper function by eating, exercising or sleeping too much or too little. This also helps us deny our emotions and our intellect because we don't have the nutrition to make our brain work well. We don't have the clarity to understand what we're feeling because our body is becoming a mess.

The Holy Spirit. We deny the prompting of the Holy Spirit. We forget that God can speak to us through a jackass (see Numbers 22:21-35), and so we don't listen to those people we consider to be "jackasses." We deny God the opportunity to bring about change by trying to control people and situations ourselves. When we do this, we put a wall around the indwelling Holy Spirit and lose our connection with God.

Reality. We create a fantasy world in our minds and act as if it is real. It's not fantasy in our minds because we are denying reality. So, basically, we deny reality in every part of our being: intellect, emotions, body, will, and spirit.

We deny God the opportunity to bring about change by trying to control people and situations ourselves. When we do this, we put a wall around the indwelling Holy Spirit and lose our connection with God.

The Results of Denial

Denial prevents change. We have to accept what is before we can change what is.

Denial keeps us from working through the grief process over the loss of a child, dreams, self-respect, prestige, job, control, health, etc. I have heard parents say that when their kids got clean and sober, they got their children back. To be able to say that means they acknowledged the loss. They did not deny it. Recognizing they had lost the child preceded their acknowledging their loss.

Denial keeps us from working through the grief process of any loss. The loss could be the loss of self-respect, a job, or the loss of health. As long as we deny it, then we can't work through it.

Denial keeps us from working through our grief so that we can't move on with our lives. We're stuck. As it relates to an addicted child, the parent is stuck with the total focus of his life being on this other person and what's happening to him. The result of that is that we don't get to live our lives.

Denial keeps us from working through our grief so that we can't move on with our lives.

> *Addicts do not wake up on a beautiful Sunday morning and say, "What a beautiful day. I think I'll quit using today. I think I'll clean up and get sober."*

Our denial prevents the addicts from experiencing the pain of the addiction. This denial eliminates the motivation to change. Addicts do not wake up on a beautiful Sunday morning and say, "What a beautiful day. I think I'll quit using today. I think I'll clean up and get sober." It doesn't happen that way. People have to hit bottom. People have to reach the end of their rope. The denial of the parent can keep them from getting to that point.

Denial feeds addiction because addiction thrives on dishonesty. Dishonesty is fuel for addiction. I believe addiction cannot continue without dishonesty. Denial is the antithesis of recovery because recovery requires honesty. So honesty is a foundation and a beginning for recovery. Denial then, is the antithesis of the honesty required for recovery.

Jesus said He is the truth (see John 14:6). Truth and lies cannot co-exist any more than light and darkness can co-exist. Denial separates us from Christ, apart from Whom we can do nothing (see John 15:5).

Defeating Denial

I want to stress the importance of defeating denial. Failing to defeat denial can result in a hardened heart toward truth. The Apostle Paul, in Ephesians 4:17-9 states,

> So I tell you this, and insist on it in the Lord, that you must no longer live as the Gentiles do, in the futility of their thinking. They are darkened in their understanding and separated from the life of God because of the ignorance that is in them due to the hardening of their hearts. Having lost all sensitivity, they have given themselves over to sensuality so as to indulge in every kind of impurity, with a continual lust for more (NIV).

Paul says they no longer live in the futility of their thinking; they're living in denial. They are separated from God, and this results in a hardened heart. They have lost all sensitivity. They have no conscience, no rationality, and their feelings are limited to lusting for more of the same. If they continue, they're trapped. So defeating denial is very important. Make a commitment to put off falsehood and speak truthfully to your neighbor, as Ephesians 4:25 says.

1. Develop a Support System

1 Corinthians 10:12 says, "So if you think you are standing firm, be careful that you don't fall!" (NIV). Don't rely on yourself alone. Seal this commitment to put off falsehood and speak truth by developing a support system of gentle and courageous people who are knowledgeable about denial. Ask them to confront your denial. We

should confess our sins to one another and be healed. We need to become the gentle and courageous people that our addicts may need when they decide to confront their denial.

2. Take Thoughts Captive

We must "take captive every thought to make it obedient to Christ" (2 Corinthians 10:5, NIV) and "be made new in the attitude of [our] minds" (Ephesians 4:23, NIV). We should remind ourselves repeatedly that interfering with the addict's pain postpones recovery. We need to capture the denial statements and correct them. It is helpful to take a sheet of paper and draw a line down the middle. On the left side, write the denial statement. On the right side write an argument against it. That trains our brains to confront automatically our own denial statements. Also helpful is to journal every day, look for irrational thoughts and denial—excuses, minimizing, and so on--and take them captive.

3. Learn to Put it into Words

Experience and express your feelings. Learn a feeling vocabulary. For a lot of people, it just hasn't been part of their lives to talk about feelings. They don't even have a "feeling" vocabulary. So learn a "feeling" vocabulary. Learn to identify "feeling" words. Look for feelings in your body. Become aware of aches, tenseness, weakness and numbness, and ask yourself what feelings are causing them. What is causing this knot in my stomach? Read your journal to look for signs of sadness, anger, fear, guilt, shame and joy, and when you find them, allow yourself to experience the feeling. Then count it all joy. "Counting it all joy" does not mean to disown your feelings. It means to experience the feelings and then "count it joy," knowing that it will produce in you perseverance.

4. Stop Self-Destructive Behavior

Stop doing things that support self-destructive behavior for yourself and others. Start practicing recovery. Attend to your physical health. Get proper nutrition, exercise, and rest, and practice good grooming. Do it, but don't overdo it. Stop any behavior that gives you a quick fix, whether it is using a drug, drinking, eating, gambling, or engaging in sexual fantasies, etc. Anything that gives you a quick fix, stop it, because that will become an addiction. Instead, as Paul told the Ephesians, we should be filled with the Spirit. Are you constantly on the go? Ask yourself, "What will catch me if I stop running?" Then deal with that. Stop reacting automatically and start responding by making conscience choices.

5. Learn to Make Deliberate, Not Destructive, Responses

Saying, "Someone pushed my buttons" is denial of responsibility for our actions. Angry, critical, condemning outbursts cannot be excused, but they can be forgiven when we acknowledge our responsibility for them. We can change by making conscious choices about how to respond to hurt and threat. What happens typically is that we develop a habitual way of responding or reacting whenever we feel threatened or hurt by someone, and that becomes automatic. Very often those ways are destructive of the relationship, so we need to put off those automatic, old habits and put on conscious choices. We think consciously, "How am I going to respond to this?" instead of just letting it go.

6. Turn it Over to God

"Let go and let God." Give Him your addiction or give Him your addict. Jesus said, "Come to Me, all you who are weary and burdened, and I will give you rest (Matthew 11:28, NIV). Give Him your burden and receive His rest. Improve your conscious contact with God. Become more aware of His presence more often and in more places. Connect with God through prayer, meditation and quiet listening. I sometimes think that we talk too much in prayer and we need to spend some time just listening quietly. I recommend trying to pray in pictures instead of words. Picture what you are praying about. Get to know God through His Word. Seek Him in every situation. Do what the kids do. Ask yourself, "What would Jesus do?" When in conflict with yourself or others, seek His peace, "which transcends all understanding" (Philippians 4:7, NIV). Peace does not mean that we should ignore unacceptable behavior. It means we may deal with it gently, without hostility.

Steps to Defeating Denial

Step One: Admit that you are powerless over your addict and that your life has become unmanageable.

Step Two: Believe that God can restore you to sanity. Insanity is doing the same thing over and over, each time expecting a different result. Denial is insanity because it is delusional thinking. It is irrational and it denies reality. And those are symptoms of psychosis.

Step Three: Turn your life and your will over to the care of God. You cannot do this and continue in denial because God is truth. Whenever you relapse back into denial, you will need to do steps one, two and three again to begin recovery. You may have to do those three steps ten times today or 100 times tomorrow.

Step Four: Take an honest look at yourself and don't deny what you see. Identify the denial methods that you have used to lie to yourself and others in this step.

Step Five: Confess to God and to one another.

Step Six: Clean up your messes. Keep working on self-improvement. Improve your conscious contact with God on a daily basis, and reach out to others who are hurting. Why is this so important? Hebrews 3:12-14 says,

> See to it, brothers, that none of you has a sinful, unbelieving heart that turns away from the living God. But encourage one another daily, as long as it is called Today, so that none of you may be hardened by sin's deceitfulness. We have come to share in Christ if we hold firmly to the end the confidence we had at first (NIV).

"Hold Firmly to the End"

The unbelieving heart turned away from God is a heart in denial, turned away from truth. Instead, the book of Hebrews says to encourage one another daily. In other words, don't go it alone. Take one day at a time. A heart hardened by deceitfulness means you're no longer open to the truth. You can be in denial so much that pretty soon you're no longer open to the truth. Paul knew that we would be tempted to give up hope. So he says that we should, "hold firmly to the end." But he doesn't say what the end is. In addiction, the end is either recovery or death. But you have to hold firmly to the end. We have become experts at using denial to make reality more tolerable. It makes the intolerable tolerable, the unacceptable acceptable. We have learned well how to stop the pain exposed by reality, not by changing our circumstances but by pretending our circumstances are something other than what they are. Now is the time to find courage and face the truth.

Chapter 10

Trusting God: Detaching from the Addict

By John Vawter

About 20 years ago, a congenital condition in my back manifested itself with lots of pain in the lower back and numbness in my legs. Little did I know that this condition would be of significant spiritual and emotional help to my wife Susan and me when drugs invaded our family years later. Let me explain.

I complained a lot about my back and legs. I would not heed Susan's advice to see the doctor. I thought I could fix it myself. I had no idea how, but I thought I could. Finally, one day Susan said to me, "If you are not going to see the doctor, do not complain to me anymore." So, I went to the doctor and got the help I needed.

Neither of us realized that Susan was practicing a principle called detachment, something everyone must consider doing with an addicted loved one. It is not easy. But those who do understand addicts tell those of us who are the loved ones that the only solution is to love the addicts but turn them over to God's care. In Susan's case, she was no longer going to be "hooked" by my complaining, spend her emotional energy helping me, or take time to try to comfort and help me when I would not take any steps to be helped by the expert, the orthopedic surgeon.

Breaking A Heart or Restoring a Life?

At first glance, detachment seems heartless. But ultimately it's the most loving, healthy and hopeful step we can take for our children. Here's one way to look at it: As Christian parents, we understand that we can model Christianity for our children or loved ones but ultimately they must accept or reject Christ for themselves. We cannot make the decision for them. So it is with drugs or alcohol. (Depending on their age, there are different pro-active stances we can take, but ultimately the addicts must decide for themselves. We'll talk more about that later in the chapter.) Detachment helps both the parents and the addicts face the responsibility for their own lives. For us parents, facing that responsibility puts us back on the path to mental and spiritual health.

While on the surface, detachment appears to be unloving, it is more unloving to deny the drug abuser the opportunity to grow by experiencing the consequences of his or her own behavior. Detaching may seem like giving up, but the only thing we give up when we break away from being controlled by loved ones who use drugs is the illusion of our being in control.

A Streak of Rebellion

Understanding that every addict or alcoholic has a rebellious streak helps us understand why it's important to practice detachment. This is why Alcoholics Anonymous programs talk about *breaking the will* of the alcoholic. Our daughter Stephanie, who is a recovering heroin addict, explained to me that addicts have chosen or continue to choose to live their lives for themselves and without consideration for loved ones. They become self-absorbed and self-focused. Usually they do not care what kind of pain or discomfort they cause those around them.

Rebels do not listen to anyone—even those who love them. Solomon gives us solid commentary on the rebel or fool in the Book of Proverbs, Chapter 15 (NASB):

Verse 1:   "A fool rejects his father's discipline…"

Verse 10: " … grievous punishment is for him who forsakes the way; he who hates reproof will die."

Verse 14: "The mind of the intelligent seeks knowledge, but the mouth of fools feeds on folly."

Verse 20b:"…a foolish man despises his mother."

Verse 21: "Folly is joy to him who lacks sense … "

Verse 26:3 "…a rod [is] for the back of fools."

Many times as parents we hide a child's addiction because we are embarrassed or afraid of people's reactions. This is a normal response to having a drug user in the family, but we must be aware that this attitude can be the enemy of our own souls and of our spiritual and emotional health. We must remember that addicts have a particular way of thinking; it is called "addict logic" and it's not the kind of logic that you and I use. The main motivation for addicts is to get that next high or fix. So, if they sense that parents will not make them face the consequences of their use and abuse, then they will manipulate their parents for their own ends—which is getting that next high or fix.

How to Detach

1. We detach first from assuming responsibility for our children's actions. As the Nar-Anon Creed states: "I did not cause it, I cannot control it and I cannot cure it." We recognize that although we are not perfect parents, our misdeeds and mistakes are not the causes for our child's use and abuse. Stephanie told us that one of her Alcoholics Anonymous discussion groups was made up of "street people, middle class people, wealthy people and people who had been wealthy but lost all their money to their addiction." She said that in spite of their socio-economic differences, they agreed that the one common denominator among them was this: *Until they quit blaming others for their addiction, they did not go get the help they needed.*

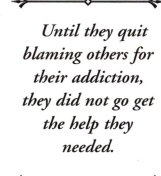

Until they quit blaming others for their addiction, they did not go get the help they needed.

2. We then begin to detach emotionally and spiritually. We put our stake in the ground as we realize that just as the addict is responsible to get clean, so we are responsible to get healthy, both spiritually and emotionally. As Nar-Anon says,

> Your role as helper is not to DO things for the person you are helping but to BE things, not to try to train and change his actions, but to train and change your actions. As you change your negatives to positives—fear to faith; contempt for what he does to respect for the potential within him; rejection to release with love…as you change in such ways as these, you change the world about you…. [1]

By detaching spiritually, we focus on our own spiritual walk with Christ and we ask and trust the Holy Spirit to work in our children's lives.

3. We then may have to detach physically from our children. This is tough. But, we must be motivated by what is best for them. Two stories from support groups for parents of addicts might illustrate the point:

- One woman asked her group if they thought she was being too permissive to allow her adult son to live in her home, where he would cook his heroin and shoot up in his bedroom. In unison the group said, "Yes!!"
- Another woman told of putting all her son's things on the front porch for him to find when he came home. He rang the doorbell, because the locks had been changed, and asked, "What is happening?" She explained that he had violated her rule of no drugs if he lived in her house. He responded by asking where he was going to sleep that night. Her response was: "That is not my worry. You made the decision not to sleep here when you used drugs again."

1. Naranon Family Group, Palos Verdes Peninsula, CA, 1971.

> ### *Why They Abuse*
>
> All the recovering addicts who have spoken at the "You're Not Alone" conferences have said that they believed their parents raised them correctly. The addicts chose to abuse. Research on this topic commissioned by "You're Not Alone" yielded interesting results. Although it was conducted among pastors' kids who have abused drugs, there are lessons for any family in the study's findings.
>
> Specifically, the study showed that children give three reasons for their use and abuse of drugs and alcohol:
> 1. rebellion against parents
> 2. peer pressure
> 3. the need to medicate themselves against emotional pain

I think it is easy to see that the woman who manifested tough love was indeed showing more love toward her son than the mother who let her son cook his heroin and shoot up in his bedroom. Genuine detachment means parents are willing to break contact with their children in order to let them assume the responsibility for their addiction.

Is detachment hard? Of course it is. Is it scary? Of course it is. Is it right? Of course it is. Solomon, in the verses cited earlier, helps us understand that not all children listen to their parents. He also helps us understand that children need to bear the consequences of their decisions. As parents we do not want to accept this. We love our kids. We want what is best for them. However, it must be their decision to get clean. It is possible that their decision to use may take years off their lives or prevent them from getting a graduate degree or keep them from landing a better job. But those are choices and decisions they make. Our ultimate goal for them must be that they become "clean" and establish a relationship with God.

Concerns about Detaching

I think we all may recoil at the word "detachment" because it seems to be so fatalistic. What if I detach from my child and he or she still does not get clean? What if my child, without my active involvement, ruins his or her life? What if my child dies? These are all legitimate questions and concerns. Detachment does not mean that we stop caring. It does not mean we violate our sense of compassion. It does not mean we stop loving our child, and it does not mean we don't take some steps to help.

Zach Whaley, a counselor in Phoenix and a popular speaker at "You're Not Alone" conferences, explains detachment this way:

When I detach from an addicted loved one, it does not mean that I am no longer interested or concerned about the welfare of the other person. It just means that I am no longer tied to the addict's emotions, thoughts or behavior. It means I have chosen to stop reacting automatically to certain stimuli and, instead, to start responding thoughtfully and deliberately. Since I am no longer attached to the other person's behavior, I am no longer under the control of the other person. Of course, my detachment also means that I can no longer control the other person. It also means I can no longer blame him or her for the things that are totally under my control, like my thoughts, my feelings and my behavior.

Giving it to God

A friend in Phoenix is the one who taught me about detachment and challenged me to put it into action. When I first met him, Stephanie had been through treatment for heroin and had been clean for 12 months. Then our son Michael told us he was smoking marijuana. Fearful for his future, I began plotting all types of strategies to help him. My friend was very matter of fact, but not lacking in compassion or faith. He reminded me that I had had a very good rational talk with my son about marijuana. I had also had a second rational conversation with my son. Both times my son had rejected my advice. There was nothing else I could say.

I had to commit my son to God in a new way, as many times as necessary every day, and let God do His work in His time, even if it meant negative consequences in my son's life. The abuser must recognize the consequences of his or her actions. My friend reminded me that God loves my son more than I do. Not only does God love our kids more than we do, but also His love and ability to work on our kids' behalf are stronger than our love and ability. I am watching that principle work and it is rewarding and humbling to watch.

Not only does God love our kids more than we do, but also His love and ability to work on our kids' behalf are stronger than our love and ability.

Degrees of Detachment

There is a vast difference between the 15-year-old who is abusing drugs or alcohol and the 30-year-old who is, so detachment takes on different forms depending on the age of the child. Remember that each parent must determine his or her own plan of action. There are no absolutes, but we can break the strategies for detachment down into three general age categories: under 18 or legal age; 18 to 30; and, beyond 30 years of age.

• Under 18

When the child is below the age of 18 and still the legal responsibility of the parent, the parent must be very proactive. Drug counseling, searching bedrooms, setting restrictions, knowing who his or her friends are and knowing his or her whereabouts are all acceptable, in my opinion. Parents are spiritually, biblically, morally and legally responsible for the child in this age bracket.

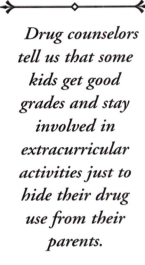

Drug counselors tell us that some kids get good grades and stay involved in extracurricular activities just to hide their drug use from their parents.

When Stephanie was 14, she got some marijuana from a young man in the church I served in Minneapolis. Susan and I knew this was not something we could ignore. We talked to the school counselor, who was also an experienced drug counselor. He advised us to take Stephanie to a drug treatment center for an evaluation. The assessment at that time was that she had experimented with but was not using or abusing marijuana or any other drug. Nevertheless, we believed it was our responsibility to help her understand the dangers of drugs. At a later date we did search her room.

Stephanie later explained that if a parent is going to search his or her kid's room, the parent needs to be prepared to have that child hate him, or at least say so. Stephanie said: "Of course the child has violated trust by bringing drugs into the home. In the way the addict thinks, the parent violates a trust, too, because kids think they have the right to their own privacy and that privacy has been violated."

However, she affirms the parents' right and need to go to any lengths to be proactive when under-age children are suspected of experimenting with, using or abusing drugs/alcohol. One of the very lowest points in my life was the day I told Stephanie in front of a drug counselor that I had searched her room and she screamed at me, "I hate you! I hate you!" Did that hurt? It hurt more than I can express or explain. But, it was the right thing to do.

When a child is at such a young age, parents cannot completely detach and let the children make their own decisions. The stakes are too high. Nevertheless, we must also be aware that our children can use and abuse if they want. We cannot be with them every minute of the day. They can buy or barter for drugs at school and use them there. Some do exactly that. Drug counselors tell us that some kids get good grades and stay involved in extracurricular activities just to hide their drug use from their parents. Todd Smoke, one of our conference speakers, says there is nothing his parents could have done to keep him from abusing drugs and alcohol in high school. He was sneaking out at night after they went to bed. He was getting good grades the entire time. He also says there is nothing they could have done to get him to stop in his adult life either. (Read more about Todd Smoke's story in Chapter 15.)

As a child gets nearer to the age of 18, the parent may have to express tough love as a part of detachment. I talked to one family who lives in a state where they could be held legally responsible—and that includes possibly going to jail—for the drug-related crimes of their 17-year-old son. Legally, they could not remove him from their property. He continued to violate their rule of no drug use anywhere. When I asked them who paid the mortgage on the house, they said they did. So, I reminded them that they had the authority to set the rules. I encouraged them to change the locks on the house and move their son's bed to the garage with the understanding that, since they were legally responsible for him until his 18th birthday, the garage was where he was going to live until he was 18. Then they would evict him from their property. He would be on his own.

This story helps us understand that detachment is not easy, clear or simple. Legal factors can enter in. Nevertheless, after our talk the parents realized that their son was running and ruining their lives as a couple. They realized they were too intertwined with their son's bad decisions. He was controlling them. They did not move him to the garage, but they did begin to detach and withdraw family favors from him. For example, they did not give him money for a major family function as they had done for the other kids. When he asked why, they told him bluntly, "We will give you nothing beyond what the law requires as long as you are using drugs." This was the start of detachment for them. They were on their way back to spiritual and mental health. Detachment got their son's attention and started him on the journey back to sobriety.

• *Between Ages 18-30*

Detaching from children ages 18-30 is a different story than when they're younger. Detachment in this age category can be more acute and definite. When our children are of this age, we have no legal right to make them do anything. We love our children, but we must understand that we cannot let them control us. Often, our detachment helps our addict children understand that they must accept responsibility for their actions. The experts in drug/alcohol rehabilitation make it very clear that only the addict can decide to get clean. Sometimes this means he or she must "hit bottom." Unfortunately, the addicts are our kids. We created or adopted them. We love them. We reared them. We would give our lives for them. We would do anything for them. And, that is exactly the problem. We would do anything for them and they know it. So, they use, abuse and manipulate us in order to spend more time with their beloved drugs or alcohol. That is why it is loving and mature to let our adult children hit bottom and face the consequences of their own actions and decisions.

One man recently wrote about his son, "My son is using drugs again. He is not using enough to hit bottom but enough not to be free to live a victorious and fulfilling life."

This man and his wife are detaching from their son to help hasten the process of his hitting bottom so he will get the help he needs.

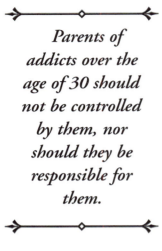

Parents of addicts over the age of 30 should not be controlled by them, nor should they be responsible for them.

• *Over 30*

By the time children who are using or abusing drugs reach 30, unless there are extraordinary circumstances, they should be living on their own and supporting themselves. There is no reason for the parents to be paying bills, giving money or providing a free place to live. This is the stage of life during which the parents should be free to pursue their own pleasures and ministry opportunities. They should not feel guilty over the choices their kids have made or continue to make. By this time there is no one to blame but the addict. It is easy to say but hard to do: Parents of addicts over the age of 30 should not be controlled by them, nor should they be responsible for them.

I just read an article about a man who ran the Los Angeles marathon. One year ago, he was living in a dumpster. His parents forbade him to come into their house until he got sober. His younger brother would leave the door unlocked so he could sneak

"Degrees of Detachment"

AGE OF CHILD	CHARACTERISTICS	STEPS FOR PARENTS
Under 18	Child remains under parents' legal, spiritual, and moral responsibility.	Parents should remain very proactive. Steps might include: • Drug counseling • Searching bedrooms • Setting restrictions • Monitoring friendships • Monitoring whereabouts • Closely supervising all activities
18-30	Parents have no legal responsibility or rights.	Parents should be willing to allow child to "hit bottom". Parents should refuse to allow child control of the parents' lives.
Over 30	Parents have no legal responsibility or rights.	Parents should offer no financial support. Parents should pursue their own pleasures and opportunities.

in during the night to get something to eat, but his parents did not know that. His parents' detachment helped bring him to the bottom. He says this about going to a Catholic treatment center: "I was so tired of being dirty and alone." It must have hurt his parents to put him out, but it was the right thing to do. At the treatment center, he met a man who introduced him to running and he used the training for the marathon as incentive to manifest the discipline needed to stay clean and sober.

Patience, Perseverance and Prayer

I have mentioned a number of times that detachment is not easy. Zach Whaley comments:

> Because detachment does not happen overnight in a once-and-for-all decision and action, we cannot just detach from the addict. We cannot just stop being enmeshed with the addict. Concentrating on detachment does not work. Paradoxically, when we focus on detachment, we remain attached. The Apostle Paul has a solution. Whenever he tells us to stop something, he tells us to do something else instead. He often used the phrases "put off" and "put on." We need to "put off" dysfunctional and unhealthy attachments and attitudes that tear us down and suck the life out of us and "put on" functional and healthy attachments that restore life. Proverbs 4:23 says, "Above all else, guard your heart, for it is the wellspring of life" (NIV).

Zach shares three helpful tactics that he used when he was learning to detach.

1. The "Serenity Prayer:" "Saying this prayer over and over helped me to focus on God and my own recovery instead of being an enabler:"

> "God grant me the serenity to accept the things I cannot change, the courage to change the things I can and the wisdom to know the difference."

2. Recalling memorized Scripture verses: "Especially helpful to me was Proverbs 3:5, which says, 'Trust in the Lord with all your heart and lean not on your own understanding,' and Philippians 4:13, which says, 'I can do everything through Him who gives me strength' (NIV)."

3. The slogan: " 'This too shall pass' helped me to develop patience and trust in God for the future of my addicted one and for my life."

In conclusion, let me reiterate that detachment is necessary for all of us who have addicts in our families. It is essential for their sobriety and our spiritual health.

Detachment does not mean we quit loving; in some cases it means we start loving.

Detachment does not mean we quit loving; in some cases it means we start loving. Detachment does not mean we are fatalistic; it just means we turn the control and future of our child over to the care of God who expresses His love to us in Jesus Christ. Detachment is not easy. We must learn to practice it every day. Relapses will occur in our journey toward detachment. As hard as it is to detach, plenty of testimonials from parents of addicts who have gone before tell us that they did not let God control the situation until they took that step.

Personality Types

The question has been asked, "Who has an easier time detaching, men or women?" I am not certain that the answer is as much related to gender as it is to temperament. How difficult we find it to detach correlates to our disposition and how well we have manifested faith in the face of trials in the past. Those with the "controlling" personality (which some might call a "driver" or "choleric temperament") find it difficult to detach because they are accustomed to being in control and solving issues independently. For those who have a "fixer" personality, detachment may be hard because they can "fix" almost anything or anyone. The loved one abusing drugs may be the first person the "fixer" cannot "fix." The amiable might find detaching difficult because they have a hard time acknowledging the depth and severity of the problem.

Especially in light of our varying personalities, it is important to recognize that detachment is all about trusting God. Tests of our faith can be unfair in that we did not create the circumstances that demand that we grow in faith, but they are necessary nevertheless. They show our need for God; they grow our dependence on God; and they unleash His power to work in the lives of our children.

Detachment: Faith in Action

Ultimately, detachment is a matter of faith in God's ability to work in the life of the addict, but such faith does not come naturally or easily. Faith grows as a muscle grows—through exertion, stress and exercise. The stress and trauma of learning a child is abusing drugs can upend our spiritual and emotional equilibrium to the point that our response to such news and trauma is more subjective and less faith-based than it should be.

Do I Have the Kind of Faith That It Takes to Detach?

Because detachment is all about trusting God in the lives of our addicted children, it is best to start with a picture of what such faith would look like and then work backwards from that picture in order to evaluate whether or not we have that level of faith. The kind of faith it takes to detach:

- Allows us to acknowledge the pain we experience as parents seeing our children involved in such self-destructive behavior
- Enables us to acknowledge our inability to work in our situation
- Makes us willing to turn our children over to the care, love and ability of God—and to trust Him to work in the lives of these whom we love so much, these whom He loves even more
- Allows us to give God the freedom to work as He knows best without our trying to manipulate Him, our children or the situation

Thus, if we find ourselves controlled and dominated by the stress of our situation; if we are trying to manipulate our circumstances; if we are trying to find "just the right word" that will bring our children back to their senses and sobriety; or if we are "bailing them out" one more time; then we have not exercised the faith to detach.

SECTION 5

Understanding Your Child, the Addict

Having drugs in your family is like walking in a deep dark forest. You stumble over roots that you cannot see and you bump into trees and objects that you did not know were there. Nothing can prepare you for the journey because you are deep into the woods before you realize it. Children who abuse drugs behave in ways that we do not understand. They were not reared or taught to act the way they do. Then, as the experts say, "Your child has become the drug," which means that the drugs are in control of your child and he or she is using "addict logic" instead of normal logic. This does not ease the pain but it does bring understanding. Even though you never wanted to know about drugs and their effects, it is important to do so, for understanding your child's addiction will bring balance and health to your family.

The next three chapters are full of knowledge and wisdom about drugs. This is necessary reading for the parent of an addict.

Chapter 11

Dealing with an Addicted Loved One

By Zach Whaley

I don't have a kid on drugs. I spent the last 12 years of my 21 years at home watching my father's alcoholism progress and watching him deteriorate. I felt shame, rejection, helplessness, loneliness, and anger. At about the time I finished college, my mom left him and he got better. He was abstinent the last 20 years of his life.

My sister's husband became an alcoholic. I don't know the whole story, but she left him and he got better. He was abstinent for the last 30 years of his life.

After three years of marriage, I saw my wife sinking deeper and deeper into alcoholism, and I spent the next 12 years trying to keep her sober. And again I felt shame, rejection, helplessness, loneliness and anger.

My response to shame was to become arrogant. Some people respond to shame by getting depressed or defeated. Then I filed for divorce, thinking she would get better, like my father and brother-in-law had. But she did not. I learned that not everyone is the same. Each person is different, unique. So at the age of 40, I was a brand-new Christian, divorced and alone. I still had to deal with shame, rejection, and helplessness. For me, helplessness frequently translated into anxiety, loneliness, anger, and a need to control.

You see, when addicts leave our lives, for whatever reason, they are still a part of us. They have become a part of who we are. So I had baggage that went all the way back to my childhood.

Emotional Bruises

Dealing with an addicted loved one leaves bruises and scars. When these are not healed, they cause us to react and overreact. For example, say I, for some reason, got a big bruise on my right arm yesterday that no one could see. Then John, in an act of friendliness, came up to me, grabbed my arm, and said, "Hey, Zach, how are you doing?" I wouldn't think, "Let's see. Yesterday I bumped into that thing and got this bruise and that is what is causing me all that pain." No, I'd probably shout, "Hey, John, that hurts!" But he wouldn't have seen the bruise. How could he have known it was there?

We can have emotional bruises on our hearts that are caused when someone we love is addicted to something. These bruises cause us to overreact, so we walk around being irritable, edgy, easily irritated, and bitter. We begin blaming. In fact, I would have blamed John for the pain that had just been inflicted, even though in reality the pain had been caused by something that had happened yesterday, not from what John had just done. But because I would have been feeling the pain, I would have to blame somebody; typically, addicts are easy to blame. We blame them for everything that is wrong in our lives.

Control for Protection

Also, when these bruises are unhealed, we get into control issues. Because we feel so helpless about this person, we try to control other people. Controlling becomes a way of life. There are a couple of methods we use to control others:

- Manipulation. By that, I mean by not being clear about what we want. Examples are when we don't tell people when we aren't satisfied and when we don't tell them what we want. We can manipulate through transmitting guilt by saying, "If you really loved me and if you were really a good person, then you wouldn't be doing this and I wouldn't be feeling this pain and frustration."
- Power. We can exert power in a number of different ways. One is physical strength. Another is intellectual strength; we can overpower people with our clever arguments. Another is financial strength; we can gain control by granting or withholding money.

Withdraw for Protection

Since we are walking around with these bruises, we don't want to get close to others because they might bump up against us. So we begin to withdraw, isolate ourselves, push people away and alienate them in order to protect ourselves.

To withdraw, we put our focus elsewhere. Work is a very convenient place to put that focus. Or we can focus on hobbies or anything that gets our minds off the problem.

Moreover, we can push people away by being arrogant and by acting like we don't need them, by becoming defeated, by moping around, and by becoming withdrawn and depressed.

Personal Story

At the age of 40, I was a brand-new Christian and alone. Twenty years later, as a pastor of counseling, I had a son who was rebellious and depressed. He experimented with drugs, but was never addicted. I know what it is like to feel like your child is ruining his life ... and also exposing me to ruin. Here are some lessons I've learned during my experiences.

Zach's Tips for Codependency and Boundaries

1. The only behavior I can control is my own.
2. Replace automatic reactions with conscious decisions about your behavior.
3. When you allow an intrusion, you have drawn a new boundary.
4. You can't require other people to honor your boundaries, but you can decide what you will do if they don't.
5. Dead people never bleed, and emotionally dead people never cry.
6. It is okay to feel what others are feeling – "Rejoice with those who rejoice; mourn with those who mourn" (Romans 12:15). It is only unhealthy when we can't separate our feelings from theirs.
7. If I stab someone and he bleeds, I can't say, "You are responsible for your bleeding." Likewise, when I do something that causes an emotional bruise, I can't ignore my part in the bruise by saying, "You are responsible for your feelings." In the first case, I am responsible for my behavior that caused the bleeding; and in the second case, I am responsible for my behavior that caused the emotional bruise. In both cases, I am responsible to change my behavior as an act of love.
8. An addict will never quit the addiction until he or she views continuing the addiction as more painful than stopping. Therefore, anything that is done to lessen the painful consequences of practicing the addiction will reduce any motivation to stop.
9. If a loved one is addicted to something, perhaps the best way to help is to concentrate on your own growth so you can become strong enough to allow the addict to experience the natural consequences of the addiction.
10. Social and emotional growth are arrested when people begin using addictive substances or behaviors to alter their feelings and percep-

tions. Therefore, treat them as if they are at the age when stay started abusing drugs or alcohol.[1]

11. Shame supports addictions, but acceptance defeats shame. Guilt has to do with behavior, which can produce repentance, forgiveness, and improved behavior. Shame has to do with identity – a deep sense of being valueless. Shame is so deep and so pervasive that it influences every thought about others and ourselves. It influences our actions, our feelings, and our interactions with others and with God. It can make us depressed or angry, defeated or arrogant. Some people only know how to deal with shame superficially by a quick fix, a drug or a behavior that causes our body to produce its own drug. The result is the same: instant relief. But that produces more shame, and another quick fix is the answer. This is part of the addictive process.

12. We can inflict shame by criticizing excessively, communicating contempt, or implying that a person's worth is determined by performance or appearance. Instead, we need to communicate that we accept the addicted person as a wonderful, lovable creation of God whose behavior is unacceptable.

13. Addicts are master manipulators. Parents can resist manipulation only when they are united. Parental unity needs to occur after both have shared their thoughts and feelings and negotiated a unified position.

14. There but for the grace of God go I.

The Great Physician

Due to this pattern of automatically reacting because of the emotional, intellectual and spiritual bruises you are carrying, you must concentrate on your own growth. The patterns become habitual. You need to consciously work on it so that you do not automatically react in those ways. We need to recognize that the Lord heals these bruises.

Healing Process Requires Patience

According to 1 Peter 5:10, "… after you have suffered a little while, [God] will himself restore you and make you strong, firm, and steadfast" (NIV). We need to be restored from these patterns that we have developed. It is very interesting that this process takes "a little while." We want to scream out, "How long is a little while?" The Bible teaches us that for God a minute is as a thousand years. We need to develop some patience.

The recovery for us as well as the addict requires a process. Part of that process

---

1. A helpful book is *Parenting Your Teen with Love and Logic* by Dr. Foster Cline and Jim Fay.

involves confessing to one another and praying for one another. The promise is that we will be healed. How do we do that? In 1986, I tried to figure out how many Alcoholics Anonymous and Ala-Anon meetings I had attended. It was about a thousand, and at that time I quit counting. We need to get involved with people who can accept us, people with whom we can share. Groups can be very helpful for that.

Couples can help each other to heal in these areas. Families can work together to bring about healing for each other. We need to heal, because if we approach addicts with irritability, blame or control, they probably won't listen.

Finding Joy in Difficulties

James 1 says, "Consider it pure joy … whenever you face trials of many kinds …" (NIV). I don't think that verse means just to put on a happy face, dance around and have fun. It means that God wants us to see these situations as opportunities to become totally dependent on Him. For the loved one, it is necessary to become totally dependent on God. We need to quit trying to control things ourselves. There is a difference between giving up and letting go. I don't advise that we give up, but we do need to let go.

"Count it all joy" also means drawing closer to your life mate and becoming more understanding, softer and more gracious in the way we minister to others. It also means that we should remain hopeful. When we do all of these things, I think we will encounter joy.

Recovery from Addiction

My basic theory about addiction recovery is stated in principle #8: Addicts will never quit the addiction until they view continuing the addiction as more painful than stopping. Therefore, anything done to lessen the painful consequences of practicing the addiction will reduce any motivation to stop.

I've never met an addict who just woke up one day and said, "Oh, this is a good day to stop using drugs." No. Instead, addicts say, "If I don't quit, I think I'm going to die." The struggle at one point is, "I'm going to die if I don't use." Then when it comes time for recovery, it is, "I'm going to die if I keep on using." That fear is the motivator. We have to allow the addicts to experience the natural consequences of their behavior.

When we take responsibility for the addicts' behavior, then the addicts don't have to. So if we take responsibility for seeing to it that no drugs are available or no alcohol is available, then the addicts or alcoholics don't have to worry about it because we're worrying about it. They can just go ahead and have fun. However, when the parent says, "If you use drugs or alcohol, you cannot live in this house," that places all the responsibility for staying clean where it should be—back on the addict.

Zach's Tips for Recovery

1. Most recovery failures come from
   - not dealing with the underlying codependency
   - not dealing with all addictions
   - not being totally honest.
2. Let go and let God! Get out of God's way so He can make things better.
3. Easy does it, but do it! Move cautiously, but move!
4. This too shall pass! Nothing stays the same. Give it time, and it will change. Relax and don't try to force it.
5. A "dry drunk" has no better excuse for bad behavior than a "wet drunk" has!
6. Just don't take the first (drink, hit, snort, look, bite, etc).
7. What works for someone else might work for me!
8. Addictive behavior must be stopped in order to make progress in recovery. For example, the addict goes to detox to get the drug out of her body. Then she goes into treatment. The first step is to stop the addictive behavior and get the addictive substances out of the system. Until that is done, you are dealing with a person whose brain is not functioning well.
9. Addictive behavior begins with focusing on the desire. Focus on God instead!
10. Addicts deceive themselves when they say, "I'm only hurting myself." That's why the "Twelve Steps to Recovery" includes five steps that focus on relationships that have been damaged by the addictive behavior.
11. This too shall pass. Two things make an addictive urge go away: practicing the addiction (using the drug of choice), and the passing of time. To avoid practicing the addiction, the addict can use the phrase "this too shall pass" as a reminder that the urge will eventually go away with the passing of time. Just be patient and trust that it will go away.
12. First things first! The first thing for an addict is RECOVERY!
13. Temptations go away when we don't give in to them. They come back when we do give in to them.
14. What causes problems is one. One addict said that she had no food in the house and hadn't paid bills in a couple of months. Yet she was using drugs? An alcoholic or addict will say, "I don't have this

or that. I've got all these problems," but he or she will never make the connection that the "using" is causing all the problems. "What causes problems is the problem." This statement can help people to take the first step of the Twelve-Step Program.

15. Our secrets keep us sick.

16. When someone else takes responsibility for an addict's behavior, the addict doesn't have to.

17. When you take responsibility for someone's drinking, he doesn't have a drinking problem. He has a drinking solution. You have the drinking problem. You have taken responsibility for this problem. Now the addict is free to use all he wants.

18. Don't argue about the details of the past. All parties' memories are selective and at least partially inaccurate, and their perceptions at the time were probably distorted. That means you are arguing over inaccurate memories of distorted perceptions. Just accept that you remember things differently and will never be able to prove it. Let go!

19. One day at a time! Jesus said that we shouldn't borrow trouble from tomorrow (Matthew 6:34), and Paul said that we should forget the past (Philippians 3:13).

First-Hand Experience

Have any of you been to a pot party? I was at one once, not knowing what was going on. Some of the counselors who worked for me had invited me and they were all smoking pot. They offered me some and, unlike some people we know, I didn't even puff, let alone inhale. I was flabbergasted. I ended up firing them all the next day. What I noticed was that the party was very quiet. No interaction at all. Every once in a while someone would say, "Wow!" "Cool!" "Look at that!" They reported the next day that they had had a ball, but I had been there. I had seen what had happened because I hadn't been stoned. The drug experience is a very internal experience.

One Perfect Parent

Remember my son who was rebellious? Applying what we learned from the book, *Parenting With Love and Logic*, my wife and I said to him, "You can choose to live here and follow this rule or you can choose to live somewhere else and keep doing what you're doing."

There is only one perfect Parent.

He said, "Oh, I'm going to live here. I'm not going to do it anymore."

That very night he did it again.

So the next day we said, "We see that you have chosen to live elsewhere. We will give you until August 1 to find a place. If you need any help with that, ask us. Maybe we could help you with it."

He moved out. He had dropped out of school at that point. Now, six years later, he has gotten his GED and he has been employed the entire time. He has been through a couple of unsatisfactory relationships. But he has said he realizes the mistakes that he made and he is getting on with his life. I wonder if he would have made all of those changes while he was still living with us. I'll never know.

There is only one perfect Parent. It is God the Father. Look at His kids. Just look around our planet and see what His kids are doing. He loves us unconditionally. And look what we are doing to each other. So, if you could be a perfect parent, your kid might still be on drugs. Therefore, don't take that responsibility on yourselves. Don't take the responsibility on yourself for your kid's drug use, because even if you were perfect, your kid still might be using.

You're not alone. God did not put 6 billion of us on this planet for each one of us to deal with our problems alone. So don't stay alone. Get help by developing a support system. Go to Al-Anon, or Nar-Anon. Go to support groups at your church. Go where you can talk to people and share with them. You need to do that, because you can't do it alone.

Growing Pains

Social and emotional growth is arrested when a people begin to use addictive substances to alter their feelings and perceptions. Therefore, whenyou're interacting with them, treat them as if they were at the age they were when they started abusing. Most start when they are teens. If an addict is 35 years old and has been using drugs all that time, you have to treat him as if he were a teenager.

Further, after he has begun using, it becomes impossible for him to have healthy relationships with other people. The drug experience is very personal and self-centered. Addiction is very self-centered. Once people start using drugs, they don't have much of a social life or interaction with other people other than scoring drugs or sharing needles, so you have to treat them as teenagers.

Chapter 12

Drugs: How They Work and What They Do

By Zach Whaley

God created us as unique human beings, and each of us has a particular response to everything that we experience. The same thing is true with drugs. In this chapter, I will discuss the symptoms and effects of various drugs, but keep in mind that each individual will experience the drugs in his or her own way. I will simply share the effects of certain drugs on most people who use them.

Types of Drugs

There are three types of drugs: uppers, downers, and hallucinogens. The uppers stimulate; downers sedate. Hallucinogens are a kind of a combination of uppers and downers; they just get people mixed up.

UPPERS

- Cocaine
- Amphetamines/Methamphetamine
- Ecstasy (also a hallucinogen)
- Dexedrine
- Ritalin
- Nicotine
- Caffeine

Some of the uppers commonly abused are cocaine, amphetamines, and meth-amphetamines. Ecstasy, a relatively new drug on the scene, is a combination of an upper and a hallucinogen. Dexedrine and Ritalin, legal drugs prescribed for weight loss, are mainly prescribed for Attention Deficit Disorder and Attention Deficit Hyperactivity Disorder, but Ritalin, when used illegally, has become a drug of choice among college students in preparing for exams. Nicotine and caffeine are also uppers.

DOWNERS

- Alcohol
- Heroin and other opiates (morphine, codeine, percadan)
- Barbiturates
- Tranquilizers
- Rohypnol (date rape drug; also a hallucinogen)
- Sleeping pills
- Pain killers

Alcohol, the most commonly used and abused downer, is one of the most destructive drugs available. Then there's heroin and other opiates: morphine, codeine, and percodan. Barbiturates are mainly prescribed for sleep and as tranquilizers, and are also prescribed to reduce anxiety. Rohipnol is the date rape drug; it's also a hallucinogen. Just as ecstasy is a combination of an upper and a hallucinogen, Rohipnol is a combination of a downer and a hallucinogen. Any kind of sleeping pills and painkillers fit into this category.

HALLUCINOGENS

- LSD, Shrooms (mushrooms)
- PCP (animal tranquilizer)
- Marijuana, Hashish
- Rohypnol (date rape drug) (also a downer)
- Ecstasy (also an upper)

What Happens When We Take Drugs

Look at the "Physical Model of Addiction" below. Notice the arrows. The "up" arrow represents increasing stimulation. The "down" arrow is increasing sedation.

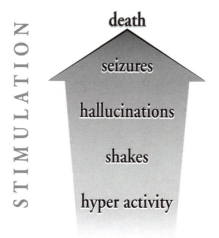

STIMULATION

death

seizures

hallucinations

shakes

hyper activity

Average Tension Level

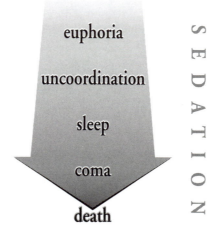

SEDATION

euphoria

uncoordination

sleep

coma

death

The center line is labeled the "average" tension level. We call it that because, as we go through the day, the amount of tension in our bodies varies. You can prove this by taking your blood pressure every hour. You'll see that it fluctuates. Sometimes it's higher; sometimes it's lower. And as long as it remains in the general area around the average tension level, we hardly notice the fluctuations in tension.

Ingesting Downers

If I were to ingest a downer, I would come out of this average tension level and come down to euphoria. This provides a feeling of goodness, like that dreamy feeling just before you fall asleep. It's a really nice feeling. It's leveling. If I were to take enough of that downer, I would come down to the point at which I would become uncoordinated, because the messengers from the brain to the muscles would be slow. Sedation slows everything down: heart rate, blood pressure, and neurological activity. If I would think, "Grab that pen," I might miss the pen because my muscles wouldn't react to what I want, because my brain wouldn't be functioning well. I might do such things as stagger when I walk, knock over objects, and crash into things with my car.

If I were to take more of a sedative, that would bring me down to sleep. When they get enough sedation, people just fall asleep. They pass out wherever they are and in whatever they're doing. I've seen people at a bar fall asleep, people fall asleep in the middle of a party, and people fall asleep while driving.

Then, if I became even more sedated, it would really start to get dangerous. At this point, people under sedation go into comas wherein everything slows down to the point that the only parts of their bodies that are functioning are the heart and lungs. Everything else goes to sleep.

And, of course, if I were to be sedated beyond that, one of those—either my heart or my lungs—would stop. I would either stop breathing or my heart would stop beating, and that's death. So sedatives can kill if we take enough of them.

Ingesting Uppers

The uppers, the stimulants, cause a reverse situation. If I were to take a stimulant, I would move out of the normal tension range and up into a hyper range. Some people experience this as excitement, as being "bright," but some people experience it as being very agitated, very nervous, and very irritated, so they don't like the uppers. They'll stick with the downers.

If I were to take more of a stimulant, I could start shaking. The shakes may begin with a shaky feeling inside, but pretty soon I would start shaking on the outside. Remember, everything would be speeding up now. My heart rate would accelerate, my blood pressure would increase, and my brain activity would be much more rapid.

Then, if I were to take even more of these stimulants, I could begin to hallucinate. The stimulant would be causing my brain to produce sensations that I normally experience through my senses by seeing something and having it register through my brain. If I took enough stimulants, something wouldn't have to be there for me to see it. My brain would create an image, a hallucination. Or, my brain might create a feeling like something was crawling on my skin or in my body, which is called "tactile hallucinations."

If I continued to add stimulants, I could go into seizures. The effect would be just like a grand mal seizure. If stimulation went beyond that, then once again, there would be death.

A Five-Dimensional Impact

As human beings, we have five dimensions: physical body, intellect, behavior, emotions and spirit. These five dimensions are interactive: each one influences and is influenced by the other four. Ingesting a drug results in alterations of the physical body. Those changes then affect the other four dimensions. So drug use creates a pretty complex process, as illustrated by the diagram below.

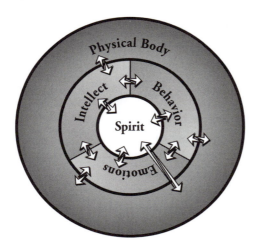

The drug goes into the physical body. It then acts on behavior, emotions, spirit and intellect.

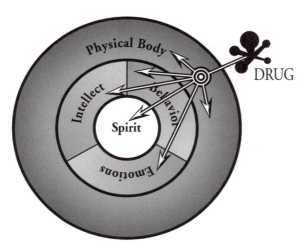

1. Physical Effects of Drug Abuse

Generally, uppers can produce shakes and make people feel jumpy. They're able to do things faster and with more strength. They sense things more quickly. Their senses become much more alert. This is why some athletes take uppers, because it helps them perform better. In World War II, the Japanese gave uppers to their pilots so they would be much more alert. A person on uppers will have eyes that sparkle. The heart rate and blood pressure increase. However, there's the increased risk of organ damage, including a potential for a massive heart attack.

As the blood pressure increases and the heart rate accelerates, people on uppers begin doing things that really test their strength and endurance. They may go on and on for days without sleep. This also improves one's chances for a heart attack, particularly for those who use uppers regularly.

Downers affect the physical dimension differently. Remember, they make you sleepy, they decrease coordination, and they decrease our sensory mechanisms. For example, many older alcoholics have burns on their fingers because they no longer have feeling in their fingers and they often smoke cigarettes down to the point where they burn their fingers. Alcohol destroys nerve cells and, generally, we can't reproduce them. However, research is beginning to show that with certain nerves and in some instances, we can reproduce them. People on downers frequently are unkempt; they don't take good care of themselves. Downers decrease pain.

Using downers also damages major organs. Alcohol is one of the most dangerous drugs that we have; it damages all organs that use blood, because it is carried in the blood. That affects just about every organ, doesn't it? We measure blood alcohol concentration to see if somebody's driving drunk. The brain is a big user of blood, so alcohol destroys a lot of brain cells. The liver is a big user of blood, so it gets cirrhosis of the liver. Any part of the body that processes food and waste is irritated and inflamed and can undergo serious damage by the alcohol.

Marijuana, we're discovering, also causes brain damage. Tobacco and marijuana damage the lungs. Researchers say that one marijuana cigarette creates about the same damage as three to five tobacco cigarettes. Pretty soon, the lungs can't take in the air.

2. Emotional Effects of Drug Use

Uppers can cause people to feel angry, fearful, and paranoid. In fact, if you're with people who are really high on methamphetamines or other stimulants, don't move too quickly around them. In fact, if you're going to go from here to there, you might say, "Hey, I'm going to get up and go over there," because they get very paranoid. You don't want to scare them. Remember, they have a lot of energy, and that energy has to go someplace. A lot of time it goes into attacking somebody. Those who use uppers also have good feelings, excitement and elation.

Downers cause many people to feel sad. You've heard of people on a crying jag; they drink alcohol and cry. Those using downers can also get angry or happy. Depressants cause people to be very uninhibited in expressing their emotions; the drugs reduce their ability to exercise much control over them.

For those who use hallucinogens, emotions are mixed. Remember, these drugs are a kind of mixture of uppers and downers. So they produce a mixed bag of emotions. For example, marijuana can make people feel mellow, or calm, but it can also make them behave in a silly way and laugh. PCP, on the other hand, can make people really wild and unpredictable.

3. Intellectual Effects of Drug Use

Drugs affect the intellect of all users. Generally, the drugs cause people to:

- **Make unwise decisions** - They make unwise decisions because the drugs hinder healthy decision-making processes.
- **Use rationalization and denial** - When I smoked, I used to say, "I really don't have to worry, because by the time I'm ready to get cancer, they'll have a cure for it." So I just continued smoking. That was my method of denial.
- **Blame others for what happens to them** - They don't take responsibility for what they're experiencing.
- **Make excuses for their own behavior** - "Well, you don't understand, I was having a bad day and therefore you have to accept what I did."
- **Lie** - People say, "The one thing I can't stand is all the lying." I say, "That's the least of all your worries." As long as a person is addicted, he has to lie. You cannot tell the truth and maintain an addiction. Lying is part of addiction. You deal with the addiction, and then you can deal with

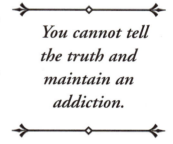

You cannot tell the truth and maintain an addiction.

the lying. The Alcoholics Anonymous *Big Book* says rarely is a person found who cannot recover following the Twelve Steps. But a few are so incapable of being truthful that they can't recover. So, lying is part of addiction.
- **Constantly focus on the next dose** - There was a time in my life when I drank a lot. When we were living in Virginia, there were dry counties and wet counties. Whenever we were going to out to dinner, our first thought was to go eat at a restaurant in a county where we could drink. The issue wasn't about finding a nice restaurant, good food, or a certain type of food; we simply wanted to go where we could drink. In planning a vacation, my first thought would be: How many cigarettes do I need to bring along? How much alcohol are we going to bring along? Are we going to bring gin or scotch? Ensuring the supply is the first thought of a person who is abusing drugs and alcohol.

- **Lower their standards of morality** - People find themselves hanging out in places where they never thought they would ever be comfortable. They find socialize with people with whom, at one time, they would have sworn they would never be comfortable.
- **Think they are powerful and omnipotent with uppers and think really slowly with downers** - People say, "I want to talk to this person who is drunk." I say, "Why bother?"

Drug abuse gives Satan a foothold with which to find his way into people's lives.

You can't talk to somebody whose brain is asleep." Basically, that's what happens. The alcohol goes to the frontal lobe immediately and starts putting it to sleep. Would you carry on a conversation with somebody who's lying there asleep? No. Just because a person has his eyes open doesn't mean he's awake if he's on downers.

How Downers Affect Memory

Downers decrease attentiveness. There are two aspects to that. One is the short-term memory. That's when the person on downers will tell a joke and then a half hour later will tell the same joke, then an hour later will repeat it. There is also the amnesia experience that we call a "blackout," which finds people waking up the next day and having no recollection of anything they had done the night before. I knew a man once who was in recovery from alcoholism for many months. He was going fishing in northern Virginia. As he was driving up to a fishing lake, he stopped at a little country store to get some food; he walked out of the store with a six-pack of beer. He had not intended to do that, but he did. He came to--six months later in Louisiana—with no recollection of anything since the time he had walked out of that store with a six-pack of beer. That's a blackout. Alcoholics think nothing of that. They say, "Well, yeah, I don't remember, but tell me how much fun I had last night." They have no recollection, and they don't see a big problem with it.

Hallucinogens Cause Psychosis

Intellectually, people who use hallucinogens, especially PCP and LSD, can act and be psychotic. With marijuana there's the a-motivational syndrome; in other words, they lose motivation. I find a marijuana user one of the most difficult people to work with in recovery. Marijuana also affects the memory and the ability to be attentive. In fact, attentiveness and memory are affected even after the marijuana abuse is stopped. Recent studies showed that 24 hours after people were no longer high, their ability to attend and to remember things was impaired.

4. Behavioral Effects of Drug Use

Most behavior of people abusing alcohol and drugs is self-serving. Their behavior is out of control. They'll do anything to get the next dose, whether it's heroin, alcohol, marijuana, or any other drug. Again, they'll behave in ways that are far below the moral standards they may have previously held. Uppers can make people attack others and make them very impulsive; they'll do things at the spur of the moment. Downers can make people aggressive because it depresses their inhibitions. If they don't like somebody or they are mad at somebody, they can be aggressive. Also, they can be behaviorally uncoordinated. The behavior of those under the influence of hallucinogens is unpredictable and of those using marijuana, it's slow. PCP causes very wild behavior. All three—uppers, downers and hallucinogens—can make people act wild, but for different reasons. The uppers make people act wild because they have so much energy. The downers make people act that way because it takes away their inhibitions. The hallucinogens make people act wild because their brains are going crazy.

5. Effect of Drugs on Spirituality

Generally, people turn away from God when they use drugs. Drug abuse gives Satan a foothold with which to find his way into people's lives. A denial of personal responsibility may be seen as a spiritual issue as well as an intellectual issue. The drug abusers are seeking a god who will make them feel good. Since the drug makes them feel good, the drug becomes their god, like an idol, and alienates them from the true God.

Social Effects of Drug Abuse

- **People who abuse drugs generally are isolated and alienated.** They don't think they are, because they have their drug buddies or their drinking buddies. But in just about every case in which somebody quits using, his or her old buddies don't miss a beat. They just keep right on going with their lives. So even though people use the drugs with other people, it's basically an isolating experience. People turn inward when they're using drugs. They can become lonely as a result.

- **People who use drugs will use people in order to get their drugs.** The commitment to drugs replaces a commitment to people; so people that they have a commitment to, like spouses and children, take second, third, or fourth priority to the drugs. Obviously, that affects social relationships.

- **People who use drugs tend to get involved in legal problems.** Most drug abuse is illegal. Those who abuse alcohol, a legal substance, can also get involved in legal problems, because of the way it causes people to act.

- **People who use drugs often have work problems.** They may have trouble getting to work on time, or they may have trouble getting work at all. Or, they may get to work and manifest some of the symptoms listed earlier, perhaps by becoming overly aggressive with a customer, for example.

Recovery

The first thing that happens when a substance abuser begins to recover is withdrawal. The person who has been using a drug stops using. What happens? Let's consider an example of a person who takes some sedative drugs and is uncoordinated. Pretty soon the liver begins to get rid of the drug. The effect of the drug wears off and the user returns to the average tension level. But there is a rebound, or secondary drug effect, and the person will jump from the sedated to the stimulated area on our diagram (page 117). On the other hand, the withdrawal from a stimulant drug is to be sedated. So a person who uses speed and goes for three days without sleep may crash and sleep for three days.

A person who has been using a downer and then stops is going to be stimulated, hyper, irritable, and easily irritated. He's going to have difficulty sleeping. A noise down the block might wake him up; he just can't get into that deep sleep because his body is up in the stimulated area on the graph. The rebound lasts longer than the initial effect.

If you understand what the drug effects are, then you understand what the withdrawal is going to be.

- **Physical Dimension:** Withdrawal from uppers causes the person to be tired, feel drowsy, and have headaches. Withdrawal from downers causes shakiness, inability to sleep, and restlessness. Withdrawal from hallucinogens mainly causes fatigue. But all of those in recovery need good nutrition, plenty of sleep and medical attention because they have not been taking care of themselves, plus they've been abusing their bodies. So they need a good physical exam, and they may need medical attention. For example, many times, recovering alcoholics need to have their teeth fixed because the alcohol has killed the pain related to any dental problems they may have had. When they stop taking the alcohol, all of a sudden those tooth problems begin hurting.
- **Behavioral Dimension:** The recovering person needs to stop taking the drug. They also need to eat right, exercise, sleep, and clean up.
- **Emotional Dimension:** The person in recovery needs "the peace that transcends all understanding," because with the uppers, emotionally he or she will be extremely depressed. This makes it difficult to help cocaine addicts. I've always been against the use of drugs to help somebody get off drugs; but I thinks it's okay to give cocaine addicts antidepressants because that deep depression in rebound really pulls them back into drug use.
- **Intellectual Dimension:** Recovering addicts have the same habits of rationalizing, excusing, denying, and lying as they did before they began the process

of recovery; they have to change that. They have to be renewed in the attitude of their mind. They have to change from rationalizing to using logic, from making excuses to taking responsibility, from denying the truth to accepting it, and from lying to telling the truth. They need to learn the lesson that pain is useful information, not something to be avoided.

- **Social Dimension:** Those in recovery need to get rid of old friends and form new friendships. Twelve-step programs provide a good source of new friends who will be supportive of their recovery. They also need to work things out with employers, the legal authorities, and anyone whom they have hurt during their times of addiction and abuse. In other words, they need to pay off any debts and make amends.

- **Spiritual Dimension:** Those who are in recovery need to claim power in Christ: "I can do everything through Him who gives me strength" (Philippians 4:13, NIV); and "… there is now no condemnation for those who are in Christ Jesus" (Romans 8:1, NIV). They need to confess their sins. They need to put off the old, put on the new, and develop a new attitude. They need to turn their lives and their wills over to the care of God, and they need to improve their conscious contact with God. They need a daily quiet time to prepare for the day and another to take stock at the end of the day.

While people are engaged in the recovery process, it's important to keep in mind that while they're trying to do all these things, their bodies, their minds, their emotions, and their natural spirits are demanding the drug. When they're in withdrawal, they know that they can stop this bad feeling just by taking their drug. Never mind that the drug caused it in the first place; they think the drug will make them feel better now. The reality is that taking the drug would just start them over again. For example, if a downer-user takes a drug to relieve the rebound, first he has to take enough to overcome the rebound, and then more to get sedated. That just starts the whole addictive process again. Some day he's going to have to just stop.

Chapter 13

Dealing with Chemical Dependency in Our Family

By Gregory and Rita Iverson

Having been in the ministry for more than 26 years, I tend to look for the deeper theological or spiritual meanings in almost everything. Chalk it up to a seminary education, maybe more significantly to the years I've spent in the ministry, perhaps more significantly yet to just experiencing the ups and downs and ins and outs of life. Whatever the reason, it seems pretty clear that the things that really matter rarely just happen. Life has meaning, theological meaning.

Not everything that happens demands theological explanation, of course. Things like my team winning a big game or overcooking the evening meal or running out of gas on the freeway probably have causes apart from God. Not that God isn't involved in the details of life. It's just that He has given us considerable latitude – freewill, most theologians would call it – over much of our lives. Some things happen because we planned them that way, or because we didn't plan at all, or because we planned poorly.

But, other things, some of life's major events, seem to call for a theological explanation – or at least an attempt at theological or spiritual understandings. Matters of life and death, human suffering and otherwise mysterious or miraculous events need a deeper theological exploration. When some event happens that has an impact upon my life and my family's life for this time and for some time to come, I seek to understand that event in theological context. What follows is my attempt to share some sort of theological perspective on something that profoundly changed my family and me as we became aware of it a couple of years ago.

—Greg Iverson

The Slings and Arrows of Misfortune

Life seemed pretty normal for us until the spring of 2000. Rita and I were in our 26th year of marriage. We had two children: Emily, 22 years old, graduating from college, and Brad, 16 years old, a sophomore in high school. Emily had gone away to college and so there were now just three in our household. To be sure, we had already faced some of life's difficulties. Our first child was stillborn. My parents divorced after 35 years of marriage. My father then died in 1996. My job as a pastor moved us from place to place, which stressed our family from time to time. The demands of ministry had occasionally made life less than completely comfortable for us. Besides that, Rita's work as a registered nurse specializing in oncology, seemingly always a matter of life and death, has not been easy. Our remaining three parents were aging and dealing with various sicknesses, including cancer. But, on balance, nothing was terribly out of the ordinary in our lives. We handled life like most people handle life. The celebrations and pains came in roughly equal numbers. Our faith in God gave us strength for the present and hope for the future. In other words, life seemed pretty normal.

Troubled Teen Years

Our son Brad, though, seemed to be going through a difficult adolescence for some reason, more difficult than that of our daughter. His grades started to drop and continued to do so fairly steadily. Little by little, he quit almost all extracurricular activities. He seemed increasingly argumentative. We wondered whether our last move, just before his seventh-grade year, had been more difficult on him than on the rest of us. We thought that being the only child at home might be making things difficult for him. We had him checked for learning disorders. We didn't have any definitive answers, just a lot of concern.

Early on, we had suspicions of drug use. Knowing what we know now, we should have acted upon those suspicions and had a chemical dependency evaluation done immediately. But Brad denied any use of drugs, and we didn't find any evidence in his room. Maybe, in retrospect, we should have searched his room more often or more thoroughly. He said that he had some friends that smoked and that's why he smelled like smoke himself. He seemed to have answers for our questions and we felt that we had to take him at his word. We trusted him, sort of.

> **Rita's Thoughts:** The whole disease of chemical dependency was new to me. I had not had any personal experience with it whatsoever. Accordingly, I went through the various stages of grief, shock, denial, anger, depression and acceptance, but not necessarily in that order. I took Brad's use personally. I wondered what had I done or not done as a parent. I was devastated. I wanted to love Brad unconditionally, but I felt deeply hurt and betrayed. I felt judgmental toward him.

Wake-Up Call?

But then things got much worse. Almost weekly, things seemed to deteriorate. Someone from school called us almost daily to let us know that he had been tardy for at least one class. Some days, he didn't even attend school. He would leave home on time and arrive at home on time, but we would find out later that he hadn't entered the school building at all. Then, one night, the night before our daughter Emily graduated from college, the police called us to come to the station to pick up our son, who had been stopped for underage consumption. He received a sentence of a little community service, which we had hoped would be a "wake-up call" for him. He also had to pay his own money to attend a lecture on drug use with other kids and their parents. But that didn't turn out to be much of a wake-up call. If things were changing, they were changing only for the worse. His grades bottomed out, literally, and he set school records, again, almost literally, in accumulating tardies and truancies.

Trying Treatment

Finally, acting on a tip we received from a school counselor, we took Brad in for a chemical dependency evaluation. He tested positive. We put him through three weeks of outpatient chemical dependency treatment. Of course, we "took the cure" along with him. The last week of that program, an intensive family-therapy week, was the most exhausting week that we have ever experienced. It required more emotional energy more than we could ever have imagined. That was the week that we found out that Brad had not used just a little "weed" now and then, the word he used for marijuana, but that he had used a lot of "weed" and also had tried just about everything else. We were shocked by the extent of our son's drug use, but he assured us that it was all in the past. We completed the program, thinking that we had "graduated" and that, with a little follow-up now and then, things would be just fine. Well, they weren't.

Car Troubles

In the meantime, Brad had been asking for a car for a long time. He worked a little bit but didn't keep his jobs for very long and didn't save much money at all. He always said, of course, that he would do better in getting to school on time and getting back and forth to work and keeping a job if he just had his own transportation. His behavior around home and his record at school were hardly worth rewarding. But, like his sister before him, he eventually wore us down. We got tired of saying "no" and eventually and reluctantly and, in retrospect, mistakenly, said "yes." So, out of money that we had saved for his college education, money he promised that he would pay back, we bought him a car a week or so before his 17th birthday.

That car lasted about a month before he totaled it. He had just picked up his paycheck at his latest place of work and reached down to pick it up off the floor on the passenger side of the car. He rear-ended a car waiting to make a left turn.

Everybody makes a mistake now and then, even though Brad's mistakes seem to have always come with large price tags and long-term consequences. So, after another month or so, with the insurance settlement and a few more bucks from his college account, we bought Brad – I hate to say it – his second car. He had that one about another month or so before he ran into a row of the most firmly planted mailboxes in human history. The mailbox posts were virtually undamaged but the car's front end had caved in badly and the frame was bent. There was no way that we could make another insurance claim so soon, so we paid cash, again out of his college account, about $5,000, to fix a $7,000 car. Before too long, he smashed that car once more for a total of three accidents in about four months. He also received two or three speeding tickets within that same period of time.

More Treatment Necessary

Our relationship with him around the house only got worse. Rita, to be perfectly honest, did better than I did at keeping communication with him open. I had a hard time reading the books that Rita was reading that explained our situation. I just wanted things to get better and was frustrated because they weren't heading in that direction.

> *I just wanted things to get better and was frustrated because they weren't heading in that direction.*

Brad lied to us again and again and again. We didn't realize at the time that chemically dependent people are liars--good liars, great liars, world-class liars, of necessity. He would tell us that he had been in school when he hadn't been, that he had done his homework when he hadn't, that he had stayed overnight with a friend we knew when he hadn't, that he hadn't used drugs when he had.

Finally, we took Brad in for another chemical dependency evaluation. He tested positive again. It seems that he thought that he could beat the odds and "handle" his drug use by just being more careful and more moderate. Well, of course, he couldn't. Care and moderation are meaningless concepts for chemically dependent and addicted people. We put him through chemical dependency treatment one more time, this time in an inpatient program. First, he spent a week in a lock-up facility where he sobered up. Then, over the next two weeks, he lived in a residential treatment facility.

Following the completion of that program, with a couple of false starts, he was admitted to Sobriety High, a small sober high school not far from where we live. As far as we know, he has been sober for the past seven months. He goes to Alcoholics Anonymous meetings somewhat regularly and, in his school, gets daily group times with all of the students who are working together on their sobriety.

The story may not be over. In fact, it probably isn't. We just hope and pray that the most traumatic parts of it are. We know that, as "the program" teaches, all you can do is to take things "one day at a time." He's still a teenager, 18 years old last month. That means that, even without using drugs, he still has all kinds of ways of driving us crazy. But he's sober now, at least he seems to be, and that's the big thing.

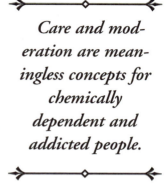

Care and moderation are meaningless concepts for chemically dependent and addicted people.

Rita's Thoughts: I knew that some of Brad's treatable problems with learning difficulties and depression had contributed to his drug use. I also knew that chemical dependency is a disease but it manifests itself in many anti-social, illegal, and I am convinced, immoral ways that compound the problem so it can be very embarrassing to discuss. But, we got help. We read books, attended meetings, talked to friends, saw counselors, went to family therapy sessions and prayed. I have tried and continue to try to turn Brad over to God to let Him handle it.

Who's Responsible?

One of my favorite episodes of M*A*S*H is when Hawkeye Pierce, the irreverent but exceedingly capable surgeon, finally "has it up to here" with the Korean War and decides to have Radar, the company clerk, send a telegram to President Harry Truman. It's a short telegram. "Dear Harry," it says. "Who's responsible?"

I've been trying to figure that out in my own life and in my family's life for the past couple of years. Just who's responsible? Not just for this event and that event, for the little things that make up our lives, but for everything, for the "big picture." Like a lot of people, back when it was a "hot" book, I read Rabbi Harold Kushner's *Why Bad Things Happen to Good People.* That never explained very well to me why relatively good people--and like most people, I've always considered myself to be a relatively good person--should ever have to suffer. I couldn't buy everything that Kushner was trying to "sell." For one thing, he's a Jew and I'm a Christian; we approach religious faith differently. He seems to suggest that there are some things that a good God just can't, or, at the very least, won't do. His argument is that if God is good (and, by definition, God must be good), then some bad things happen because God just has no control or chooses not to have control over those things. God, Kushner says, wouldn't be good if he could exercise control over some of the bad things in life but then chose not to do so. Like I say, I can't buy that. God is omnipotent, omniscient and omnipresent: all-powerful, all-knowing and everywhere present. I can't believe that God is responsible for what happened to my family and me, or that it "just happened." So, like Hawkeye, I've been trying to figure out just who's responsible.

The Existence of the Devil

Interestingly enough, 26 years of experience in the ministry and 51 years of age, much more than my formal theological education, have finally taught me what others have known for a long time: that there is a real personification of evil in the world traditionally called the devil or Satan. I'm a slow learner, apparently. However, much of what I have learned about life and the influences of evil has taught me that someone is in charge of evil in this world.

You've probably heard him called everything from Lucifer to the man downstairs, but no matter what label you stick on him, the devil is real. If you've been around church very long, you've probably heard that Lucifer, whose name means "star of the morning," was actually one of God's angels (Isaiah 14:12-15). He wanted to be God, but God wouldn't have it so He cast the devil out of heaven (2 Peter 2:4).

Satan again appears on the pages of history as a serpent who tempted Adam and Eve to disobey God. That resulted in the three of them being thrown out of the garden. (Boy, Satan keeps getting thrown out of places, doesn't he?) Even though Satan thought he won, he was—and is—a defeated foe actually on God's leash. Think about Job! Satan had to ask God's permission to mess with Job's family and farm (Job 1-2).

For now, the devil "prowls around like a roaring lion seeking someone to devour" (2 Peter 5:8, 9). We need to be on the alert, acknowledge that he's really there, and resist the traps he throws our way.

Now, please don't misunderstand me. I'm not suggesting that there is a devil behind every bush. Not everything can be blamed on the devil. Sometimes, at least, Pogo was right. "We have met the enemy and he is us." We need to take responsibility for our own actions and the mistakes and sins that we commit. We have been created with a free will, and our willful misuse of that freedom sometimes brings about a just punishment. It does no good to be irrationally fearful or unreasonably blameful. The devil is not under each and every rock.

However, the devil may be behind more bushes than we think! We cannot explain away every destructive act as mere deviant behavior. We cannot dismiss hatred and hate crimes as diversity. True, we need to take responsibility for the evil things that we do. Nonetheless, some evil things happen because they are a part of a master plan by a master evildoer.

In other words, I have to believe that evil is a reality in this world, both in its larger worldwide manifestations and in its much smaller and more personal and yet, still exceedingly hurtful manifestations, like what has happened to my family and me over the past couple of years.

The Devil in the Bottle

When I was about 12 years old, I went on a fishing trip to Canada with my father and some of his friends and their sons. It was a great trip. We were gone for about a week and we caught lots of fish. While the boys drank all the soft drinks they could consume over the course of a week without their mothers around, the men drank beer and, occasionally something stronger. I don't recall that any of the dads drank way too much or that they had so much to drink that they became sick or belligerent or falling-down drunk. They were just behaving like a lot of men felt that they could behave in front of their sons without their wives around: a little rowdy but not too rowdy. However, I remember one conversation when my father's old high school classmate Wayne took another swig of beer and said to the men and the boys sitting around the campfire, "You know, if there ever was a devil, he lived in a bottle." Everybody laughed at that.

What I remembered for decades as a joke was visited upon me as a reality a couple of years ago. Although the devil is alive and well in many different circumstances, certainly one of the places where he lives, I am convinced, is in the bottles and the joints and the capsules and the syringes that we sometimes use to numb our pain or somehow to relax us or to enhance our lives. For me, it's no longer a joke. It's no longer something to be mocked. The devil does live in a bottle, among other places, where he waits for us and lures us into destruction.

I don't know what your experience with chemical dependency may be, but I simply have no other way to explain the kind of havoc and destruction visited upon my family and me through my son's use of chemicals. There is simply no question in my mind when it comes to who's responsible. When it comes to chemical dependency, the devil is responsible.

I need to say that. I need to admit that. I need to identify the enemy. You can't fight an enemy until you know who that enemy is. For me, it's perfectly obvious that not only Rita and I, but also Brad, more than either of us, have all been fighting the devil.

Why Me, Lord?

The question of responsibility leads to yet another question: Why me, Lord? So the devil is behind all kinds of destruction on global levels and on personal levels. Why me? Why has this particular form of evil, chemical dependency, been visited upon my family and me instead of someone else and his or her family? Is it a purely random, an accidental kind of thing like contracting some dread disease over which we have no control? Is it a kind of "out of the blue" experience that no one had any way of foretelling? Or, is it in some way according to some plan perhaps not entirely understood by us, an intentional bit of evil specifically designed for a specific person at a specific time and in a specific way?

For some reason, through the chemical dependency of my son, Satan chose to attack my family, my ministry, and me. In all honesty, it was potentially a lethal attack. He knew that my wife and I would be embarrassed by our son's behavior. He knew that some people would have doubts about my ability to be a leader of a congregation when it appeared that I couldn't be a leader in my own family. He knew that some people might even discover what Paul says in 1 Timothy 3:4-5, that a spiritual leader "must manage his own family well and see that his children obey him with proper respect" (NIV). In other words, if anyone does not know how to manage his own family, how can he take care of God's church?

The devil knew that people would gossip about my parenting abilities or about my being preoccupied too much with family matters to be a good pastor, or about my "worthiness" to teach them or their children. I have always taken seriously the words that were said to me when I was ordained: "Go and take thou authority to preach the Gospel." I think that the devil knew that the place to attack and wound me was through my family, which would seem to undermine that authority. The method, the instrument, the tool that he chose was the chemical dependency of our son.

We Methodists generally aren't taught much about spiritual warfare. I didn't learn about spiritual warfare in seminary. I learned about it in the heat of battle. It wasn't something that came to me out of a book, but rather out of my personal experience. The devil is strong, much stronger than I am in my own strength. Apart from God, I have no strength to stand against the evil that I have faced. I am powerless as a human being to stand against him whose plan it is to destroy everyone. The devil chose this one way to destroy my family and me and, through that personal destruction, to destroy my ministry. I had only one hope.

No Easy Answers

Looking back, it seems like the answer was so simple. But at the time, it was anything but simple. It was a mass destruction that resulted in confusion, chaos, despair, fear and hopelessness. I have found that I have always been pretty good at helping people discover what's wrong with their lives and at writing out prescriptions on what they could take that could fix their lives. Somehow, I was spiritually blinded about the things messed up in my own life and what I could do and needed to do to remedy those issues.

Part of the problem with being in a state of hopelessness is that you don't see what you can do to stop being hopeless. Telling someone who is confused to stop being confused is like telling someone to pick himself up by his own bootstraps. Rarely do you ever get very high above the ground doing that. No, you need strength and a power outside yourself to exert a force upon you to lift you up. That strength to us is God. It seems so simple. When going through that "dark night of the soul," the answer is anything but simple.

I would like to tell you that I just turned my life over to God once again and immediately He healed my family and me of all that we were facing. I'd like to be able to tell you my story as some sort of normative experience that you could take and apply to your life. I wish I had a miraculous cure for the chemical dependency of your son or your daughter. There's nothing I'd like more than to be able to stand here and to share a magic and miraculous cure that we experienced and which would surely work for you in the same way.

The programs that deal with chemical dependency – programs like Alcoholics Anonymous, Al-Anon, Narcotics Anonymous, Families Anonymous, and Alateen, etc. are right when they say the road to wellness happens just "one day at a time." That's why no one talks about being fully recovered or cured from chemical dependency. It's also why no family members or other loved ones talk about having recovered from the illness that comes from the chemical use of another family member. We're all recovering in this experience. We're all in the process of getting better.

Rita's Thoughts: I try to take one day at a time and have used various techniques in order to cope. It is still a daily struggle to let go and let God. I have grown in this experience though. I find myself really listening to people more and having a greater sensitivity toward others. I am learning no longer to expect or to need life to be perfect or like a fairy tale.

Voice of Experience

I want to tell you a few things that I have found to be helpful in my own personal and professional life regarding the chemical dependency of our son.

1. Don't try to carry the burden alone. After the initial shock and embarrassment and the accompanying confusion, chaos, despair, fear and hopelessness, I decided to take the advice that I had given to so many others and not to "go it alone" anymore. I told my personnel committee about my son's chemical dependency, about our family's struggle with it, and about the personal hurt it was causing us. I wanted to take the matter to them instead of running the risk of having one or more of them bring the matter to me. I also chose to talk with one or two close friends in the congregation about what we were facing. I needed friends and I found them.

> *A lot of information in the right hands can be exceedingly helpful. A little information in the wrong hands can be unbelievably hurtful.*

2. Use discernment in choosing confidants. On the other hand, I purposely did not speak publicly about what was happening in our family nor with just anyone. A lot of information in the right hands can be exceedingly helpful. A little information in the wrong hands can be unbelievably hurtful.

3. Make connections with support groups and professionals. Rita and I sought help from others who had faced similar circumstances. We went to Al-Anon and read their literature as a part of our daily devotional time. Rita has been much better and much more faithful in that exercise than I have been, but we approach our devotional lives in different ways – she more formally, me less formally. Nevertheless, we have both found help in being in groups of people who have "been there." We have attended meetings at Brad's schools. One advantage of his being kicked out of so many schools before finally landing at his present school is that we have lots of contacts with teachers and support staff in lots of locations. Every time somebody decides to hold a meeting about kids and chemical dependency, we put it on our calendar. We're there. We admit it. We can't face this alone. We need all the help we can get. In short, the way that we have chosen to take care of the business of getting healthy has been to make as many connections as possible with others and, through them, with God.

Epilogue

Some people have struggled with chemical dependency in their families for decades and even lifetimes. It would be presumptuous for my wife or me to suggest that we are experts and have this thing "licked" because of our experience of just a couple of years. We hope that it's over. We pray that it will be over. Yet, we know that it will never be completely over and that life will continue to be a struggle in this or some other ways until the day we die. We have found strength in the ability to share with others and encourage you to do the same.

Brad has been sober for about seven months now. We celebrate that. But we live with the reality that it could end at any time, even tonight while we are here, and that we may need to start the process all over again. What we have learned through the experience of the past couple of years, however, is that God will be with us as we work to beat the devil.

Rita's Thoughts: Obviously, we would never in a thousand years anticipated or wanted to go through this particular kind of experience. It has been and to a lesser degree continues to be the most traumatic experience I have ever faced. But again the events of the past couple of years have tested my faith and my patience and have brought me closer to God and deepened my faith. God has made it possible for me to get where I am today. I am convinced that He will make it possible for me to get through whatever happens in the future.

SECTION 6

Listening to the Recovering Addicts

There would be no pain for parents nor would there be any reason for a book had our kids not felt the need to use and abuse drugs. In the next three chapters such kids have been willing to talk freely about their descent into the world of drug and alcohol use and abuse. They are different people with different stories and different motivations. They help us parents understand that we can do a good job of parenting and still have our kids abuse drugs.

Chapter 14

A Young Addict's Perspective

By Evan Hodge

I had loving parents who were always there for me. They didn't always understand what I was going through, but that wasn't their fault. It was mine because of my lack of communication. The openness and the willingness from them were always there. I just didn't know about all the struggles my parents went through behind closed doors.

The Power of Peer Pressure

In fifth grade, while at a Christian School, I went through the drug abuse program DARE (Drug Abuse Resistance Education). The program taught that drugs are bad and you should never do them. In sixth grade, I hung around with my friends, including my best friend, who came from a loving Christian family. We did everything together. One night, we decided to sneak out to meet some other kids. We ended up at one of the schools, where some of the older kids were smoking weed. I had never really been exposed to it before. This was the first time I had ever seen it outside of what I had learned about it from the DARE program. At this time, the stuff I had heard the year before in the DARE program meant nothing to me.

I would have never tried marijuana if my friend had not done it first. I looked up to the other kids who were there, but if my best friend had said, "No," I probably would have said, "No," too. When I saw him go ahead and take that first hit, I felt compelled to do the same. "He did it," I figured, "It can't be that bad!" I am not blaming this on my friends, not at all. It was completely my responsibility of choosing to do this.

I would have never tried marijuana if my friend had not done it first.

Consequences? What Consequences?

They had taught us in the DARE program that drugs would make your teeth fall out and make other horrible things happen. Yet, every day at school, I would see my friends high, going to class, getting straight A's, and doing all the things they wanted to do – at least at the beginning. Many were excelling in sports and academics. I just didn't see any consequences at that time. I could not relate what the DARE program had taught me with what I saw happening around me.

Me, Me, Me

Throughout the next few years, I kept on doing my own thing. I did not realize what this was beginning to do to my family. However, when I was in the 8th grade, my Dad told me he was seriously considering quitting the ministry because of the question raised in the Bible that if you can't take care of your own household, how can you be a shepherd to a flock? That Dad might be screwed over because of something I was doing just didn't make any sense to me. It ticked me off because this was my life, my decision. It had nothing to do with him; but yet, it was affecting him.

It was ME who was getting high. It was ME who was hanging out with my friends. I was oblivious, mostly because I was selfish.

I just became angrier. Still, I did not realize at any time the full impact of the effect my choices were having on them, ever. It was ME who was getting high. It was ME who was hanging out with my friends. I was oblivious, mostly because I was selfish. That is the biggest thing about getting high; it is all about "Me" and is pure selfishness. A lot of kids don't have a clue that they are being so selfish and hurting their families, for they do not understand drug abuse affects the whole family. To me, this was about just doing my thing; it was no different from playing soccer or football.

In Plain Sight

It would take a few Jerry Springer episodes to explain all that I went through during that time. But all the time, I knew what I was doing was wrong. The desire in my heart was to continue getting high, not to do what God wanted me to do.

My parents were really naive, or so I thought, since both had been raised in good homes. Neither one had been exposed to the culture in which I was living. They had no idea that I could be high right in front of them, because they didn't know what to look for. I was high in front of my parents all the time; but I covered it up with my eye drops, breath mints, etc. I had everything under control, or so I thought. I thought that they had no idea, until the abuse was out of control and was clearly visible.

Cue in to Your Kid's Culture

I encourage you to understand the culture and the lifestyle your child is involved in. Weed was my choice of drug. Using it placed me in a whole culture, a lifestyle. Everyone I ended up being friends with smoked pot; all they did was get high. I also liked people who didn't smoke; that wasn't an issue. It was just that I liked to be high and I wanted to be with people who liked to be high.

Blind to the Consequences

There is a huge haze over this generation that blocks its ability to see the effects their drug use is having on others. All kids see is just a different way of living. They don't see the consequences of choosing this lifestyle. They don't understand that years down the road they might be fighting with their families, flunking out of school, or losing their relationships with husbands and wives. If I could have just realized the true effects my choices would have on my life and the lives of those around me, I would have thought a lot more about what I was doing.

Love That Sticks

My mom used to take me to the beach all the time. I was heavy into skateboarding and really loved it. Skateboarding was one of the key things that kept me from doing drugs after I had quit. When I was active and determined, my mind had to be clear. My body had to be in good shape and I didn't want to do drugs when I was skating.

I would often get arrested for skating in the wrong spot. Once I was arrested where my mom worked. The university had just built a multi-million-dollar complex with great skateboarding places and brand new cement everywhere. When the security guards called my home, Dad came down with his motor home, picked up about ten of us, and took us to a place where it was legal to skate. He stuck with us. Those kinds of things are what I remember about my folks, being there for me. But it was the Lord that brought me back. I always had knowledge of Him. I was raised as I should have been raised. I was loved; I was accepted; but it was the Lord who brought me back.

"What If's" Don't Help

Maybe it would have helped for my folks to explain to me how much I was hurting them, how much I was destroying them on the inside as they were watching me get into this kind of trouble. But I don't know if this would have helped, because I was so totally oblivious. These were my parents. Parents are supposed to be strong and stable, and always there for me. I just don't know. There is no way to know what would have gotten through to me.

When my dad said that he was seriously thinking about giving up the ministry, it severely crushed me. Did I get high that night? Yes, I did; but did that stick in my mind forever? Yes, it did. It crushed my soul that I was hurting the guy who loved me so much and was always there for me. I was killing him with my own selfishness. Yet, I couldn't understand that fully at the time; it took me a while to get to that point.

Unconditional Love

Because of the love and openness that was always in my home, I knew that at any time, I could come back. If I needed that comfort, if I needed a place to be, if I needed to come back, I had a home.

The Grip of God

The Lord brought me out of my drug abuse through an odd circumstance. I had just been in a big car accident, which had left me sick and sore. I had been out of work for a month and a half. One day, I was sitting in my chair watching a program that featured a story about a guy whom God convicted to give up his selfishness. The man was sick of living for himself. God prompted him to quit working so much and to meet with his friend to pray. Within three years, this man was a pastor whose church was over 3,000 members strong. God had given him a vision. Because the man had been willing to get past himself and listen, God had used him and amazing things happened.

Sometime during the program, I literally was thrown out of my chair. I found myself kneeling on the floor, where I started to bawl, uncontrollably. I heard a voice saying, "Evan, it is time. It's time to stop running." It was God. I immediately went to my parent's house and told them that I knew the Lord had forgiven me.

Chapter 15

A Sober View after 20 Years of Drinking and Drugs

By Todd Smoke

My name is Todd and I am an alcoholic. I say that not as much for you as I do for me because I have accepted the fact that I am an alcoholic. I have to remind myself of that all the time. I am an alcoholic before I am a father to my children. I am an alcoholic before I am a son to my father, and I am an alcoholic before I am any sort of employee to my employer.

Just for Fun

I started drinking and using drugs when I was 14. I started by smoking pot and drinking beer. My use was caused by nothing my parents did. I didn't drink and use drugs because of pain. I wasn't hiding from anything. I wasn't running from anything. I drank and used alcohol because it sounded like fun. That's my excuse. I looked for the people who were drinking and using because I wanted to have fun.

Alcoholics are selfish and self-centered. We think about us. I thought about me before anybody else. I thought about what I could get for me--as much as I could and as fast as possible; I thought about what was going to make me feel good or make me feel different. Eventually, I drank to take away the feelings, but that is not why I started.

Dealing Parents Dishonesty

My parents knew pretty much right away that I was using drugs when they found a big bag of pot in my room. I wasn't hiding it real well from them. So they didn't go through denial.

It did take them a while to understand the lengths I would go to in order to keep using drugs and alcohol. They were tough on me, and set boundaries from the beginning. They said, "You cannot use and stay here. If you do, you will be confined to this house." They stuck to that. But I still drank and continued to use because that is what I wanted to do. They would put me on restriction after school, saying, "You can't go anywhere." I would say, "Fine." But as soon as they went to bed, I would leave. I went through most of my high school years like that. I would always find a way to get away with it. I would say anything to get them off my back; I would just tell them what they wanted to hear: "Yes, sir." "Okay. I'll do that." And then, bam, I would go out the back door.

It got to the point that I wouldn't even listen to what my dad was saying, because the whole time he was talking, I would be thinking: "What does he want me to tell him? What is the answer he is looking for?"

Sinking into a Rough Scene

Surprisingly, I did real well in school through all of this. I wasn't at school much, but I pulled off good grades. When I got out of high school, I decided to take some time off for me. I decided to take a summer off to surf, skate, and do all the things that kids like to do because I was young and I could do that. The fact was I took that time off to drink and use. I became heavily involved in the early underground punk rock scene in Hollywood during the late seventies and early eighties. That subculture gave me more opportunities to use drugs. I was still able to work. I found an interest in the medical field and began working, which helped me support my habit.

First Dose of Reality

I got my first shock of reality when I was about 21 and I woke up in an ambulance after a heroin overdose. You can't scare an alcoholic sober, but the experience did scare me enough to slow down. With some help from my father, I was able to get through a trade school for training so I could do more medical work. But I continued to use and drink during the whole period. I couldn't stop at that time.

Right around that time, my dad took me to see a counselor because he knew I had a drinking problem. The counselor talked to us for about ten minutes and said, "He's not done. It's working for him. Leave him alone." I'm sure my dad didn't like those words, but it was true; I was enjoying myself.

A Turn for the Worse

From that point on, things got worse. I would get a job for a year and a half, then I would become too comfortable, my use would get out of control, and I would lose the job. Losing jobs didn't matter to me, though. I was living the way I wanted. I thought I had it good: I always had a beautiful girl, a halfway decent job, and popularity around the scene in Orange County. It was cool.

I moved to my parents' house in Phoenix in 1987. At that point I was already really strung out on heroin. I had already had an overdose and spent some time in jail, but that hadn't been a big deal to me. But now I had become unhealthy, really skinny, and tired of working; I wanted to get off the heroin. So I did. But after I quit using the drugs, I would just drink more.

I went on methadone and kicked the heroin, but my parents almost immediately kicked me out because of my drinking. I stayed with some friends, then got an apartment, got a job and lost a job – my regular routine. I lived in a car that didn't run for a couple of months. I took a series of beatings. All I did was drink. I pretty much lived to drink. I was living outdoors, so I had to drink to sleep. All day long I had nothing to do but drink.

Doing Detox

I went to my first detox in Phoenix. After the detox, I got into a 30-day quick-fix program. I thought I wanted to stop, but I didn't hear a word the counselors said. Now when I look back, I see it wasn't that I wanted to stop drinking. It was that I wanted all the stuff that went with the drinking to stop. I wanted to stop going to jail. I wanted to stop living outdoors. I wanted a paycheck--not necessarily a job, but a paycheck. I wasn't ready to get sober, but I was tired of all the bad things that went with drinking.

I moved back to California in early 1990, then began making a career of entering detoxes and staying in recovery homes. I would go to detox when things got bad. I didn't go because I wanted to stop, but because I was trying to get out of trouble with my folks or my boss. After detox, I would say, "Look at me. I got two weeks sober. Things are great." Then I'd go back to drinking.

A bad thing about alcoholics is that we clean up quick. A drunk can come off the streets--puking his guts out, shaking like a leaf, and totally delusional—and enter detox. Within in four days--after a couple of showers, a little bit of sleep, and a couple of good meals--he starts thinking, "I've got it going on." Things just don't seem that bad after a week or two. I ran in that cycle for years.

Managing or Adapting?

About this time, I realized that I was an alcoholic. That is a very small part of the first step of the AA's Twelve Steps. For me, it became an excuse. I blamed all my bad behavior and way of living on that fact. "I am an alcoholic. That is why I do what I do," I said.

The second half of the statement in the first step is to admit that my life had become unmanageable. I didn't get that part. I thought I was managing just fine. But I wasn't managing, I was adapting. First, I thought I was managing because I still had a job. Then I got to the point where I thought I was managing because even though I couldn't work, I wasn't going to jail. Then I thought I was managing because even though I was living on the streets, I wasn't in jail. Then I did go to jail. But I believed I was managing just fine there since I hadn't gotten into any fights or trouble with the guards.

Needing Hopelessness

By the time I was 37, I was constantly on and off the streets, in and out of jail. In my drinking career, I have managed to pick up three drunk-driving charges, two drunk on a bicycle charges, and countless public drunkenness charges. I've overdosed on heroin three times, each time waking up to the paramedics pumping on my chest. You would think that kind of stuff would scare me sober.

Unfortunately, as I said before, you cannot scare an alcoholic sober. I found out that I needed to get that second part of The AA First Step. I had to believe that my life was unmanageable. I had to get hopeless. But all the trouble I got in did not make me hopeless.

> *The biggest thought in my whole world was to find a bridge.*

At one point, I was sleeping outdoors in the canyons where I used to go run and hide. It was raining and it was January and it was cold. My best thought was, "Find a bridge." The biggest thought in my whole world was to find a bridge. I was sleeping outdoors in the canyon because my head was telling me that I wasn't homeless and I wasn't a bum. To the mind of an alcoholic, even living in a canyon outdoors meant that I was handling things. I was calling myself a "camper." I would remember the homeless people with their dirty clothes and dirty bags, sleeping behind dumpsters, behind buildings or behind car washes where they had set up their camps. "I'm not like them," I would say. "I'm a camper, I'm not a homeless person." Talk about denial.

Finding Hopelessness

What does it take to get make an addict or alcoholic willing to stop using drugs and drinking? I know my story is depressing and you are probably hoping your child doesn't have to live a life like mine before he gets sober. God bless him, I hope he doesn't either.

An alcoholic or a drug addict has to become hopeless enough to be willing to do what it takes to stay sober. As Zach Whaley says, the pain of getting sober must be less than the pain of staying drunk before one decides to get help. I have seen people come in for treatment because their boss told them they were going to be fired. That is what got them hopeless. Then they became willing to work the program and stay sober. For me, sleeping under a tree in the rain still didn't make me hopeless enough.

What got me hopeless? I ended up going to the state penitentiary, "the big house." Certainly that would scare me sober and make me feel hopeless enough to stop drinking. The whole time I was there, I thought that it would be enough. But it wasn't. I was going to Bible studies, reading my Bible, reading the *Big Book of Alcoholics Anonymous*, and thinking that when I got out I was not going to do that again. During my last month there, I began thinking that prison really wasn't that bad. When I got out, I was really healthy, because in prison all I had done was eat, work out, sleep and read a lot of books.

As I sat on the bus leaving the penitentiary, I began to think a pint of vodka wouldn't be that bad. It wasn't bad that first night, until I woke up the next morning needing more. That was a real short trip back to hell. I spent the next three weeks drinking.

I had been released from prison five days before Christmas. My dad had said I could stay at his house through the holidays and then move into a recovery home. But two days after I moved in, he found a bottle in my backpack and told me I had to go.

"Daddy, it is three days before Christmas. You can't kick me out," I said.

He wasn't angry. He didn't get mad, yell, or throw things. I wasn't drunk. I hadn't caused any problems. He had simply found the bottle, and he knew what that would lead to.

Dad had built up all of his hopes for me again. Seeing the dejection on his face was painful. That was the first time I really saw the pain in his face.

I left and continued to drink for another week or so. The week after that, I found myself outdoors again under a tree. It was raining and it was January and it was cold. I was drunk. I said to myself: "This has to stop. What's wrong with me?" Of course, just being out of prison, I was on parole at the time and I had a little bit of fear of going back to prison hanging over me. That was enough fear to get me to beg my way into a hotel room so I could clean up to see my parole officer. But when I got into that hotel room, I drank for two straight days until I got to the point where I couldn't drink any longer. Then God saw fit to stop my drinking.

I was so physically sick from drinking that I could not drink any more. Detox was hell in that hotel room. I was shaking, itching, and sweating; and I hadn't slept in a week. I was drifting in and out of consciousness. I couldn't drink the alcohol and I knew I had to get it down or I was going to be really sick. I got to that point of hopelessness, that hopelessness deep inside. I prayed to God, "Please help me get three swallows down, so I can stop shaking and feeling like this. Please take this obsession away from me to drink. Help me stop, but let me drink."

That is when it really hit me how hopeless I really was. I couldn't imagine my life with alcohol and I couldn't imagine life without alcohol. That is when I finally found that hopelessness.

Reaching for Recovery

While I was lying there, I was trying to decide whether I should go back to detox again or to the hospital. My alcoholic thinking was telling me I should go to the hospital to get drugs and be weaned off of the alcohol. That would have been the easy way.

Fortunately, I decided instead to go to detox one more time, my ninth time. Thankfully, they let me in. They could have said, "Yeah, you've been to this one four different times. We can't do anything for you." They didn't know that I was going into detox that time with a willingness that I had never had before because I was hopeless.

I had an AA sponsor I had known for years. I would call him every time I got to jail or to detox. I would kind of do what he said to do, but not really, because I just didn't want to stop drinking. This time I called him and he came down again. He laughed at me, which is what he did every time that he showed up at detox when I was there.

"Are you done fighting AA?" he asked.

"I don't know," I said, "but I'm done today."

I had been in and out of Alcoholics Anonymous for years hearing this motto: "One day at a time." I had thought that was the corniest thing I had ever heard, along with all those other cutesy things they say in Alcoholics Anonymous. I didn't understand it that day, but I was willing to do it that day because I was so sick.

> I could look in my Dad's eyes and see the hurt. For a long time it did not matter to me because drugs and alcohol were what I did. I could see my dad in pain. He would tell me how much it hurt him. He would talk to me about the times he and Mom would stay up all night crying, wondering where I was. At the time, it didn't touch me. I can look back on it now and see with clearer eyes what they were going through and how they were there for me.

A Greater Power

The first tool I was given in the Big Book was that its main object was to enable me to find a "Power" greater than myself to help solve my problem. Remember, I am selfish and self-centered. I think of me. I want my way. How was I supposed to put my trust and power in God? I had grown up in a church family, but my prayers to God had been, "God, get me out of this one. I'll do something, if You get me out of it this time."

But this time, I humbly offered myself to God. It was real simple. That was enough for me to make a start. We need God. I've heard about people shying away from Alcoholics Anonymous because they don't talk about religion and Jesus Christ. They have a purpose for that. They want to be open to everybody who just can't quite hear. But if you have any notion that Alcoholics Anonymous is not a spiritual program, you are wrong. It plainly states in that book that we have to find and live by a "Power" greater than ourselves. It isn't about just stopping drinking. It is about a way of life. You see I stopped drinking; but my life is still unmanageable. I've got to have God.

Finding a way to live is what the AA steps are about, because I had never lived. I just did what I wanted to do. You mean I have to work every day? I have to pay bills? Come to find out, it is not even my money. Imagine that! I am still cleaning all that wreckage up and it is probably going to be a life-long process.

A Family Disease

The alcoholic's actions affect the whole family one way or another. I can't take away the hurt I have caused my family by saying, "I'm sober now. I'm sorry." My actions on a daily basis are part of the amends to my family. If you can't fix the alcoholic, what can you do? You can work on yourselves and your relationships with each other and your other kids.

Experience: An Asset

One of the things that I learned in Alcoholics Anonymous is that my most valuable asset is my experience with all my drinking and drugging and staying sober. How could all that bad stuff that happened to me be the best thing I've got going? I needed every drink and every drug to get me to the point that I was willing to do what it took to stay sober. Now I've got all of this experience of staying sober. What good is that? Why do I have all of this experience? To help somebody else. It's simple. I can help another man who has suffered just like me because I have had that experience.

That means I kind of have a purpose for living today. That is pretty cool. You see, I didn't come to Alcoholics Anonymous to get a purpose. I came to Alcoholics Anonymous to stop drinking and get on with my life. I've gotten so much more than that. I do have a purpose: to work with others.

How You Can Help Your Kids

Not everyone has to go to the lengths that I did in order to work this program. If you have kids who are 16, 18, or 19, you certainly don't want to sit around and wait until they get 37 for them to get sober.

The problem is that you can't make them hopeless. You can't make them willing, but they don't have to go through what I went through. What should you do? First, I tell parents to give their kids "one freebie." By a freebie I don't mean a free ride. I mean a serious effort to help them the first time they get caught. If they are getting a jail sentence, help them get an alternative sentence or into a program of recovery, if they are willing. After that, all bets are off. Take care of #1. You have wives and husbands. You have your other children. Take care of yourselves and your other kids before you worry about your alcoholic kid. It's easy to say, but not easy to do.

He never said he didn't love me.

Second, I can tell you what worked for my dad. He kept just enough contact with me to show he loved me. He gave me enough love and support to keep me alive so I could get to that hopelessness. He never said he didn't love me. He always said he didn't like my actions and he always showed me he loved me, but to the best of his ability, he tried not to enable me.

Here are some more specific things my parents did that were helpful. These ideas might help you with your own kids:

- **My parents didn't like my actions, but they were still there for me.** They let me know this even though they were pretty hurt the first time they found that pot in my room and the first time I came home smelling like alcohol.

- **My dad didn't mind being seen with me.** When I became involved in the underground punk rock scene, my hair was blue or white or black, whatever that week's color was. I had the earrings and all the funny clothes. But my dad still would pick me up on the weekends to play racquetball. My blue hair didn't faze him a bit. In spite of all that I was doing, he was still showing up with me because I was his son. At the time, I didn't see it, but I can look back on it now and see how cool it was.

- **My dad helped me without enabling me.** He was there in times of need to help out with some phone change, a sandwich, a ride to detox, or a ride to a recovery home. He was willing to give me a ride to a meeting, but he wasn't willing to say, "Come in and stay on our couch for another month and we'll watch you slowly kill yourself."

- **My parents always made me feel welcome in their home** and they included me in holiday celebrations and family events, but they set guidelines. They wouldn't give me keys to their house or let me be there alone, but they told me I was welcome as long as I wasn't drinking or loaded. They never stopped doing that through all the years, whether I was in jail, living on the streets or going through all the other things I went through.

- **My dad was there for me every time I went to jail.** He would take my phone calls and give me a little bit of money each time I was there so I could buy the things I needed. He would write me letters and send me Bibles, self-help books, whatever he could do. He arranged for friends that I could call when I needed help.

- **My dad didn't hide the fact that I had problems.** He was real open with his family, with his congregation, and with his friends about what I was going through. I have a lot of respect for him for that, because it would have been easy for him to just put me on the back burner. He could have said, "Come back when you're better." But he never did. He was there for me even though I can't say I was always there for him. There were periods when I didn't talk to him for months, but every time that happened there was something missing in my heart. I missed my dad. No matter how much I knew I was messing up, no matter how bad I was doing, I missed that contact with him.

- **My dad didn't even give up on me when I went to state prison.** He took my phone calls and sent me money there.
- **My father always had hope.** He always had faith in God that somehow I would recover if he just persevered long enough. In fact, one time during the year before my prison sentence, I was living under a bridge down at the beach. I was stealing my bottle every morning; I would drink all day long until I was too physically ill to drink. I had a quarter in my pocket for about a week and when I couldn't drink any longer I called my dad. I hadn't had a shower in a couple weeks and I was filthy, but when he showed up he still got out of his car and gave me a big hug. I wanted to go to my sister's, but he took me to detox one more time. He was there to help. He wasn't there to assist me or enable me. He was saying by his love, "I'm here. I have faith that you will change some day." He never gave up on me. And I didn't see that for so long. In fact, some of it I didn't see until I was a couple of years sober. My sisters had pretty much given up on me. My mom never gave up on me but for her the pain was just so bad that she couldn't have contact with me after a while. It wasn't that she gave up but she just couldn't handle the pain. I don't blame her, but for some reason my dad kept persevering with me.
- **My dad always kept the communication lines open.** This was probably the most important thing he did. He kept in contact. I've heard people say, "Kick 'em to the curb." He didn't do that. He would keep talking to me. He found that balance between loving me the whole time and not enabling me. He never shut me off. I knew I was loved. I knew he had faith and hope that some day I would recover, even though he was scared that I might die. He kept trying.

Staying Sober

I wasn't struck sober. It involves a lot of work. Today I go to meetings. I work with other alcoholics. I share my experience. I go through those steps. I keep reading the *AA Big Book*. But I have found that staying sober is easier than the games I had to play to stay loaded and to hide out and to stay out of jail.

I have a routine today. If you have kids who are getting into early recovery, they have to establish a routine. Ask them what they are doing to stay sober each day. Get involved in their recovery. Ask where they're going to meetings and whether they have a sponsor. Find out if they're working the steps. Are they working with other alcoholics?

You are not going to fix them. You are not going to change them. But you can give them some assistance and you can watch. And if you can't fix your son or daughter, work on YOU. You are going to get experience that will enable you to help another family. Our experience is a vital asset, of supreme value. It's no good unless we use it. Use it for God's glory. Wow! What a concept!

Finding Faith in God

I found God in Alcoholics Anonymous. I didn't see Him in a blinding flash. I got that faith by walking through pain, by walking through fear. I followed the steps of Alcoholics Anonymous and those steps led me to God. They put life in front of me, gave me ways to walk through it, and told me to put my trust in God, even if I wasn't too sure about God.

I know there is a God today and He is working in my life. I have a message to carry. What a gift!

Chapter 16

Putting Drug Use Behind You

Stephanie Vawter
Interview with Mark Halvorsen

Mark Halverson is the host of a radio talk show "Front Page" on WWIB in Chippewa Falls, WI. Mark invited Stephanie to be a guest on his show...and this interview is the result. Mark asks penetrating and poignant questions. Stephanie shows a vulnerability and honesty in her answers that will help the parent of the addict and challenge the addict that now is the time to come back to God and get clean.

Mark: When did you get introduced to drugs? When did that temptation enter your life?

Stephanie: Probably the first introduction would have been when I was about 14. That was to marijuana. I was introduced to marijuana and I really enjoyed it.

Mark: Do you remember at all anything passing through your mind, like, "I shouldn't do this"? What were the reasons that might have kept you from doing it?

Stephanie: I don't know if anything would have kept me from doing it. I think it was my curiosity. I wanted to see what it was like, and once I did try marijuana I sort of felt relieved from the internal pain I was feeling.

Mark: Were there any mental obstacles that ran through your mind to possibly say no to drugs? You said you don't think anything would have kept you from that.

Stephanie: I don't think so. I think that's my makeup. I don't deny that "Say No to Drugs" program works. I think it does work for a lot of kids. But I think I had to push the envelope and part of that was doing things that people said I shouldn't. I wanted to test it for myself. If someone tells me something's black, then I want to try to say it's white.

Mark: Some people dismiss concern about marijuana because they say it is "just" an entry drug. But a lot of experts and active anti-drug speakers point out that this entry level drug can lead to the use of more dangerous drugs down the road. Is that what happened in your life?

Stephanie: That was the case with me. I started using marijuana and at that time I enjoyed it. I enjoyed the high. I want to explain that. I believe and I know to this day that I am an alcoholic and a drug addict. Part of being an alcoholic and a drug addict is not really feeling like you fit in your body. When I smoked that marijuana, I felt like I fit. I felt like I was whole and I didn't have the worries that I did. But, not everyone is like that. I don't believe that every kid who smokes marijuana is going to end up becoming a heroin addict. That's not the case at all. But for me, I think it was inevitable that I would eventually go on to bigger and "better" drugs, as it were.

Mark: You pretty much kept that from your parents. They didn't know that?

Stephanie: Oh, no. I was very good at hiding it.

Mark: Some people might say, "How naive must they have been! How could they not have known?" Didn't they see the redness of your eyes or smell your clothing? How did you conceal all that?

Stephanie: Addicts are very good liars. As I told my dad when he asked how he could have been so stupid (his term) to miss my addiction, "You cannot be a successful addict unless you are a great liar."

Mark: Because you're lying to yourself first and foremost. You're lying to yourself saying, "This isn't hurting me."

Stephanie: Right. And you believe it yourself. I think you become such a good liar

I think you become such a good liar because you need to hide your use, because that is what is giving you your only joy.

because you need to hide your use, because that is what is giving you your only joy. "Joy" is not the right word, but for lack of a better word, it will work. It is joy at that point. You'll do anything to hide your use and abuse in order to have that joy. I think that if you believe the lie, then it's easier to make other people believe the lie.

Mark: Take us through the Reader's Digest version of your experience: You used marijuana at 14; your parents didn't discover that you were doing drugs. What happened after high school?

Stephanie: I moved out about a week after I turned 18 and moved to another state to work. I met some people who were a little older than I was, a little more experienced and little bit more on the edge. I started experimenting with other drugs: LSD, speed, and cocaine. Crystal meth wasn't around when I was 18 or 19, but I experimented with that later as well.

> *One of the dangers with marijuana is that, because it's a depressant, it lulls you into a "not caring" attitude. You think you're enjoying it. But it really zaps you of any desire to do anything.*

Mark: So you started to use a variety of different drugs. Where were you working?

Stephanie: Different odd jobs: pizza delivery, receptionist and a waitress.

Mark: How did you get your drugs?

Stephanie: From people I knew. Once you get into those circles, it's very easy to get drugs. Drug dealers are friendly with the drug users.

Mark: At which point, if at all, did you get into dealing?

Stephanie: It's interesting that you ask. I never thought that I dealt drugs until I got sober. That's when someone asked me whether I had ever taken money for drugs. I said, "Well, sure." He said, "Well, then you've dealt."

Mark: Why didn't it occur to you that taking money for drugs was dealing?

Stephanie: Well, it's the attitude. I thought that to be considered a dealer, you had to be selling large quantities and having people come to your house day and night. You had to be driving a flashy car, having a cell phone, that type of thing. I had just sold drugs to my friends. If I had drugs and someone wanted some, then I would sell to them. It didn't cross my mind at that point to think that I was dealing drugs.

Mark: Now take us into your 20's.

Stephanie: Interestingly enough, the entire time from when I was 19 up until I was 23 or 24, I had been using marijuana daily. For people who say that marijuana is not harmful and that you can't become addicted to it, I was addicted. I don't believe it was a physical addiction, but a mental addiction. I was dependent on that marijuana. One of the dangers with marijuana is that, because it's a depressant, it lulls you into a "not caring" attitude. You think you're enjoying it. But it really zaps you of any desire to do anything. I didn't want to go to school. I didn't want to work. I basically just wanted to stay at home and smoke pot.

That's what I did for three years. I worked off and on, but had no ambition. So, I had been smoking pot and experimenting with other drugs when they were available. When I was 23, someone introduced me to heroin. I don't want people to think that their kid is smoking pot so instantly he is going to start shooting heroin. For me, it resulted after a progression of several years of searching for a bigger and better high, which I wasn't getting with any of the drugs that I had been trying. I was looking for an escape. That's what I wanted, something to make me not feel. I think that's what every addict wants: They don't want to have to feel. They just want to be numb.

I tried the heroin and it gave me that feeling of numbness. I wasn't thinking about anything, I wasn't worried about anything. Nothing hurt; I was just numb. That was the feeling I had been looking for my whole life. From that moment, I wanted to do it again.

At first, I just did it on the weekends. Then I started doing it during the week. This progression spanned about three months. I went from using it on the weekends to saying, "Well, it's Thursday so I think I'll do it today," to saying, "Let's do it Wednesday, Thursday, Friday, Saturday, Sunday." Then, even though I was doing it every day, I wasn't addicted to it, in my way of thinking. I was just choosing to do it because it made me feel so good. I was smoking it in the beginning, but that only lasted about three weeks. Then the person I was using it with said, "You should try using a needle. It's a lot better." I did and that was all it took.

Mark: Is this tough for you to share?

Stephanie: I don't want to glorify it in any way. I want to make sure that people don't think that I'm sharing it to get any accolades. I'm just doing this to try to make some difference and to help other people.

Mark: So more and more you injected the heroin. Then what?

Stephanie: Then it was a year of madness. About the first six months that I was using heroin, I was still able to function somewhat. I wasn't working, but I was still seeing my friends. I was active. I was doing things. I even went on a trip with my family. Then about six months into it, I stopped caring. Then I was all-out using and trying to be high all the time, searching for that high, trying to find the drugs, and trying to find the money to get the drugs.

Mark: All this time your parents didn't know?

Stephanie: Correct.

Mark: And people again can say, "How could they not know?"

Stephanie: Well, here's what I did. They lived in Arizona. I lived in another state at the time. I had turned 24, so it wasn't like we talked every day. They would call once a week, but I wouldn't answer the phone. I would have my answering machine on so they'd call and I'd call them back when I was relatively coherent. I would talk to them 15 minutes or so, tell them that everything was fine, tell them what they wanted to hear, and hang up. That kept my secret going.

Mark: But along came a trip to Mexico that your brother Michael knew about. When did he find out about your drug use?

Stephanie: He had known that I had been using drugs, but he didn't know the extent. I would lay down my life for my brother, that's just how it is. We had secrets from our parents and we kept them like any siblings would. He had known I was using marijuana. When Michael came to visit me about six months before I got sober, it was obvious to him that I was completely hooked on drugs. But I convinced him that I was going to stop, that it was going to be over, and that everything was going to be fine; I was not going to use drugs anymore. He didn't have any reason not to believe me, so he thought that was the end of it. He thought it was a phase and that I was going to quit. Why shouldn't he believe me? Who wants to think his sister is a junkie?

Mark: So how did he find out about the trip to Mexico?

Stephanie: I had moved a drug dealer into my house. He was living in the basement apartment. We went to Mexico to buy drugs.

Mark: At this point you did not have a job? This was what you were doing?

Stephanie: Correct. And we ran out of money. I didn't have any money to get home, so I called Michael from Mexico and asked him to wire me some money. He asked me why I was in Mexico and what was I doing. Being a smart kid, he thought, "Hmmm, Mexico; there's a lot of heroin there." He did wire me money to get home, but he knew that I had been lying to him at that point. He wasn't happy about it. I think he realized that I really was in danger. I believe he was worried about me. But I also believe he didn't know what to do. He lived in another state than where I lived. He was a college student at the time and he knew that no matter what he said, I wasn't going to change my mind. I'm his older sister and he's always looked up to me, and there I was, strung out on heroin in Mexico. He didn't know what he could do, so he sent me the money because he wanted me to get home and be safe.

But what happened is that I spent that money on drugs and didn't end up getting home. Then I called my aunt to wire me some money. I gave her some song and dance story. She did send me the money, which I did use to get home, but she also called my dad, her brother, and said, "I think something is wrong."

Mark: I thought there was a phone call from your brother, too, to your parents.

Stephanie: After my aunt called my mom and dad, they called my brother. They said, "We don't want to break any confidences between you two; but if something is wrong with Stephanie, you really need to tell us because we're worried for her life." Michael did some checking to confirm my addiction, and then he called my parents and told them. The drug dealer I was with at the time and I got into an argument. I left and drove home from Mexico--about a 16-hour drive--all by myself. I didn't have a stereo in my car because I had sold it in Mexico for money to buy drugs. I barely had enough money for gas to get home. During this entire drive home, I was thinking, and I realized that I had to do something. But I didn't know what I needed to do.

At this point, I just was broken. My spirit was broken; I felt like my soul was gone.

Mark: Safe to say there were a lot of tears in the car on the way home?

Stephanie: Tears inside. I still wasn't ready to let those tears out on the outside. I didn't know what to do. I was thinking on the way home, "I've got to get some help. Maybe when I get home, I can go get help for drugs." But interestingly enough, I didn't ever think once, "Maybe I'll call my mom and dad and say, 'I have a problem.'"

Mark: Why didn't you think that?

Stephanie: Because I was ashamed that I had a problem with drugs and I didn't want to burden them with it.

Mark: But somebody might say, "They're your parents and you know they love you unconditionally."

Stephanie: Right. But I thought the worse thing for me to wish upon them was to let them know that their child was a drug addict. I didn't want to put them through that. I thought they'd be ashamed, which is exactly the opposite of how they responded when they discovered I was addicted to heroin.

I was obviously at a crossroads and I had to do something. I couldn't go on the way I was going. I had been home for about an hour when the front door to my house opened and in walked my mom and dad.

Mark: They lived in Arizona and you lived in Colorado?

Stephanie: Yes. You have to understand my dismay that they had just walked through the door. I was in my bedroom. They came in, sat down on my bed, and my dad said, "Stephanie, we know you're on drugs. We want you to come get help."

And just like that I said, "All right." I believe that it was a "God moment." God put them there at the right moment; I was ready at that moment. Had it been a day earlier or a day later, I don't know if I would have said, "Yes."

It's important to know that when you do intervene with people, they're not always going to be willing to get help.

Mark: We hear about the difficulties of trying to overcome cigarette addiction. What is behind trying to overcome heroin addiction?

Stephanie: First, you have to go through detox for the physical addiction. I recommend going to a detox center for that. It's difficult to do it on your own in your home. People can do that, but you need, I believe, some supervision for that.

Mark: How long does it take?

Stephanie: It depends on the person. I had tried several times to do it by myself. Usually I got to the 24-hour mark and then just started using again because the pain was so great. Interestingly enough, the time I went into detox, I didn't have any of the usual or expected symptoms. None. I kept waiting to get sick. I kept waiting for the pain and it never happened. I believe that was God's intervention. I believe He touched me and said, "Look, I'm giving you this chance. Take it."

Mark: From the sound of it, some of your closer moments with God, at least up to that point, came during that week.

Stephanie: Yes, they did.

Mark: So are you saying that God meets us at our lowest place?

Stephanie: I believe so. I think everything happens for a reason. I don't think God makes things happen, but I think He comes to us at certain points. You can choose to listen to Him and say, "Wow, thanks," or you can damn Him, as it were, which a lot of people do. And I chose to see Him in that situation when I was desperate and my parents walked into my bedroom.

Mark: How did your recovery progress after that?

Stephanie: From detox I went to get professional treatment. I began attending twelve-step meetings daily for the first two years and then every other day after that. I have been sober 44 months now. By sober, I mean that I haven't had any alcohol or used any drugs since then.

Mark: That's a long time. I mean it all happens one day at a time, but there was a point in your life when that would have sounded ludicrous to say.

Stephanie: Definitely. There are points today when I say "Wow, will I stay sober the rest of my life?" I can't look at it that way. I have to look at it as staying sober today. All I have is today.

Mark: It's kind of like walking a tightrope between two very tall buildings. You're way up, you can't look to the left, you can't look to the right and you can't really look behind you. You've got to keep your eye in front of you, don't you?

Stephanie: Correct.

Mark: I'm just saying that it seems you can get distracted. Even Stephanie Vawter gets elevated by thinking, "Wow, I've made it a long time." But if you allow that to happen, it seems like that would be the entry point for failure.

Stephanie: Right. And that's the danger of saying, "I am cured." Just the other day I was thinking, "Oh, wow! I've been sober this long. I wonder if I had a drink, what would happen?" That's the addiction talk. That's the addiction saying, "Sure you can have one drink and that won't lead to drugs and that won't lead you right back into the depths of despair."

Mark: As you know, because it sounds like you've worked recovery pretty extensively, sobriety and recovery are different things. It is one thing to be sober. But are you moving ahead? Are you growing in character change?

Stephanie: That's true. I didn't get sober just to stay the same, to be the same person I was when I was using drugs. I need my life to have a purpose and to work towards something. I have finished college and work in a residential treatment center for teenage girls who have abused drugs or alcohol and broken the law.

Mark: Who are drug users? Before you answer, let me say it seems to me that people think they're the troublemakers. They're the "bad" kids. They're the ones who were the "freaks" in high school. Yet as I hear your story, you didn't come from a bad home.

Stephanie: Drug users can be anyone. College graduates, high school dropouts, anyone. It's not the "bad" kids. Drug users are people who are hurting; they're not just the delinquents. It's not just the kids who are from single parent families. It's not just the kids who live in the poor side of town. It's everyone. It's mothers, fathers, and it's kids. Addiction is not about how good you are or what you've accomplished or how much money you have or how thin you are, or anything like that.

Mark: What can you say to parents who may have a concern that their child is a user or maybe, as was your case, parents who just don't know.

Stephanie: I would say if you suspect a problem and ask your kid about it, a lot of the time your kid is not going to tell you the truth. Try some sort of intervening, counseling, or talking to your school guidance counselor or a drug counselor. Talk to someone who's been there.

If you have a friend whose child has gone through using drugs, ask him or her about that experience. If you suspect your child is using, don't ignore it. That's the biggest thing to remember.

SECTION 7

Hoping the Best for the Future

Having a child on drugs/alcohol can take away every bit of hope and faith a parent has for the future. The pain and despair of today can be overpowering. Tomorrow looks even bleaker, if we have the energy to think that there is a tomorrow. The parent is the victim and has to do the hard work of recovery by living by faith one day at a time to regain personal, marital and family health. This journey is not an easy one, or a simple one. But it is one that must be taken.

It is honest for parents to say, "It is not fair! It is not fair that my kid uses drugs and I have to do the hard work of getting healthy, regardless of whether my child chooses to get sober and clean." This is not fair, but it is reality.

Parents of abusers often say, "I did not use drugs. In fact, I modelled abstinence and warned my kids against drugs/alcohol experimentation, use and abuse. Now here I am—angry at a 'phantom' drug dealer, angry at having to go to support group meetings, angry at having to pay for my kid's drug treatment program, and I am scared for my child's future. It just does not seem fair." It is not fair, but it is reality.

Plenty have walked the road before us who have learned to live one day at a time, who have met God in a new way and seen Him work. Not all stories end positively. Some kids die, some continue to use drugs, some go to jail and some never return to be the people they once were. We cannot dictate their future to them or to God. As one recovering addict says, "I had to dance with the devil to come back to God." But the good news is that often they do come back.

Our research shows that most kids abuse drugs for five years before they realize they have a problem and go for help. The answers for all involved usually are not simple or short-term. So, we have to learn how to be healthy and give the future to God. We have to trust in God—one day at a time. This is the only way we can survive the pain of today and have hope for the future of the child we love so much. That is what this section is about.

Jim Smoke tells his journey of 20 years with his son Todd on the streets and in and out of jail. (Read Todd's story, p.145). Dr. Terry Zuehlke is prescriptive and direct in helping the parent of the addict to know how to trust God and get back on the road to spiritual, mental, emotional, and marital health. And Pat Boris points to the future by sharing her research on how parents can regain health in the face of their kids' drug use.

John Vawter summarizes by reminding you that God can be close when you are hit by a ton of bricks.

Chapter 17

Persevering When You Feel Debilitated

By Jim Smoke

More than four years ago, my wife Carol and I emerged from a black hole that had lasted for 20 years--our son Todd's addiction to drugs/alcohol. He was finally clean and sober. We felt as though we had gotten our son and our lives back.

Our journey started when Todd, our oldest child, was in high school and began doing drugs while maintaining a relationship with the church and youth ministry group. Slowly but surely, the strength of his group of friendships outside of the church began to pull him in their direction.

I had worked in Youth for Christ for 12 years in the 1960s when the drug culture was thriving. Our ministry had run a coffeehouse, where we worked with many kids who were picked up off the curb and hauled to the hospital. This topic was not foreign to us. However, we were in denial. We didn't want to believe or accept that our son was in the same situation as those kids we had seen years ago.

First Offense

When my son was 16, he was picked up by the police for the first time and found to be in possession of drugs. I waited for his case to be called up in the Orange County Juvenile Court. When it was his turn, the judge read the riot act to him. He said, "Son, we're going to try to teach you a lesson. We are going to lock you up in jail for a long weekend, and see if that will bring some consciousness to you."

The sheriff's deputy said, "Give your father your watch, your ring, your wallet."

Todd did that. Then the deputy hauled him off in one direction and I walked out the door alone in another direction.

That was on a Friday morning. On Sunday I taught two singles classes in the church. That Sunday was our time to bring all the classes together, which meant 800 singles. Knowing I had to teach the next Sunday morning, I thought I had one of two choices: I could forget what had happened in juvenile court, just plod my way through and fake it, until I was finished. Or I could tell the people what was really going on.

I thought, *"Okay, how do I do this, God? Just go the denial route and be cool, calm, collected, teach the lesson, and go home? Or share the pain inside of me?"* I decided I was just going to rock through the teaching that morning and go home. Everything would be fine. I thought what they didn't know wouldn't hurt them or me.

But toward the end of the teaching time, it was as if God said, *"Share your experience with them."*

After I finished teaching, I said, "In essence, we're family here. I want to tell you what happened to me on Friday morning, what I have gone through this week, and what I feel in my heart." A holy hush fell over that auditorium. As briefly as I could, I shared what was happening and how I felt. Then I prayed and dismissed them. But nobody moved. A few people started to get up and move in my direction. I thought, "What's going on?" Soon almost everyone in that room who could get close formed a circle around me and said, "We want you to know we love you, we care about you, and we're with you. We're praying for you." There was a viable teaching that Sunday morning of the authenticity of a thing called community in the family of God. I've experienced it during my 40 years of ministry in anything and everything I've ever done, but never more profoundly than that Sunday morning.

From that morning on, people in my class would ask me how Todd was doing. Sometimes I would have to say "Not good," and other times, I would be able to say, "Well, right now, he's okay." But they would always say, "We're praying for him."

Times of Trials

The years rocked on. When Todd moved out of the house at age 18, he moved into a drug culture. Kids in that type of culture always seem to band together. We never knew quite where he was living or what he was doing. He pretty much dropped out of church when he made that choice, except when we asked him to come with us on Christmas and Easter. He would come to family gatherings, but his life just sort of faded into oblivion.

In the 21 years of his addictive processes, we have gone through about everything that a parent can go through. We've been in court; we've been in jail; we've been in the sheriff's office; we've been in counselors' offices; we've been in drug rehabilitation programs. You name it; we've been there.

I have no secrets about how we endured these trials because, in fact, we lived a marathon that just ground on. Eventually, we came to that final stage of acceptance, but acceptance didn't mean we said, "We like this and we're not concerned about it."

Acceptance meant we simply gave it up to God.

You do come to a place, I believe, where you say, "God, we dedicate our kids to You. We gave them to You, but we repossessed them along the way. Now, God, the only way we are going to live with this problem is to give this child back to You, in totality. You be God in his life."

Faithful Friendships

One way we endured our situation was through the faith of close friends. My best friend is a psychologist. His son also got involved in drugs the same as our son did. We used to sit together in restaurants and share "the most bizarre story of the month" with each other. At some of our sessions, we would cry and shed a lot of tears. At others we would laugh. Our wives and we had met in college and formed a close bond that allowed us to share our laughter, tears and struggles. We knew we were probably going to be in this experience for a long time.

Change of Scenery

In 1987, after we had spent 16 years in Orange County, we moved to Tempe, Arizona, because we wanted to get away from some of the memories and pain. We thought it would be a good place to live for a while or maybe even permanently. Consequently, we disconnected from some of the events that were going on in Todd's life. Periodically, we would hear news about him from our girls.

At times when I would ask my son about some of the things the girls had told us, he would respond, "Dad, you don't want to know."

I would say, "You're right, I don't want to know."

Then he would look at me, smile, and say, "In fact, Dad, there is a lot of stuff you don't want to know. I'm never going to tell you because it won't help you."

About every time Todd came to see us in Tempe, he was stoned or drunk, but he had learned how to cover it up pretty well. He smelled rotten, but he walked straight. At one point, he moved into a drug rehab place on the edge of Tempe. He spent about two months there, but when he came out, nothing dramatic happened. He got right back into using drugs.

A Series of Bad Decisions

Todd did eventually get off drugs because of several bad experiences, but he traded drug abuse for alcohol abuse and he continued to make bad decisions. He began to steal, and also along the way, he began living with his girlfriend, a situation we were not too happy about. She became pregnant, and twins were born into his life during the panorama of his struggle. The last thing that he needed, we thought, was to be a father. He would live in the house, then move out; he would disappear, he would reappear. He lived a ragtag existence, and it was tough on the mother of his two children.

As I drove him to the Salvation Army the morning he was going to check in, I told him, "I hope this really works for you. We are praying for you. We want this to work."
He said, "Dad, I want this to work, too."

In 1995, we moved back to Orange County to be closer to our eight grandkids and to help in Todd's situation, as best and as much as we could. The move put us back in Todd's life in an "in-your-face" kind of way.

When we had been back about a year, the court system began to catch up with his probation violations and DUIs. In court again, the judge said, "I'm going to give you a choice. You've either got to go into the Salvation Army program or I'm going to pack you off to prison."

I sat there in the courtroom that day thinking, *"Thank You, God. At least he is going to be compelled to go into a program."* As I drove him to the Salvation Army the morning he was going to check in, I told him, "I hope this really works for you. We are praying for you. We want this to work."

He said, "Dad, I want this to work, too."

It was a six-month program. For four months, he hit home runs everywhere he went. His counselor told us he was a great kid, and said he had high expectations for Todd. The Salvation Army even wanted to hire Todd after he finished the program. Relieved that he was doing so well, our hopes began to grow. We thought that finally, after all of these years of pain, suffering, anguish, trial and struggle, he was "connecting."

But somehow, on a weekend pass, Todd decided to drink. When he returned to the program, they tested him, found out that he had been drinking, and booted him out.

Punishment in Prison

That began another part of his journey downhill to the place where, in the spring of 1997, the judge finally said to him in another court appearance, "Son, I'm sorry.

... when the judge said, "prison," my heart just about stopped beating.

You just don't understand how things work. When you keep violating court appointed probation situations, we send you to a place called state prison." When I had been in youth ministry, I had visited kids in a lot of different penal institutions, including the Florida state prison, many times. So when the judge said, "prison," my heart just about stopped beating.

"This can't be happening," I thought. My wife and I thought this might be the wake-up call that would finally bring Todd into recovery. We also thought this

> ### *The Wounded Healer*
>
> Henry Nouwen, in his great book, The Wounded Healer, says, "We're all wounded healers." I look at my son now and say, "Okay, we went through a 20-year block of garbage, but what came out of the experience is that he is now able to help other people who are hurting. That is Romans 8:28 in action: "...in all things God works for the good of those who love him, who have been called according to his purpose" (NIV). God took tough stuff and brought good stuff out of it.

might be the last chapter of the book.

Todd was first sent to the Orange County jail and then was processed in a holding place up in the middle of California. From there, he went to Ironwood State Prison in Blythe, California. We had prayed that he would be close enough that we could contact and visit him.

Todd called us once a week. We would write to him and try to keep regular contact. We found out that he was involved in a number of Bible studies there, which made me very happy. But I learned that the one thing everyone gets in prison is religious. Todd told us that inmates go to Bible study because there is nothing else to do.

One day, I opened a letter from Todd asking if I would come visit him, so I found myself on a Friday morning making the long drive from Orange County to Blythe, California. Turning into the prison parking lot, seeing how ominous the place was, and realizing somebody I love was locked up here hit me hard.

We spent about three hours together. It was a tough conversation. We didn't know what to talk about. We struggled for words. But we filled the time, and we hugged each other.

Todd told me that if things worked out, he would be released December 21, 1997, and he asked if I could arrange to pick him up. I said, "Yes," and he was indeed released about that time.

As I drove to the bus station to pick him up, I remember thinking, "Wow, it's been a long, long time, but he's out now and hasn't had any alcohol for five months. Maybe we are on the right road."

He asked if he could stay with his mom and me over the Christmas holiday, and I said, "Sure, no problem."

When he had been home for just two days, I found a bottle of vodka in his backpack. I don't know why I even looked; maybe it was my suspicious nature. I confronted him. "Where did this come from?"

He said, "Gee, I have no idea."

I said, "Yeah, right. You have no idea. What's going on?"

He said, "I just had a couple drinks, Dad. It's no big deal. I'll dump it out. Don't worry about it."

I said, "Okay. Rule number one: You can't live here if you are going to drink."

He said, "Okay, I understand that. I'll go stay with my sister."

He spent the next couple of days with her. Obviously, that was a very difficult Christmas. I thought, "We are back in this all over again."

Raised Hopes

After Christmas, Todd drifted around a bit; nothing constructive happened.

Finally, he called me one day and asked if I could pick him up.

I said, "What's going on?"

He said, "I can't do this any more. I just don't know what to do."

I said, "What do you want to do?"

He said, "I think I want to go into detox."

Over the 20-year span of his drug and alcohol addiction, I had dropped him off at detox so many times that the staff there knew my car.

I said, "Okay, I'll take you."

"Can I spend a night at the motel by the detox center in Stanton?" he asked. "I just want to get my thoughts together before I go in there."

I checked him into a Budget Motel and paid his room. The next morning when I went to pick him up to take him to detox, he wasn't there.

He had gone on another drinking binge, and called me again in a couple of days.

"I need to be driven straight to detox," he said. "Can you come and pick me up?"

Again, I picked him up and drove him to the Stanton detox. Although I have always been an optimist, when I took him in that day, I thought, *I don't understand this anymore, Lord. This just keeps going round and round like a merry-go-round. Where do we get off of this thing? When does this all end? This kid is in his late-30s now. We have been at this a very long time.*

To get into detox, you have to smell like alcohol, and he was really reeking of it that morning. I literally had to walk him to the door. He looked pretty ratty. I patted him on the back and said, "Okay, call me if I can do anything." The door closed behind him and I drove home.

I prayed all the way home, "God, this has to end somewhere. We have prayed our hearts out over 20 years. Please." The Scripture says, "The prayer of a righteous man is powerful and effective" (James 5:16, NIV). I decided my prayers weren't working because I wasn't righteous.

I came home and my wife said, "Here we go again."

Realized Hopes

An incredible thing happened the next day. Some guys from a recovery house called Bookhouse in Orange County came to the detox facility. They are called that because they work the *Alcoholics Anonymous Big Book*. These guys decided Todd was a project that they wanted to take on.

They picked him up and took him to a placed called Bookhouse 2 in Costa Mesa, California. Now, we had been through the in-and-out routine a lot of times. We prayed that this would work. Bookhouse 2 included a bunch of guys who were recovering alcoholics and addicts--about as gnarly and tough a group as you would find anywhere. Todd became a challenge to a couple of the guys in that house. They somehow decided that they were either going to beat his brains out or get him clean and sober permanently.

We watched something happening in his life. We watched him growing stronger.

Days and weeks passed. Todd called me one day and said he needed a job.

"Dad, I have got to find work," he said. "You can't stay if you don't work."

I called a man in our church who had a company with a big warehouse and asked if he could give Todd a job.

He said, "You got it. Bring him in, no problem."

Todd started working there and going back and forth on the bus each day from the recovery house to work. As the weeks began to roll by, we began to think, "Wow, he

---

Everyday Life

I call Todd all the time and he knows I'm checking on him, so the first thing he always says is "I'm okay, I'm okay."

I called him last night and I said, "How was your week?"

He said, "It's really a busy week. I think I did about eight meetings and I spent a lot of time at detox. I picked up a couple of guys I'm going to be working with who are hard-core cases, but things are going good."

Todd has been back with his children since he got out of Bookhouse; his twins are eight and he has another little boy who is six. He is an awesome dad. He spends a lot of time doing stuff with his kids and for his kids.

hasn't flipped out yet." We watched something happening in his life. We watched him growing stronger.

Todd began to inch his way along. I began to watch the weeks go by and my friend at the church for whom he was working said, "This kid has the whole warehouse organized. He really knows what he is doing. He is going 100 miles an hour!" Slowly, Todd was pulling his life back together. We watched our son return to wholeness.

After he finished a year in Bookhouse, the staff said they needed his bed for someone else, but they asked him to remain on their governing board. And shortly after that, his mom and I were ecstatic about his decision to become a certified drug and alcohol rehabilitation counselor. He has helped others in this counseling position for four years now.

Wish Lists

When Todd had been in prison and was scheduled to get out for the Christmas season, I had written each of my three kids. They had always asked me what I wanted for Christmas, and I had traditionally answered that I just wanted them to be okay and to do well.

But that year, I had decided to write a wish list for them. I wrote a list for each of the girls and one to my son. Todd's had four wishes on it.

The girls responded to their letters; we talked and laughed about them. But I never had heard a word from my son. He never had even acknowledged that he had received the letter.

The Christmas after he had been involved in Bookhouse, he handed me an envelope and said, "This is my Christmas gift for you and Mom." I opened it up. It was the letter of wishes I had sent to him in prison, with each of my wishes checked off.

Powerful moment.

> Life goes on in recovery. Todd has told me he's probably going to be in recovery for the rest of his life.
> "But it's cool," he says. "I want to help other people and I want to keep helping myself."

Power of Pray-ers

Perseverance has been a factor in all of this. I don't know any magic formula, but I do know that one thing that has worked for us, as I mentioned earlier, is to be with Christian friends. I would encourage you to ask God, if you don't already have them, to give you some people with whom you can lock arms and hearts, and who will be there with you on the mat no matter what happens.

A lot of my friends have been praying for my son over the years. If you have people around you who can raise the candle of hope, it makes life a lot brighter.

Do some of you have kids who aren't where you want them to be today? You may be in this for the long haul and in the journey you need to have some wagons circled around you. You need to have some people praying for you and for your child. You desperately need to have some people love you up close. You need to have some

> *If you have peo-ple around you who can raise the candle of hope, it makes life a lot brighter.*

Caring Through Weakness

We have grown a lot through all of this. I think when God pounds on your heart enough, you become really sensitive to the needs of other hurting people. For many years, I was involved in a ministry called "Faith at Work" with Bruce Larson and Keith Miller. Those guys taught me something: The Christian leads best when he or she leads from weakness, not from strength. Nobody cares about my strength. They don't give a hoot. However, the minute I mention weakness, everybody jumps on board. I don't run around and tell everybody else on the planet that my son is an alcoholic and what we have gone through. But the occasion is there at times, and I can use those occasions to share my experience and help somebody.

When I do, people say, "Thank you for sharing. You have no idea how helpful that is to me." There is a point of identity in that and a point of care in that.

people who are there when things are really bad and really hard and really tough who just say, "We love you."

That's pretty strong and powerful. We don't need to be the Christian army that shoots its wounded. We need to be the Christian army that's in a healing ministry and helping ministry for people who need our help.

God has been faithful. My son is 41 and grew up in the church. The Bible says, "Bring up a child in the way he should go and when he is old he will not depart from it." It has been a long time but it's been worth the journey; it's been worth the wait.

Chapter 18

Moving from Denial to Dependence on God

By Dr. Terry E. Zuehlke

The story is told of a wise old sea captain who used to pilot one of the huge iron ore ships on Lake Superior. Every morning he would come to the bridge to take control of the ship. As he got to the bridge, he would take a key from his pocket, go to a drawer, unlock it, take out and read some notes on a small piece of paper. The crew was quite puzzled by this routine, but allowed him his privacy.

The day after the sea captain died, the crew immediately got that key and went to the drawer to see what was written on that paper. They were quite surprised by what they read: "Port is left; starboard is right."

***

In my view, that captain had the right idea because he wanted to keep himself keenly aware of the basics of his circumstances. In this chapter, I want to discuss some of the basics of how to move from disbelief to trust in God when your young adult family member is struggling with substance abuse.

I will address common reactions families have to the discovery that substance abuse has invaded their homes and I will explain some steps to help you deal with this kind of disruption. I'll point out some things to watch out for and offer specific actions you can take to promote the process of recovery.

A Biblical Snapshot of a Family in Crisis

When a calamity such as substance abuse hits a family, dysfunction either develops or preexisting struggles intensify. We know a fair amount about what to expect from dysfunctional families. Chuck Swindoll has spoken about this condition by using King David's family dynamics as an example. His description closely matches the struggles of families I see in my counseling practice. For example, in David's family, we see second marriages, deaths of spouses and young children, blended families, incest, rebellion, addiction and even murder! The details may vary, but what happened in David's family in 900 BC is very similar to what happens in families today. So, when possible, I'm going to use biblical examples to illustrate my points.

Co-Dependence: A Family Disease

One of the most important new developments in dealing with families in substance abuse crisis is to look at the problem as a family disease. Some experts call this family disease co-dependence because the family members suffer just as much psychological damage and become just as emotionally distressed as the chemically dependent person does. In fact, I can't think of a way in which family members couldn't help but be drawn into the sickness of the situation.

Most parents are initially vulnerable to some kind of co-dependent response to their child's addiction. That's because most parents are vulnerable to the false assumption that they can control themselves and others so well that they can solve all the problems caused by chemical dependence.

Let's look at some characteristics of family reactions to the crisis of substance abuse by a child or young adult. This will familiarize you with what to expect as you move toward becoming strong enough to turn the struggle over to God, rather than crashing and burning while you try to solve the addict's problems yourselves.

1. Shock

There is a common denominator of shock or disbelief when the reality of a child's substance abuse hit home. Most families I know were quite shocked when that "ton of bricks" fell into their living rooms. Despite a vast amount of literature available through schools, doctors' offices and churches that lists the warning signs of child and adolescent substance abuse, a general mindset that "this will never happen to us" sets in. That makes it easy to ignore or overlook small clues left by substance-abusing children:

- Missing appointments
- Receiving lower grades
- Forgetting obligations
- Having a lack of money
- Showing a diminished regard for personal hygiene
- Withdrawing from the family

When the hints can no longer be denied and it's time to accept reality, most families are quite disrupted and become dysfunctional. One pastor has used the word picture of a hand grenade going off to describe the initial shock; another has spoken of a child's substance abuse inflicting "emotional bruises on our hearts."

2. Denial

As the shock of the circumstances begins to wear off, most families try to handle the pain by avoiding or denying it. By doing so, they fall into the same defensive strategy their child has employed to continue using substances, even in the face of major physical, social, and emotional problems.

Co-dependent parents live in a world of pretend. Denial enables them to make a bad situation look good and an intolerable situation look hopeful.

As Gene Bourland, a pastor and conference speaker who has struggled with his son's drug abuse, has said, "I was rarely in touch with my feelings that God had created in me. The words of my mom sometimes colored my somewhat naïve and often-superficial approach to life. 'Smile. Everything is okay.'" (See Gene and Norma Bourland's story, page 3.)

Families touched by co-dependent behavior often have what is described as a loyalty expectation. This is what causes them to defend family members with problems, because image is so important. The needs of the family come first and family appearances or reputation can be extremely important.

Denial of the substance abuse problem often has three effects. Sometimes, parents consciously push uncomfortable thoughts and feelings out of awareness. This is **suppression**. Or, the parents filter out these uncomfortable thoughts and feelings before they even have a chance to come into conscious thought. This is **repression.** Other times, the parents try to substitute reasonable explanations for actual causes. This is **rationalization**. If one parent is more inclined to react in a way that is different from the way the other parent reacts, increased marital and family tension often develops.

Usually, however, both parents try to smooth things over and dismiss the substance abuse, maybe thinking about it as a one-time incident. This is the *"it won't happen again"* thinking that takes over, blinding parents from seeing the truth. For example, they might say:

- "He got drunk because of being tired, rather than because of how much he drank."
- "Well, the drinking is probably a once-in-a-while event. Maybe if we ignore it and don't get too upset, the abuse will go away. Besides, she has promised it won't happen again. Next time she'll resist – just a beer or two – nothing to excess."

These little phrases and others like them represent what is often called wishful thinking, which involves unrealistic hopes that somehow things will get better and that time will heal. Let me tell you something. Time doesn't heal!

3. Blame and Guilt

Another common response to substance abuse in the family is the tendency for the parents to take full responsibility for the problem. Many parents take on a firm belief that they should have been able to prevent the substance abuse or, now that it's occurred, that they should be able to change their child's behavior. Personalizing the failure offers hope that by increasing or improving their efforts, they can keep the addiction from getting further out of control. Some parents have said:

- "In those early moments of discovery that our child was chemically dependent, we felt paralyzed. Everything we dreaded, wondered about, and feared happened."
- "When the realization hit, our bodies shut down. We didn't want to move; we wanted to sit, hands folded, engulfed in the feeling that weights are tied to each limb. But our minds, filled with incriminations, accusations, anger, frustration, embarrassment, anxiety, and fear, were whirling. When we discovered our child, our wonderful child, was chemically dependent, we felt a mental outpouring of blame and guilt."

Not uncommonly, parents quickly begin to question their parenting skills and abilities. One parent said, "I didn't make the decision to abuse drugs; my son did. Yet, something deep inside of me as a parent wanted to protect my son too much from his decision and therefore take the responsibility for his drug abuse."

Parents often think, *"If only I had done this or that, this problem wouldn't exist."* Self-incrimination can be mixed in with lashing out and blaming the other parent. Common accusations parents may make against one another include:

- Pushing too much for academic, athletic, or social success
- Overworking, and therefore failing to spend enough time with the child
- Offering too much leniency regarding household rules and responsibilities

4. Scapegoats

One mother in this situation has spoken about being left with the question: "How am I going to deal with this?" She describes the reality of her son's alcoholism as "one of life's interruptions that I didn't want." Characteristic of others in similar circumstances, this mother said she and her husband started to look for what they could do to explain their son's problems. He was taken to the doctor and found to have a "chemical imbalance."

She said:

> So we think, "Okay, so it's that." That is the reason. We're always looking for those reasons and in our shock we don't want to think that it is really as bad as it is. *How can it be that bad?* How can he drink that much? We began to read some books about adult Attention Deficit Disorder. We showed him those. Maybe that's it. He identified with 16 out of 18 characteristics. That's the issue! It wasn't that we were totally in denial or that he was, but you know you keep hoping you can find the answer so that you can fix the addict. You want to be able to help them. You want to be able to fix them.

Usually the effort to look for a scapegoat is an early way to deal with the problem as shock and denial begins to wear off. It's as though parents say to themselves, *"Okay, we've heard the bad news and have to accept it. But now how do we explain it? Because it couldn't possibly be deliberate."* So they look for physiological explanations, learning disabilities, or perhaps another person who has driven their child to chemical abuse. Many times in my practice, parents have requested an evaluation for their teenagers, seeking answers for why they are abusing controlled substances. While we do sometimes find unexpected difficulties that could explain the chemical abuse, a manic depressive illness or psychosis, for example, the answer almost always points the finger of responsibility directly at the addict and, to a lesser degree, the family that raised him or her.

5. Distorted Sense of Willpower
Like chemical dependents, co-dependents believe it's possible to control their lives by using the sheer force of their will. Parents show this attitude every time they try to control the feelings and behavior of the addicts, as well as their own feelings and behavior. "If only we all try hard enough and pull together, we can get our son to stop drinking."

6. Confusion of Identities
This condition exists in a dysfunctional family when one or both parents' self-worth rises or falls with the success or failure of the child. For example, if the substance-abusing child promises his parents he's not going to drink or smoke pot anymore but does, the co-dependent parents feels like they have failed. Their identity becomes so enmeshed with those close to them that they lose themselves and tend to think they are really only an extension of something or someone else. Wives of pastors are especially vulnerable to this kind of distorted thinking.

7. Low Self-Esteem
We're all social creatures, and people tend to make judgments based on what they see and hear, even though their impressions may be inaccurate. We've all been told our actions reflect on one another. Growing up, what Mom and Dad did for a living, where we went to school, and our last names all made a difference.

So, if the neighbors, family members or members of the congregation get the wrong impression, then what do we do? If they learn our child is dependent on drugs, how do we convince them we're really a nice family, nevertheless?

Impression management is very important. It's more important than reality. Co-dependent parents are approval junkies who can't live with the idea that they aren't admired and everything doesn't look in place.

But here's the problem with impression management: When we start trying to protect our image, we can no longer be honest about what's happening in our lives. By hiding the truth, we hide our true identity and problems develop anyway. So, a mask becomes a powerful prison where no one really knows the real you.

However, co-dependent parents fail to see this logic and invest their self-worth into how others want them to act. They are totally reactive to what others want. For example, one parent said, "...my coping skills were highly affected by my emotional attachment and glaring need to have people like me."

Addressing the Facts

Let's talk now about some healthier ways to address the fact that your child is a substance abuser or addict. If you don't face your fear of change, recovery will be that much more difficult, if not impossible. Denial and all the other defensive coping strategies we have been reviewing are deadly. If you remain defensive, you're going to lose hope. You can't be aching inside and then put on a happy face each morning. You can't lean on your own understanding of the problem and expect to completely resolve the trouble.

STEP 1. Acknowledge the problem and identify your fears. Jesus spoke of this with the Jews who were living in denial in Palestine (see John 8:32). He was talking about the freedom to allow God in their lives and to stop living by the ridiculous rules and regulations that they had built: "Then you will know the truth, and the truth will set you free" (John 8:32, NIV).

> *Sharing your problems is absolutely necessary because it puts your fears into perspective and reduces their strength.*

We need to understand, as people of the early 21st century, that we don't have to be slaves to anything or anyone. We don't have to be addicted to any lifestyle or any substance unless we choose to do so. The word "choice" needs to be underlined in your vocabulary. Denial is deadly. Sharing your problems is absolutely necessary because it puts your fears into perspective and reduces their strength. There's no sweeter feeling than to discover you're not alone or crazy regarding these events in your life. You can move beyond denial and begin to trust in the Lord by acknowledging your fears. You'll find they're not as big or as powerful as you once thought because you will discover others who have experienced the same things.

Commit yourselves to total acceptance of all of the problems, including your part in some of them. It's one thing to acknowledge that your child is chemically dependent. It can be much more difficult to look honestly at yourself to search for any part you may have contributed to the family's dysfunction—past or present. Look to the

Lord in prayer and thank Him for the triggers He is giving you. They reveal areas in your life from the past where lie-based thinking continues to exist. Ask Him to bring His truth about the weaknesses in your past so that you will be strong in dealing with the issues before you.

STEP 2. Realize that it isn't your fault. Even though you want to remain important in your children's lives, you can't make that happen. Your job as a parent is to do all you can to get your children to the point in life where they can make their own decisions and live with the natural consequences of those decisions. You can't decide for them or think for them; you can't take responsibility for their lives. Your job is to get them ready to leave you.

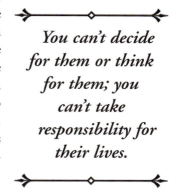

You can't decide for them or think for them; you can't take responsibility for their lives.

You didn't give your child the illness of chemical dependency. It isn't your fault that they have it any more than it would be your fault if they were diagnosed with cancer or heart disease. No one knows who will become ill with an addiction, and no one knows who will become chemically dependent. There is no perfected test we can take to determine if an individual is more or less likely to have these kinds of problems. The addiction, not you, made your children ill. Accept the first of the Alcoholics Anonymous' Twelve Steps, which states that we are powerless over another person's use of alcohol or other drugs. They have to be willing to work for their own recovery.

STEP 3. Detach. When you do this, you accomplish a temporary emotional distance from the situation your child has created. Detachment doesn't mean abandonment, nor does it mean running away. The idea of detachment is represented by the well-known phrase, *"Let go and let God."*

Jesus, in Mark 1:35, showed us a perfect example of detachment. He often went alone out into the wilderness to pray (see also Matthew 14:22-23). After feeding the 5,000 people and ministering for an entire day, He detached—he went up on a mountainside alone to pray. He knew where His responsibilities started and stopped. Co-dependent parents blur the boundaries.

Jesus' ministry shows us an important principle: The more you do for others, the more you need to understand the need for boundaries and the more recharging that you need. No matter how much you give to your chemically dependent child, no matter how much you give and give and give, all that will be expected of you is more and more and more. The point here is this: If Jesus wouldn't take care of everybody, then neither should you. If He needed to detach, so do you. If we don't detach, we not only destroy ourselves; we destroy the people to whom we're attached.

There is an often-told story of a young man who was walking home from school one day and found a cocoon attached to a stick on the sidewalk. Not wanting it to die, he picked it up, brought it home and put it in a jar with food and water. As he waited for the butterfly in the cocoon to hatch, he noticed that it seemed to be struggling to get out. Wanting to help, he took a small knife and cut a slit in the cocoon. The butterfly emerged and walked around and around the jar. It looked just fine, but it never did fly. In fact, it soon died.

Puzzled by what had happened, the boy asked his next-door neighbor, a science teacher, why the butterfly had died. He told him what had been done to help, and then the teacher said, "Well, that's your problem. It's the struggle that gives the butterfly strength to fly."

When you try to eliminate the struggles in the lives of your children, you run a big risk of crippling them. Excessive parental efforts to control and care for and help are counterproductive. You've got to keep your boundaries and temporarily detach when your kids are working out their recovery programs. Let Jesus work with them. He's the Wonderful Counselor, the Great Physician, and the bondage breaker, not you. (For further discussion on the subject of detachment, see chapter 10).

STEP 4. Care for yourself. You can't help others if you're running on empty. Let yourselves grow and do the things you have wanted to do but haven't done because of the energy you have been using to hold on to your child. Focus your efforts on returning a sense of normalcy to your life and the lives of other family members. It's okay to talk about the problems facing the family, but there is no need to make them the focus of every day. Feel those bruised emotions, but then get rid of them.

> *Until you have peace with yourself, you're not going to be at peace with those around you.*

One pastor said: "We need to recognize that the Lord heals these bruises. 1 Peter 5:10 says, '... After you have suffered a little while, [Christ] will himself restore you and make you strong, firm and steadfast' (NIV). It is very interesting that it says: 'after you have suffered a little while.' We want to scream out, 'How long is a little while?' The Bible teaches us that for God a minute is as a thousand years. We need to develop some patience."

Don't continue to waste good time dwelling on past disappointments. Let yourselves develop and give yourselves permission to go on with your lives. Support groups such as Al-Anon, Nar-Anon and Families Anonymous can greatly enhance your freedom for personal growth.

In Matthew 19:19, Jesus said, "... love your neighbor as yourself." You see, the point here is that you can't effectively love anybody else until you first love yourself.

That's not an invitation, of course, to be selfish and self-centered. It's an instruction to love yourself in a healthy way. Seek His truth about the source of your own wounds and get healing.[1] As you become healthier and happier, you will be a better resource for others. Matthew 23:39 and several other verses say the same thing. The Bible only has to say something once to make it true, but God emphasizes this point by mentioning it several times in Scripture. Until you have peace with yourself, you're not going to be at peace with those around you.

STEP 5. Work closely with a partner. If you are married, that obviously means your spouse. When chemical dependency infects a family, you can expect that one of its negative consequences will be marital distress. Harsh words will be spoken because each of you will feel some responsibility for the struggles of your child. When you're angry at your child, you are quite likely to take it out on each other. Preoccupation with your child's problems will hamper your ability to listen to each other.

To protect your marriage, establish your priorities. You must not allow your child's addiction to ruin your marital relationship. Your marriage commitment to your spouse should come before your commitment to your child's recovery. Healing is the child's responsibility. Preservation of the marriage and family is the parents' responsibility.

One father said to his son, "We will not let your decisions ruin our marriage. I don't think you are making wise decisions here. Your mother is more important to me than you are. If you don't quit using, I'm not going to let your decision to use marijuana ruin my relationship with your mother."

His son said, "I understand that."

So, do what you have to do to regain your love and respect for each other. Sit down together and talk about what is needed to renew your reliance on each other. Talk about your future together. Don't make excuses. Acknowledge your true feelings. Look closely at your individual personality styles and get help if necessary in understanding what to expect from each other during times of high stress. Learning about each other's needs will help each of you be more sensitive and sharing.

A pastor said,

> As we have continued to have this commitment to one another that we are not going to let this ruin our marriage relationship, we are learning that what may be right for her may not be right for me and what is right for me may not be right for her. I may be stressed, but I have to respect her right to be peaceful. It is not that we have this peaceful co-existence, but it has deepened our appreciation for who each other is. It has also deepened our respect of how God made us.

1. For more information, see Anderson, Neil T., Zuehlke, Terry, Zuehlke, Julianne. *Christ-Centered Therapy: The Practical Integration of Theology and Psychology*, Zondervan, 2000.

STEP 6. Make peace with God. Most parents of chemically dependent children become angry at God because they've prayed for Him to intervene. They've been deeply disappointed because He didn't step in and fix their child and the family dysfunction.

Here's the problem with that: This kind of prayer is erroneous. It's a mistake to believe that God will step in and override the free will of your child and fix him for your sake. The truth is, God will not do that. God is a gentleman. He never forces anything on anyone. God is not in the control business, unless you'd like Him to help you. So, when God doesn't come through by fixing your child, disappointment often turns to bitterness.

We also need to remember that God has not promised to fix all people and their problems. Some sickness is used for the glory of God, as is pointed out in John 11:4. As far as I know, Paul's thorn never was removed.

What God has promised, however, is that when we do experience adversity, He will go through it with us. In Isaiah 43:2-5, He tells us He'll be there when we are in deep water and great trouble.

So, parents, doesn't it make sense to drop your denial and instead, trust in God for your child's future? Romans 8:28 offers a powerful promise: God will cause everything to work together for the good. Paul knew it. Do you?

Listen to another pastor's thoughts: "Often we do not go on to verse 29 where He is describing His eternal plan. It says that He is sovereignly working to 'conform us to the likeness of His Son.' Even the most difficult of circumstances, such as the struggle with a wayward child, is used by God to conform and shape us, as we trust Him in the situation."

Have you come to the place in your life where you can let God be the God of your life? As Ephesians 3:20-21 points out, "to Him be the glory." He's able to accomplish infinitely more than we could ever dare to ask or hope if we let Him. If we'll let Him love us and let Him walk with us, then we don't have to be responsible for our child's recovery. God is able, which means we can all let go and let God be God in our lives and in the lives of our children.

Chapter 19

Recovery Parenting

By Pat Boris

I find that parents in recovery have concerns in four core areas: physical, emotional, social and spiritual. Each area contributes to the whole picture. On any given day, one area may be more important than another. For example, when you wonder how you will pay for treatment, it's a tangible, physical problem. On another day, the stress of wondering if your child will ever get to treatment is an emotional problem you face.

So often, we use all of our energy on our problems without replenishing that energy. We martyr ourselves for the worthy cause of our children who are in such pain and trouble when martyrdom is not necessary or even helpful. A big part of our jobs as parents is to stay healthy. But it's hard to stay healthy when our children may be dying on drugs. We are worried sick and direct most of our resources towards our children.

It is vital that we look at our problems and our energy in light of our renewable resources. Are we using up our resources without renewing them? Are we forgetting to eat, exercise, and laugh with family and friends? More importantly, are we relating to God? If we are not, then we are sacrificing our lives. This won't bring about recovery to our children.

The main objective of this chapter is to help us find power to begin or continue our recovery. If we muster the courage and faith to work on our own recovery, we will be more whole and available to our children if or when they begin their own recovery. But that is not the main reason for us to recover. Not to recover is to choose to be ill. Illness will not bring our children recovery, but it will sacrifice other valuable people to addiction – us.

Learn to Respond, Not React

Doing something with our children usually makes us parents feel good about ourselves. It's great when we have a nice product at the end of our activity, like a science project. But when something goes wrong, parents feel disappointed, even guilty, that they couldn't make it turn out better. Some parents feel sad, others get angry, and others try to talk the child into better behavior with humor or treats.

In the first case, the vibes are good, our plans work out well, and the activity may have seemed effortless. In the second case, even a lot of effort might not salvage our plans. We could be the best parents on the planet and still argue with our children about that science project. At times like these, it had better be clear who the grown-up is. When the child has a tantrum, the parents must resist having one, too. Parents must RESPOND to tantrums as maturely as they respond to smiling cooperation. Parents must RESPOND to an oppositional, drug-using child from a mature center rich in resources and God, rather than REACT out of fatigue, guilt, or self-doubt.

Parents must recover to become, or remain, responsive in a terrible situation like teen drug use. Failing to work our own recovery will result in raw emotional reactions to a child's drug use. Recovering parents will still have strong emotions like fear, but they will not have to respond to them every time.

> *Parents must RESPOND to tantrums as maturely as they respond to smiling cooperation. Parents must RESPOND to an oppositional, drug-using child from a mature center rich in resources and God, rather than REACT out of fatigue, guilt, or self-doubt.*

Who—or What—is Your Center?

Recovering parents have resources in addition to emotional and spiritual fuel. They have a center source of spiritual power in Jesus Christ that is full even when everything else seems empty. What is fueling our parental tanks today? Are we going on emotions? Are events driving us? Before we go any further, reflect on where your strength is today. Is it coming from Christ? Can you name who or what is at your center today? Is it your child? Addiction? Emotional confusion? Finances? God?

Before or sometime during the addictive process, the addicted children usually become the center of our lives. We increasingly direct all of our emotional strength, physical endurance, spiritual energy and social momentum towards our addicted children. Going to work becomes a sham. Meals lose their taste, marital intimacy disappears, and we set the other children aside. How much of our physical, social, emotional, and spiritual lives are tied up in our addicted children?

We may ask why this is important, since we believe we can't do anything about our energy expenditure towards our children right now. Or we may wish we had even more energy to devote to the cause. We must be very honest as we think about our personal energy, ability, and resources, especially where they come from and where we are spending them, because we cannot make good choices if we don't consider what they are or how they might be different.

For example, in a race we pace ourselves so we have some kick at the end. Some parents use all their energy on their drug-using child as if it was a sprint. Addicts routinely run over sprinters. Some parents use the family resources on their addict child like a credit card. Addicts routinely max out resources.

Take a moment to write down who or what you are focusing on today. Don't analyze yourself. Just put down who or what is in your focus. Your energy is going out into these places or being restored by them. It's important. Naming what is in your focus gives you a place to begin to focus on healing and recovery.

However, wherever we start, ultimately we want to focus on God as our source of strength.   What consumes your physical, emotional, social and spiritual energy? What restores your energy in these areas? Where is God in relation to all of this?

Part I: Parenting and Responsibility

Can we ever forget the day we brought our children home for the very first time? Whether these were our firstborn or our fifth, our families would never be the same. We wanted these children to be all they could possibly be. We were responsible for making the possibilities happen, and we were more than a little nervous when we couldn't.   As sure as we all counted fingers and toes on our newborns, we thought about the day our kids would reach adolescence. Would these innocent babies someday be beautiful, talented, and brilliant?   Or would they do scary things we could hardly think about: abuse drugs, rebel against us and others in authority, become promiscuous, or run away from home?

Recently our son went overseas to study. The night before this now mature 21-year old left for Japan, I begged him to let me fold something. I yearned for a physical duty to connect me to his adventure. We parents are inextricably linked to the physical lives of our children. As our children grow up, we have to learn how to let go appropriately: not too quickly and not too slowly. We second-guess ourselves, get scared, and pull back after giving out privileges. It happens to most parents, and it starts from day one.   We meet their helplessness with varying degrees of our own helplessness. Providing for our addicted children begins with the physical questions and concerns.

Physical Concerns

Physical concerns account for many of our problems and unanswered questions about our child's addictions. We worry that our children will keep their feet dry and get enough to eat at the same time, we hope they won't be shot in a drug deal, or we fear that they might cause a fatal car accident. As a mother, I have found these physical concerns irrationally washing over me. I couldn't separate the important (food) from the urgent (bad drug deal). Where did my son end and where did I begin? Many of my concerns, rational or otherwise, stemmed from questions concerning my larger parental responsibilities. In addition, it was not always easy to bring God into the equation. Sometimes He seemed distant.

You may be asking some of these questions:

_____ What is addiction? Did I cause it? Can I fix it? How soon?

_____ Will the addiction last forever? Is there a cure? If so, what is it?

_____ If there is no cure, will he/she die?

_____ Is my child brain damaged or dangerous to him/herself/others?

_____ Is there a skill, information, or service that I need?

_____ How will I pay for help? Who will help me get it?

_____ Have I turned my child over to God's care?

_____ Am I trusting God to meet my needs?

Social Concerns

Families want to be close and proud of one another. Parents expect to be proud of their children, in part because parents expect that they have contributed something besides good genes to their children's success. After all, Mom helped with the spelling homework, Dad taught the curve ball, and they both cared...a lot. While I have met lots of parents with regrets, I have never met parents who raised their children badly on purpose. The pressure to do a good job is just too strong. Women contemplating pregnancy stop smoking and begin taking folic acid. Couples talk, sing and play music to the unborn children. Perfect babies are quite an accomplishment for which new parents take pride (and some credit).

Parents who have disabled children often blame themselves for the disabilities as they grieve the loss of perfect children. These loving parents may have done the same things the parents of healthy children did to ensure their babies' health; but the unexpected happened anyway. Parents of children who become injured, ill or have behavior problems feel guilty, sometimes reliving over and over decisions which led up to the discovery of the problem. With guilt comes the social stigma of having children who are "different."

Guilt-Prone Parents

Recently, a young woman arrived unannounced at my office door. Her story helps us understand how prone we parents are to feeling guilty about issues and situations in our children's lives. She was in her early 30s, of medium build, with shiny blond hair and a furrowed brow. She looked around, and because my door was ajar, she stepped inside.

"Are you ... No, how could you be?" she began. She had tears in her eyes.

I told her that I would help her if I could. She was looking for a nurse practition-er she had called at random some weeks before regarding her son. Yes, I was the one she wanted.

Thirteen years prior to this day, she had been a high school senior, ready for col-lege, and pregnant with her football star boyfriend's child. They had cared about each other a great deal, but had known they couldn't provide a home for their child. They had placed their beautiful baby boy in a loving adoptive home. It had been a difficult decision, but one that they believed was right. The day she made the phone call (and got me), she had received information that her son was in a home for delinquent boys. The agency that had placed her son with his adoptive family wanted to know more about the backgrounds of the boy's biological parents. There were obvious questions about physical lineage, but there was no problem there.

The more immediate concerns of this young woman just blew me away. She had a wonderful husband and two little preschoolers. She had not married the father of the boy, but someone she had met and fallen in love with in college. He knew all about her past, even about her continued friendship with members of the old boyfriend's family. I sensed that these were very loving people. But on this day she was wonder-ing about the implications for her new little family. Was it possible that she had passed on some impulsiveness to her boy, the impulsiveness that had led to her pregnancy in the first place? And if she did, could she have also passed it on to these new babies? What did the future hold for her as the mother of delinquent children?

These are normal questions. What surprised me was the sense of responsibility this mom had for the trouble the boy was in. She both wanted to know if there was any hope for him (and her other children), and was ashamed of what had made him that way. She felt stigmatized and afraid.

An Unhealthy Entanglement

Rebellious substance-abusing children have very different values and lifestyles than those of "normal" adolescents. It is extremely confounding and distressing when an adolescent chooses drugs and a wayward path. As we saw in the physical concerns sec-tion previously, we have such a sense of responsibility for our children that it is hard to separate where we end and they begin. Part of the distress parents feel is social dis-tress or social stigma. We "own" the successes or failures of our children, even to the extent that our own self-definitions are reshaped by it. Our society cultivates parental ownership even as we pass laws that hold parents responsible for their children's misdeeds.

I believe that parents whose identity and worth are tied up in the successes or failures of their children will be the most confused and devastated of all parents when their children rebel and abuse drugs and/or alcohol. This is not to say that parents don't influence rebellion, only that taking such total credit or blame for our children's independent actions represent two sides of a counterfeit coin.

Taking credit for their successes leaves our children without the dignity of their own good judgment, while taking blame for their failures relieves the burden of their acts. Our job as parents is rather to teach and love and stand back while our adolescents learn through as many natural consequences as possible about normal successes and failures.

Our society has misinterpreted high parental involvement for parental responsibility for every outcome. One writer makes the distinction between being increasingly "responsible to" versus "responsible for" the adolescent. Social stigma has to do with the judgment of society that a parent (or a child in the parent's care) has failed to reflect the values of that society. It's a type of banishment, and the fear of it keeps us from making hard decisions, such as letting children take responsibilities that they may not seem ready to take.

Social concerns are all about social stigma, about questions from friends, family or employers regarding our responsibilities as parents to our children. Ultimately, we must parent according to God's standards and allow Him—and only Him—to be our judge.

Check the Social Concerns You Have:

_____ Are people avoiding me, my spouse and my other children?
_____ Am I avoiding people?
_____ Do I need counseling to be able to parent this child?
_____ Who has to know about this?
_____ Some of My Other Social Concerns Are: _____

_____

_____

As you begin your own recovery, take time to think about what brought you to where you are today. Your child is abusing drugs or alcohol or is in chemical dependency treatment. Does this say something about you? What? If you make changes in your life, will it be because you want this child to change? If your child does not change, can you still grow to be the person you want to be anyway? Can you still become the person God wants you to become?

Research shows that strong social support is a key factor in successful recovery. Find it for yourself. We invited a few other parents to our home for informal support each week for over two years. We helped each other cope with runaways, drug overdoses, insurance denials, and those terrible calls from the police. You must have support to get healthy, and your child needs healthy parents as a main source of social support when he or she chooses recovery.

Part II: Our Inner Lives

A good deal of what we think about is connected to our expectations of "how it ought to be." One way psychologists look at how resilient people are is by finding their "locus of control." Locus of control means to make good decisions after taking in all relevant information, and not being unduly swayed by others. We must make our decisions based on faith, facts, and wise counsel. As followers of Christ, we know He is in charge of our lives, and works out the circumstances for good as we depend on Him.

Locus of Control

We are always responsible *to* our children, but less and less responsible *for* them. For example, I tied the shoelaces until my daughter could do it for herself. It was a test of wills to potty train her because she wanted to have big girl pants on from day one, and had a tantrum every time she had an accident. I learned how to walk away from tantrums and she learned how to use a toilet. It was very embarrassing to have a screaming two year old with wet clothes at the mall, but as I figured out just who had the wet pants, I could figure out what was the appropriate response to them in that pre-Pampers era.

I loved this child more than life. How could this happen?

I was able to see that she would train more easily if she could make the connection between her wet pants and how to use a potty without my emotional input responding too much to her emotional output. I was able to see that she didn't make me lose my cool when she lost hers. This is an example of internal locus of control. My power to *control* my circumstances is limited, but my power to respond to my circumstances is limited only by my internal ability to separate myself from them. No one can make me lose my control without my permission. Galatians 5:22-23 tells us that the fruit of the Spirit includes self-control.

Fast forward to my snarly, teenage child sneaking out of the house at 10 o'clock on a school night to meet some "druggie" friends. I was much more invested in this outcome than I was with potty training. I was actually feeling a creeping insanity as I looked into those hate-filled eyes. I loved this child more than life. How could this happen? Suddenly, I realized that my child could die, that he could die alone with his addiction...or he could take me with him. I'd seen it happen with other parents I knew. One had aged 10 years in six months. Her marriage was shaky, her other children were emotionally at risk, and her job was on the line for all the time off she needed because of her child's addiction.

Maybe I was just a bad parent. I felt so terrible that I just wanted to isolate myself until the problem went away. I let his state define mine...an external locus of control. I let his circumstances define what mine would be. I learned to let go, and to separate his actions from mine. This is the meaning of "letting go and letting God." Think about your circumstances, whose problems these are, and what you may do about them.

Who's Responsible?

One of the hardest things parents must do is to shift the burden of responsibility for their children's decisions to the children. Oh, sure, when the child forgets his lunch money, a good "lesson" is a lunchless lunch period. But when a child is picked up high or intoxicated by the police, will the child understand that this is his own responsibility, or will his parents pay the fine and cover for him so he won't be thrown off the hockey team?

When parents take responsibility for their children's decisions, it's really natural because parents see most things related to their children in a " big picture" way. Our dreams are wrapped up in the hopes and plans we've dreamt for them from before they were born. Parents see their children's lives in such a long-term way that we find it hard to employ short-term lessons.

Write out your own problem list and see if you can assign the problem to the right person and decide what to do about it. You may need a spouse, friend or counselor to help you.

Having a substance-abusing adolescent is so heart wrenching, so stressful, so emotionally draining that we sometimes turn inward, get depressed, and blame ourselves for all the things that inevitably went wrong. We have an emotional crisis and do not have the ability to deal with it.

Parents tell me they feel so guilty they can't have fun. They eat or drink too much, yell a lot, isolate themselves, and do not deal with their own recovery.

We struggle with issues such as:

_____ I feel so ashamed. Am I a bad parent?

_____ Why am I so sad and worried about myself?

_____ I can't admit I don't like my child right now.

_____ I feel like I can't trust anyone anymore.

_____ Is God punishing me for something I did?

_____ Sometimes I feel abandoned by God and bewildered. Am I normal?

_____ Some of my other spiritual concerns: _____

_____

_____

_____

Addiction: A Family Disease

Every one in the family is touched or affected in some way by a member's drug or alcohol abuse. Parents of substance-abusing adolescents often feel vulnerable and defensive. Some say it's as if other normal parents got a more complete set of directions for parenting than they did.

But we have to ask this: What is my definition of a normal family and how closely does my definition compare with God's definition?

The Role of Insecurity

The truth is, all parents feel insecure at times. The insecurity of parenting a substance-abusing child is tied to "not knowing." We don't know how to parent a child who comes home stoned, fails in school or steals our stuff. There is no parent manual for us for these situations. Even the "experts" are relieved and happy when their own kids don't use drugs. But when their kids do, the experts are just as confused as we "non-experts" are. They don't have all the answers either.

Insecure or not, we need to be the adults in our families. Our kids will not make us secure in our decisions. It is not their job to make us feel secure. When our kids use drugs, we have very little positive feedback about how we are doing our job, so it's important that we find good ways to learn what we need, and find some models in other parents.

Stress and Confusion

Actually, stress and confusion add to guilt. Most of us experience guilt because we think we should have known the answers to our questions. The result of the mix of stress, confusion, and guilt is to become paralyzed and not ask for help. For the same reason, people don't ask directions when they know they are lost. They think it's temporary. They think they know where north, south, east and west are. They may feel guilty that they took a shortcut. Besides, they've gotten out of worse jams than this, and they'll have to admit they might even have contributed to the problem. If we have difficulty admitting we need help in finding directions, then it follows that we will have trouble asking for help when drugs and/or alcohol hit our families.

- What are the other sources of stress in my life that contribute to my confusion?
- What else causes confusion for me?
- What do I feel guilty about?
- Should I have known more or done more?
- What help do I need or what person should I see to do a better job as a parent of a substance-using kid?
- How can I rely more on God to remove or deal with the stress and confusion in my life?
- Is guilt getting in the way of asking for help?
- Have I tried to take a shortcut in my life or my parenting that I now regret?

On the Road to Recovery

It's okay to ask directions on the road to recovery. We couldn't have known about this stressful, confusing road. Few people talk about being here even though a lot of people have been. We want to leave it behind, not put up detours or draw maps for other frightened travelers. We certainly didn't come here on purpose. We need directions to an exit, detour or bridge to get our families and ourselves to a safe highway.

Where We Think We Are

Take some time to do one of these thought-provoking exercises. Do it again with another adult, your spouse, your parent, or a trusted friend who is accompanying you in recovery.

1. "Serenity Prayer" Exercise

Do you already know the "Serenity Prayer"? Read it now, and think about it as you do this little exercise. "God, grant me the serenity to accept the things I cannot change, the courage to change the things I can, and the wisdom to know the difference. Amen."

● **God grant me the serenity to accept...**

Where I am, and that it's a good place to start even if I am a confused traveler on a strange road. I'm not sure how I got here, or how to leave, but I know I didn't intend to take this turn. I'm really lost. I need Your love, wisdom, direction and strength to get out of this mess.

● **Some things I cannot change:** _____

_____

● **Courage to change:** _____

_____

_____

It's hard to change me. I'll start changing but I don't know where to start because I'm stressed and confused. I need Jesus Christ because He knows the road and where the off ramp is. Lord, strengthen me to change the things I can.

● **Some things I need the courage to change:** _____

_____

_____

● **Wisdom to know the difference...**

I need to know if this is a straight and narrow road to recovery, or another crazy ride over a cliff. I must admit that it is impossible for me to change my child. Write down some areas where I have trouble knowing the difference among things I can change, things I cannot and the things God can change. _____

_____

_____

2. Picture yourself talking to God in person.

What would you say? Are you angry? Disappointed? Sad? Contented? Fearful? Faithful? Below, take a moment to write a few words to God, telling Him how you feel and how you are recovering today. Tell Him how much you need Him to be working in your life. If you are angry at Him, tell Him. He can handle it. He responds with love when we are honest with Him. _____

_____

_____

_____

Self Care

We parents all know we have to eat and sleep to live. Yet we don't feel right about spending time on ourselves when our children are using drugs. It seems selfish to worry about ourselves when our children could die.

Let's stop here a minute, because poor self care is a side street of the guilty road that we parents often take to Martyrdom Drive.

What do I need to do to take care of myself and allow God to care for me?

We can get confused on Martyrdom Drive and stop taking care of ourselves. Instead, we must get back our courage. It's not courageous or faithful to be exhausted and thin. It won't make the user stop using drugs. Martyrdom is self inflicted and lonely, and it prevents God from working in our lives. It takes real courage and faith to thrive. Getting well takes courage and acceptance of God's love for us.

We parents get confused when our kids use drugs, because nothing seems to be working predictably except the numerous paths that take us to guilt. This is why it is so important to have God working in our lives.

What do I need to do to take care of myself and allow God to care for me?

Probably all attempts at recovery are real, but not all are successful. The martyrdom - guilt connection is a good example. There are many others, and they have things in common. Let's look at some ways people take care of themselves. These are called coping strategies.

Coping Skills: Responses that Deal with a Problem

Some coping skills are appropriate and positive; some are not. For example, an appropriate way to deal with someone stealing your wallet is to call 911. It's not appropriate to excuse it, even if the thief is your son.

Positive coping means to choose actively, not reactively, a good and justly motivated response. For example, when your daughter is an hour late for curfew, a positive coping skill is to respond, calmly applying the consequences previously agreed and go back to bed. A negative coping response would be to open the door, yell and scream until you have a headache, and ground her for a month, which should not be an option. It is hard to trust God when we manifest such behavior.

Contracts are good ways to help yourself and your child define consequences. They help reduce stress by choosing strategies and making choices ahead of time with appropriate consequences. The contract may be as detailed as you and your child want. But you must both agree to the terms and sign it. You may make changes any time, but you both must agree on the change, and sign it.

Contracts help build trust, negotiation skills, and communication at a very fragile time. Some items for a contract might include:

- chores
- times for waking up and going to bed
- a list or description of acceptable friends
- a list of who can call, and when
- where and with whom the adolescent may go
- curfews

Each item should have a consequence that should relate, if possible, to the offense. Parents should spell out their responsibilities to the adolescent as well. For example, our contract said, "I (parent) will drive either to or from one AA meeting a week. You (son) will find a ride the other way. If I fail to drive one way any week, I will drive both ways another week."

Which coping strategies do you use, and which ones are helpful?

Which coping strategies do you use, and which ones are helpful?

Some coping strategies are helpful, and some are not helpful. For example, taking a walk is a positive coping strategy. Being honest with God about your fears is a positive coping strategy. Kicking the dog, criticizing your spouse or drinking to inebriation is a negative strategy. It might be helpful to make a coping strategies inventory. You may be using any one regularly, but you must accept that a negative strategy cannot possibly bring the positive changes you desire. Reflect on how often you use the coping strategies, then evaluate the need to change. Be honest about where God is in all of this.

Trust in God

Of all the ways I learned to cope with the stress of our child's addiction, learning greater trust in God was one of the most powerful for me. Psalm 56:3 says when I am afraid I will trust in Him. Being afraid drew me closer to God. Addiction is scary. We used to say it was as if aliens had come and swapped bodies with our son, he was so different. Isn't it a joy to know that God's not afraid? I saw a bumper sticker that says GOD NEVER PANICS. He always says "Don't be afraid," over and over in His word. He always says to trust Him when we can't trust ourselves. He made us, He understands us. Read over Psalm 139. Meditate on the fact that He knows you better than you know yourself. He also knows your child. He knows about this addiction, and He is not afraid. He has a plan to bring your child and you to wholeness. I think of that wholeness as recovery.

It's been eight years since I decided to begin my own recovery. The Lord has blessed me with much greater reliance on Him, and even a better understanding of parenthood based on His unconditional yet tough love for me. I work on my recovery every day. Begin yours today. I'm praying for you.

Chapter 20

Hope: The Last Word

By John Vawter

Hope. It's an important word, but a tough one to put into action. It is difficult to have hope when your kid is abusing drugs and/or alcohol. But, without hope you have no sense that the future can be better. We often say that the addicts or alcoholics have to come to the place where they can admit they are powerless over their drug of choice. It is also true that the parents of the addicts must come to the same place of powerlessness as it relates to hope. When we get to this place, then we can declare our need for God in our lives and for Him to be working in the terrible situations we face. For the parents who like to be in control, it is hard to assume a position of dependence on God because we have become skilled at solving problems. It is difficult to admit that the issue of our children abusing drugs is way beyond our ability to control it. Those parents who are more amiable in temperament and easygoing in personality probably tend to become skilled in avoiding situations or "letting nature take its course." In both cases, our refined skills are not enough. We must bring God into the equation.

As we have seen in the previous three chapters, and in fact throughout the whole book, hope does not happen naturally. We must be honest with ourselves and with God that we are frightened for the future of our kids. We must be honest that the situation of drug/alcohol abuse is beyond our ability to control. That fear and lack of control are what motivate us to depend on God.

Unfortunately, it is not always easy to cast our dependence on Him. Sometimes we feel that He has failed us. Or, we conclude that He has turned his back on us and that is why our kids have decided to abuse drugs/alcohol. Neither is true, but such thinking moves us away from God, not closer to Him.

God at Work: Yesterday, Today, and Tomorrow

In the entire situation you may have been involved in, God has not changed. He is always the same—loving, caring, and working. But, He does not override or subvert our free will or the free will of our children. He is working in the addicts' lives even though we parents may not see it. Many addicts who have been raised in Christian homes but who have moved away from the values of their parents have said their awareness of God never left them in spite of the choices they have made. I believe that is God's way of continuing to work in the lives of our kids.

In all the turmoil we parents face when our kids are abusing, it seems that God is trying to turn our attention to Him in a more dependent way. We may have already met Him…or we may be in the process of meeting Him. I met Him as a sophomore in college. I came to understand that He had expressed his love to me through Jesus Christ coming to earth. I asked Jesus Christ to forgive my sin, to come into my life and to empower me to become the kind of person that He wants me to become. At that time, I began the life long process of "becoming conformed to the image of Jesus Christ." Every time I have faced a crisis or challenge since then—and drugs invading my family was the worst crisis I have faced—I have had to remember that God wants to be a part of my life through my relationship with Jesus Christ. It is not always easy to rely on Him because of my free will. To ask Him to work in a situation is to acknowledge that He is more capable of working than I am and that He loves the person more than I do. Because of my fear or my stubbornness, sometimes that is difficult to acknowledge. If you have never taken the "final Step" of becoming a follower of Christ, let me encourage you to do so now. It is as easy as saying, "Jesus Christ, I believe in you. I have sinned. I am imperfect. I ask you to forgive my sin and come into my life"

Step by Step

Thus, my relationship with God through Christ has involved a lifelong series of "taking the next step" in my spiritual pilgrimage. The first step is to acknowledge our sinfulness and invite Him into our lives. After that decision, the next step is always similar—even though the situations may vary and the issues can be more and more severe—in that we must continue to acknowledge God's love for us and our loved one and His ability and willingness to work in their lives. Making this "next step" decision allows us the honesty to acknowledge the bad days, the frightening days and the days we feel as though God has abandoned us.

God has a magnificent way of using these situations to build more faith in us as parents. Our fears and insecurities about the future of our kids point out our need for Him on a daily basis. This is why many of the contributors to this book have mentioned their own experience in re-evaluating their faith—or lack of faith—and have said that the experience deepened their faith in God.

Tomorrow may look bleak. We may be worn out. There may be no more stones to turn over relative to helping our beloved children become sober and clean. But, our continued dependence on God can give us the hope that gives us strength for today. Many years ago, a man in the church I pastored in Minnesota asked me if I was "going to give up on him?" I told him that I might but God would not. When this man finally placed his faith in

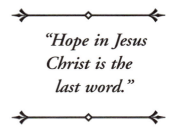

"Hope in Jesus Christ is the last word."

God through Jesus Christ, he contacted me to remind me of our conversation. He said to me, " I realize that I wore you out but I did not wear God out. He kept after me. I finally gave Him my life.' So it can be with our kids. They may wear us out, but God will still be working. That is why I say, "Hope in Jesus Christ is the last word."

ADDENDUM #1

The Path to Parental Health:
Eight Responses Many Parents Express

Dr. Steve Nicholson, an anthropologist and former college president, did follow-up interviews with You're Not Alone conferees. As he talked to parents and listened to what they were saying, he began to discover a process of recovery and growth for parents whose kids abuse drugs or alcohol. In some ways, this process is similar to what Elizabeth Kubler-Ross discovered about the process of death and dying.

Our initial research suggests eight common responses that parents of an abuser of alcohol or drugs may have on their way to becoming healthy enough to leave the issue in God's hands and quit ruining their own emotional and spiritual health. Granted, every parent does not follow the same path or even experience all of these responses. But the research has validity and can help parents understand where they are and where they need to go for the sake of their own health. Furthermore, depending on the age of the child, responses can be different for each parent. In fact, parents may experience two or three responses at the same time. Here are the eight responses recognized as being common for parents of abusers:

1. Denial

Denial is not seeing or admitting the evidence of our children's abuse of drugs or alcohol. Certainly any denial is exacerbated by the intense feelings of grief and loss the parents experience.

2. Realization

Accepting that our kids are abusing drugs or alcohol is very difficult. We did not rear them this way. We are afraid for their future. However, accepting the reality allows us to get the help we need for our own emotional and spiritual health.

3. Shock

The shock of the reality can be described as a huge, energy-draining phenomenon that has a tremendous impact on the parents. The shock is so intense that it often immobilizes the parents and keeps them from fulfilling normal family and work responsibilities. In some cases, the pain and shock are so debilitating that the parents feel like quitting on God, quitting on life, or lashing out at God in anger.

4. Enabling

Parents of drug/alcohol abusers often enable because they love their children and want the best for them. We enable when we cover and make excuses for the abusers and don't let them face the consequences of their actions. However, we must stop enabling because, although our motives in doing so may be pure, the effect denies the abusers the responsibility of seeing the error of their ways.

5. Anger

Anger—or misdirected anger—can be directed at many targets: the child, the drug dealer, society, one's spouse, or friends who are not sensitive to the pain of the parents. Nevertheless, the parents must assume responsibility for their own anger, and then deal with it. If left unchecked, the anger is very destructive. It has been said, "Hurt feelings only hurt us in the end." The same is true with our anger.

6. Acceptance

Acceptance means we begin to apply the three C's: (1) I did not **cause** this; (2) I cannot **cure** this; and (3) I cannot **control** this. When we get to this stage, we begin to reach out to God and ask for His intervention in the lives of our children. The parents begin to realize what they can and cannot control. We accept the fact of our children's abuse. This realization allows us to pray harder and focus more of our energy on our own spiritual, emotional and mental health, while asking and trusting God for His intervention in the lives of our children.

7. Marital Tension

Often parents are challenged in relating to one another. Our basic temperaments cause us to respond or react to our kids' abuse in different ways. One may be calm and practicing faith while the other wants to control everything. If these temperament differences are not dealt with as soon as possible, the parents' marriage can suffer.

8. Faith: Loving the Addicts but Leaving Them in God's Hands

We begin to get our lives in order; we realize that we can trust God with the lives of our children. Reaching the stage of trusting God is a tortuous journey, but we cannot give up hope. Some call this response "detachment." The parents do not quit loving or caring for the children. Detachment simply means the parents learn to trust God and learn how not to be controlled by the abusers' actions. We find we may take one step forward and two steps backward along the path to this response of faith. As long as we understand that this is a goal, then we have something concrete to hang on to when the pain and grief become particularly intense or when we are not doing so well in trusting God. When we reach the highest level of this response, peace returns and anxiety, fear, and hostility melt away. We trust the God Who loves our children more than we do to keep working in their lives.

In conclusion, these eight responses were taken from the voices of experience of parents who have traveled or are traveling this road. Their words pave a path of understanding for those parents involved with children who are abusing. No definite time frame exists for these parents. They all follow their own pace and must be careful not to let others force them into an artificial time sequence. Marriage partners must be careful not to project their responses onto their spouses. Recognizing that others have walked the road and have achieved some balance and faith in their lives will help those now on the journey.

Addendum #2

Questions Parent Ask

This section is designed to answer some frequently asked questions by parents whose kids are using illicit drugs, alcohol, or any mood-altering chemicals. We make no differentiation, because addiction can be deadly in many ways and addicts will use whatever gets them high. In many cases, there is not one universally accepted answer. In those cases, we will give dissenting views with the knowledge that parents ultimately must make their own decisions.

Action Steps

What is the first thing parents should do when they find out their children have been using?

- The first thing is not to panic. Remember, you're not alone. As clearly as you can, think carefully. Do not overreact. Call your pastor, a close friend, or a person you know will pray for you. Get to a counselor who understands the implications of drug/alcohol use.
- The age of the child is a factor in what you do. But do not wait. Get to work on finding help and support for the rest of the family and the addict.
- It is important to be with someone who understands drugs or alcohol. You need expertise at this point. Try to avoid those who will meddle, preach, or ask why instead of helping you find answers.
- Some families have found great help and wisdom in having a drug counselor perform an evaluation on the child. The counselor can tell if there is experimentation, use, or abuse, and whether the child is "at risk." The counselor can explain the differences among experimentation, using, and abusing, and can tell the parent whether a treatment program is necessary.

My child is in junior or senior high and using. What do I do?

- Find out how much he or she is using, as well as when, where and with whom.
- Tough love is not a cliché. When a child is still living under your authority, you must take action.
- One father says, "It's not a time to caretake, negotiate or rationalize, or be a wimp. Figure out a plan and work it. The plan has to be thought out objectively, maybe with a friend or counselor, because addicted kids can be so manipulative. We never want to think our kids lie to us. In the midst of emotions, we lose objectivity and the impact of the decisions we need to make and maintain."

I feel helpless knowing my child might be an addict. How do I start getting help?

- Some parents find great help in talking to the school counselor.
- Again, we cannot emphasize enough the value of seeing a drug counselor.
- Remember, abuse is not always addiction; it can be the result of succumbing to peer pressure.
- Join a support group for parents of addicts.

My child is not yet an adult and is living in my home. The police say that I will go to jail if I do not control him/her. What do I do?

- This is a very real issue in some states. We recently advised a couple to reiterate the rules of the home, which included NO use whatsoever of drugs or alcohol. Further, we advised the parents to tell the child that if use continued, the garage would become his/her bedroom until he/she were of legal age, at which time he/she would be escorted from the property.
- Parents have the right to retain their dignity and standards.

Parental Pain

How do I deal with the pain that I experience when I learn that my child is experimenting or using drugs or alcohol?

- The expression, "One day at a time," applies here. Our fear can immobilize us. Get through the first day. Break it down into smaller units if need be.
- Do not stuff the pain; be honest with it because the pain is real and it can become debilitating very quickly.
- Do not deny your feelings. What are you and other family members feeling? Focus on your feelings and the reality of your child's behavior.
- Guilt and shame paralyze; anger and rage consume energy and solve nothing. If you experience these emotions, ask where they come from.

Where is God when I'm in all this pain?

- Remember that God is close by, even if He seems far away.
- God knows your pain. Reading the Psalms of David has helped some parents. The Psalms express sorrow and despair, but also show David turning his focus back to God.
- One father said about finding his son abusing drugs, "Prayer helped us realize that our son's salvation and relationship with God were more important than his relationship with the family. I would pray for that and keep the 'self ' at a healthier distance."

How do I see God helping my child when he or she is hooked on drugs?

- One parent says he prays every day with a picture in mind of Jesus Christ standing behind the child saying to the parent, "I'm still at work. Don't give up on Me. I love your child even more than you do. In fact, I died for your child."

How does talking to friends help when I'm in such pain? Frankly, I don't feel like talking to anyone.

- Talk to someone you trust, preferably someone who is experienced in this sort of thing. If he/she is a person who will hug you, that will be even better. A person of compassion who can cry with you and not preach at you will work wonders in your soul. Do not keep the news inside.
- Have a friend, counselor or pastor to whom you can talk at any time. Also, remember that the pain is real. We cannot deny it. But, after a while, it begins to dissipate; although when you are in the midst of it, that is hard to believe.
- What scares you? Be honest about this fear. Discuss it with God and others.

The stress and conflicting ideas about our child's use is hurting our marriage. What do I do about this situation?

- We must accept the fact that marriage partners may have different temperaments. These different temperaments mean that often our responses to situations will differ. It is important to talk about these differences and acknowledge them. This helps us understand that our mates are not necessarily being cruel or insensitive to us. They just have a different response.

I am a single parent. I feel all alone, tired, overwhelmed, and depressed. Where do I go for help?

- We empathize with you. As a healthy, married couple we often ask ourselves, "How do single parents get through this pain?"

- We cannot emphasize strongly enough the need for support groups, Ala-Non, Nar-Anon, prayer partners and compassionate friends on whose shoulders you can cry.
- Again, the expression, "One day at a time," applies, because you need to manifest faith just to get through the day. Worry about tomorrow when tomorrow comes.

Does the fear for my child's safety ever go away?

- There is probably no right answer, but we say "No."
- This question was asked of a man who had three of his four children go through treatment, the last over 14 years ago. He said, "No. Every time the phone rings late at night, I think it is related to drugs."
- The addict husband of a friend returned to cocaine after being clean for 11 years. The loved one should never stop praying.
- The principle, "One day at a time," is true here as well. The parent must give the daily fear to God, never get cocky, and continue to ask God to be working in the life of the recovering addict or alcoholic so that he or she may stay drug-free and sober.

Does the pain you experience as a parent ever go away?

- Yes, but like scars for our own sins that seem to surface from time to time, we do not forget. I can now, after 12 years, laugh at some of the incidents, even when it involved lies and tricks that I fell for. The joy of seeing a healthy son who is married with two children and who has made a recommitment of his life to Christ, far surpasses any pain that I suffered. I am still amazed at the way I remember things versus the way my son remembers things. The Lord is so good about deflecting some of the bad times from our memories. These are opportunities to live, learn and practice being God's children.
- One father says, "We learned from our daughter, who had learned it from AA, that 'I will not regret the past or seek to change it.' When asked how she could not think of the past, her answer was, 'I am forgiven by God. If I keep looking to the past, then I will not have the energy to focus on accomplishing something in my future.' This has helped me deal with the pain that still exists."
- The behavior is always hateful, but the child needs to be forgiven and the parent needs to forgive. You forgive but you do not forget because you will be vigilant the rest of your life. As sobriety grows, you can talk about it as real history.

How do I deal with the guilt I feel over my child being an addict?

- Welcome to the club!! Not one of us hasn't wondered, "What did I do wrong?" Be encouraged by these words from a recovering addict who said to her parents, "Tonight in my AA discussion group there were people from the streets, middle class people such as myself, people who have fortunes and people who have had fortunes and lost them through drugs or alcohol. We agreed that the common denominator among us is that until we stopped blaming others for our use and abuse of drugs or alcohol, we did not get the help we needed."

- Most addicts, when they go through treatment and do Steps 8 and 9 that lead them to make amends with the people they have hurt, go to their parents and acknowledge that nothing their parents did or did not do caused them to use drugs or alcohol.

- If we know of areas where we failed our child, we can ask their forgiveness and God's forgiveness. At times when we know we did the best we knew how, we have to leave it in God's hands, knowing we are not responsible for the child's choices. Then we move ahead to build a healthy and positive relationship with the child and with each other.

- We must remember that there are no perfect parents. It is only a sign of our lack of understanding of drugs and/or alcohol as parents that we would blame ourselves for our children's use or continue to let them blame us for their use.

Sometimes I feel as though I have lost hope for the future of my child. Can you help me?

- It is important to remember that we are all human. We are not concerned about the parent who does lose hope from time to time; our concern is for the parent who always seems to be strong. That does not seem to be realistic.

- It is important to remember to be realistic but not fatalistic. The truth is that some of our adult children never come back to God and get drug-free or sober. There are no guarantees. However, this fact should not preclude our praying and asking God to work in the life of our loved one. For example, we just dealt with a 41-year-old man whose life has been ruined by alcohol. He has thrown away everything his Christian parents taught him in his pursuit of drugs and alcohol. He may be returned to prison for 16-21 years. Maybe another sentence in prison will make him hit bottom and get serious about getting sober.

- Be encouraged by this letter from a mother who writes about her addict son. "I recently saw the youth pastor who ministered to my son (or tried to) when he was a teenager. My son is now 32. It was interesting to get the pastor's perspective on those tough teen years. Our son will never know how much pain he caused us because of his lifestyle and his rebellion against God. We finally got to the point where we had to realize that faith is a gift from God and nothing we could do would make our son have it. Praying for him was a daily thing; it was at most times an hourly event. Then, all we could do was leave it in God's hands, realizing that He loves our son more than we do. He was 30 when he finally gave his life to God. I will tell you he is sold out for God! All four of our kids are walking with Christ, but he is the most committed. Who would ever have thought this? God knew when he would be ready. Our son is an example of a miracle and God can do more of them in others' lives."

Sometimes my mental responses to having drugs in our family are not indicative of a follower of Christ. I find myself hating the drug dealer who supplied my kid drugs. Do you have any advice or experience that will help me?

- It is common to have deep feelings of hatred toward the drug dealer who gave our kids drugs. It would be unhealthy to deny that hatred, for God cannot work when we are denying sin in our lives.

- It seems to be a "father (or man) thing" to want to bring retribution on the heads of drug dealers. We know of one father who sat outside his kid's school with a baseball bat looking for the dealer. We know of another father who was making plans to kill the dealer who supplied his kid. In both cases, the fathers ultimately recognized that: (1) the battle for sobriety is not theirs but their children's; (2) they cannot take the law into their own hands; (3) they must confess hatred as a sin and let God do a new work in their life.

- It is important to recognize that parental response also differs based on the age of the child. If the child is a teenager, then the parent must be more vigilant to make certain there is no contact with the dealer. If the child is an adult, sobriety and staying away from the dealer is the child's responsibility because there will always be another drug dealer or opportunity to buy or use. The recovering addicts need to decide how serious they are about sobriety and being clean.

Tough Love / Denial, Enabling

It is tough to be tough with my child. I think I must give him/her another chance. What do you say?

- We parents are in this bind because we love our children; we created them; we want what is best for them. On the other hand, we must remember that there is normal logic and then there is "addict logic." Addict logic is not something we parents can understand. Of course, we want to give "one more chance." However, the addict should not be enabled.

- One more chance may be enabling. Get help. Your kid's drug is his or her "beloved."
- Kids do not need another reprieve. They need contracts with consequences.
- Unless your child is experimenting with drugs or alcohol, he/she is probably lying to you. Remember, illicit drugs are of the devil, who is the agent of lies, not truth. So, if you are expecting truth from a kid who is using drugs, you are being naïve. They do not want the drugs taken away and they do not want to say "no" to their friends.
- Also, if you are like most parents to whom we talk, you are not experienced in this sort of thing. You do not need to feel guilty about that. There is no way all of us can know about drugs. Therefore, deal with it like any other ignorance.

How do I know if I am enabling my child?

- Enabling is making excuses, covering up, or giving "one more chance" without forcing the addict to assume responsibility for his or her actions.
- If we as the parents keep repeating the same actions toward the child and giving more chances, but we see the same response or non-response, then we are probably enabling.
- Know the signs of addiction: changes from normal behavior, changes in grades, poor behavior at home. If you see any of these signs, act.

What is denial?

- Denial is not admitting the truth of the situation and actually making an effort to avoid the truth.
- Denial is easy for Christians because we say we "give everything to God," and that "Christians are not supposed to worry." Often these are games we play to avoid the truth of the issue we should admit and deal with.
- When asked about feelings, we often shift to thoughts. But if we're feeling pain over our child's behavior, this is a step beyond denial.

My spouse is in denial about our child's use. What advice do you have?

- It is not unusual for parents to deny their kids are using. Try to talk with them about what you see.
- We must be responsible for our own feelings and our own level of understanding of the problem.
- We must try to respect our mates' feelings. We may have to agree to disagree.
- When parents agree on a problem and a course of action to take, they can rely on and draw strength from one another.
- When parents disagree or one is in denial, tensions arise. At this point counseling, support groups and leaning on a compassionate friend are strongly recommended.

Addict Behavior

Can you explain "addict logic" to me?

- Addict logic is different from normal logic.
- Addict logic rationalizes any action that continues the use or abuse of drugs or alcohol.
- Addict logic is a selfish logic. It is only interested in the use or abuse of drugs. Trying to be rational with an addict who has not hit bottom is a waste of time because he/she will simply use addict logic in dealing with you.

I think my addict child is lying to me. Why would he/she do that?

- As one addict told her parents, "You cannot be a successful addict unless you are a great liar." We non-addicts do not understand the drive to use and the willingness to lie, steal, cheat or beg to get drugs or alcohol. Remember, for the addict, nothing is too great a risk in order to get high once again.
- Addiction seems to be triggered in a euphoric experience early in use that is planted deep in the memory.

I think my addict child is stealing from me. What do I do?

- Do not be surprised that your child might be stealing. Remember that once drugs are used, they become the highest priority in life. Drugs are the antithesis of truth; so it is naïve to assume the child would not steal in order to get drugs.
- We know of parents who have hidden things of value so they would not be stolen. The parents' sentimental attachment will not preclude the addict from taking something of value if the body is craving drugs.
- Watch as closely as you can the "cash flow" of your kids. Also, many addicts are minor suppliers (not pushers) to friends. They may have a stash somewhere.

What are some behaviors associated with drugs?

- Changes--in moods, spending habits, possessions, hygiene, clothing, and their bedroom.
- Mentally—They may have a fuzzy recall of yesterday, a loss of focus, and offer alibis and "tall tales."
- Socially--unusual risk taking, change in friends, being alone or out of sight.
- These behaviors can be some of the potential signs of drug/alcohol use. But it is important to remember that "one can't be a successful addict without being a great liar," so these behaviors are not always present.

Support Groups

I am uncertain about attending a support group that is not overtly Christian. How would you advise me?

- This is a very sensitive area on which we will never all agree. However, many of us have discovered that there is much to learn about drugs, the behavior of those using drugs, and how we respond to that. That information is not Christian or non-Christian; it is just information that the parent of the addict needs to know. Therefore, it does not matter where you get that information. It needs to be learned.
- John and Susan Vawter, who are the sponsors of the *"You're Not Alone"* conferences, found great help at Nar-Anon, the sister organization to Al-Anon. They say that in spite of coarse language and the taking of the Lord's name in vain on the part of a few, every meeting they attended had some specific information that they thought they needed to hear and that came directly from God.
- Addiction is no respecter of persons or families, Christian or non-Christian, just as heart disease, cancer or diabetes are not. Hopefully, Christian people can take sound advice and use God's power to implement it. Who asks a heart specialist about his/her religion or credo? Get help!

What is the value of a support group?

- There is strength in numbers; we understand we are not going crazy and that our feelings and fears are common to others.
- It is therapeutic to share with compassionate and understanding people.
- There is relief in actually speaking our pain and feelings aloud to others.
- Hearing others talk about their fears, struggles and problems gives us the courage to admit what our fears, struggles and problems are. This also helps us admit our behaviors, good and bad.
- One father says, "The value of a support group for me was learning the real damage and behavior of addicts and chemically dependent children. I was one of those who did not know much about chemical dependency and it blew me away."

Is it hard to walk into a support group when, as a minister or missionary, you are used to giving answers to people?

- Of course it is hard. Sometimes it is very hard. But that is just our ego and we have to surmount it for the sake of our child's welfare. When our daughter checked into treatment at the hospital where her uncle had been Chief of Staff of Cardiology, many people asked if we were related to him. It was embarrassing for a while until I realized her health was important, not what other people thought.

- The first time we went to Nar-Anon, it was extremely difficult. I am a pastor. I give answers to people. But, interestingly enough, when I go to the doctor, be it proctologist, dentist or surgeon, I go for answers, not to give them. I quickly learned that the people at Nar-Anon were experienced and knew more than I did. I needed to be quiet and listen, and at every meeting God spoke to me.

What is Al-Non? What is Nar-Anon? What happens if people do not respect my faith at one of those meetings?

- These are support groups for family members whose loved ones use alcohol or narcotics. They are based on the Twelve Step Principles.
- Just as addicts are advised to find a support group that meets their comfort level, so the family member must do the same. Al-Anon relates to alcohol and Nar-Anon relates to narcotics.
- One of the principles of the groups is that people rely on their "Higher Power," as they perceive Him. As followers of Christ, we do not call Him "Our Higher Power." However, some of us have found great help at these meetings. Our intention was not to discuss theology, convert others, or struggle when others did not honor God; our purpose was to learn about drugs and alcohol and get help for ourselves.

Advice from Veterans

I have heard the phrase, "Let go and let God." What does it mean?

- I cannot be responsible for another's choices.
- I must let the other person be responsible to God. I must pray diligently for God to work in his/her life.
- I must accept the fact that my worrying will not accomplish anything; my prayers will, but not my worrying.

What does the phrase, "You did not cause it, you cannot control it, you cannot cure it" mean?

- Nothing the parent did caused the addict to use and nothing the parent does can stop the addict from using.
- Only God can change and bring about a cure in another's life as he/she turns to Him.
- I am not God; therefore, I quit trying to control the addict and ask Him to work in his/her life.

- Read the words of the parents who had three of their kids go through treatment. "With our first chemically dependent child (C.D.C.), we thrashed, rationalized and deluded ourselves for three years before we insisted on treatment. Finally, one of the school counselors phoned to say our son was out of control and should go into a treatment center immediately, not "let's talk about it" but "get him there today even if you have to tie him up and carry him. With our next C.D.C., we waited three months until school was out. With our last C.D.C. we waited three days. She was 'turned in' by her then-and-still best friend. The treatment time to get back to a sober life was proportional to the delay before we took action, about 1 1/2 years, about 2 months, and a couple of weeks."

General Questions

Would having a child drug or alcohol addicted disqualify a pastor, according to 1 Timothy 3:4-5?

- Our understanding of that issue is that an adult child away from home certainly would not disqualify a pastor. One pastor's son was a model child through high school. He got into drinking in college.

At what point would a younger child's disobedience or loss of control to chemicals disqualify a pastor?

- We are not certain. The board of each church would have to rule on those cases individually. We understand that not every theological or ecclesiastical system agrees on this matter. However, we think God does not intend to disqualify ministers as often as people do. Probably the best we can say is to make certain you are with people who will be gracious and helpful, not harsh and judgmental.

I have heard it said that a born-again Christian cannot be an alcoholic or addict. Would you comment on this?

- I have a friend who is a recovering alcoholic. She relates, "After I went through treatment, one Thanksgiving some friends said to me at dinner, 'Since you are born-again, you cannot be alcoholic. Have a glass of wine with us.' I assumed they were right; so I had the glass and over the next few months fell completely off the wagon. I lost EVERYTHING in my life." Remarkably, she does not blame those friends but now knows they were naïve.
- A pastor explains, "I spent one Christmas with my brother in a drug rehab center as he finally admitted his problem. I watched him struggle as a number of

well-meaning people asked him how he could be a Christian and struggle with drug addiction. 'I do not understand. How can you say you follow God? Look where you are.' I watched my brother doubt and suffer in trying to reconcile his relationship with God and his addiction."

- A missionary explains, "Saying Christians cannot be addicts is tantamount to saying that born-again Christians don't/can't sin or that they will always be free from 'serious' sin. This 'assumption' is both foolish and foolhardy. Christians and Christian ministers/missionaries have been adulterers, homosexuals, embezzlers, etc. So claiming that a born-again Christian cannot be an alcoholic or drug addict is simply not true. However, the Christian community's penchant to stigmatize and ostracize those caught in serious sin, means one is hard put to find 'safe' groups in the church where help and support are extended to those struggling and to those affected. At the same time, this does not change the message of the Gospel but strengthens it. When we sin, we have indeed forgotten our own powerlessness and the necessity of an hourly and daily reliance on His power and the strength of His people as burden bearers. Our need for Christ does not stop when we become Christians. Our need for His people is intensified because none of us is strong enough to stand on our own."

- I am always amazed that people who still lust, get angry, are impatient, gossip, are overweight and so forth, even though they are born again, somehow think they have the right to proclaim that one cannot be a Christian and an addict. Just because someone is a follower of Christ does not give him the right to intrude into the life of the addict or his/her family with their opinions on things of which he/she knows very little.

How do I deal with the "well-meaning" family members and friends who intrude and ask too many questions?

- Each family system is different, but the very life and future of the addict must be of highest importance. If that means telling people half of the story, if that means telling them you cannot be with them unless they say encouraging things, if that means cutting some people out of your life who will drain what little energy you have out of you, then so be it.
- If possible, get the family members or friends involved in treatment, Al-Anon, etc.
- The message has to be this: When we are at our most vulnerable point, we must surround ourselves with those people who will be empathetic, sympathetic, understanding, supportive, convicting and confronting. We need to distance ourselves from those who want to make proclamations about something of which they are naïve and ignorant. Usually, recovering addicts must find new friends. Sometimes their family members must do the same.

Do I need to feel guilt about my child's addiction?

- Chemically dependent people are great at making others believe they are the cause of the dependent behavior. Don't be hooked by this guilt-producing talk.

Does addiction stunt emotional growth?

- The time between the first use and intervention indicates how much "loss of growing up" has happened. The addict simply does not learn coping skills, except for medicating.
- If the child started using at age twelve and has used for three years, he/she has the maturity of a 12-year-old, not a 15-year-old.
- This is one reason why treatment of adults who become addicted in their 20s will focus more on abstinence, while treatment of juveniles will focus more on learning coping skills.

Do parents do something wrong when their kids use?

- One successful pastor warned his child against drugs/alcohol, told him of the high possibility of "alcoholic genes" in the family, and was aware of the child's behavior and peers. The child still abused alcohol/drugs in high school and college. Rebellion can be subtle and hard to define. The parent did nothing wrong. The child chose to rebel.

Treatment Programs

Why should I consider a treatment center for my child?

- If you found out your child had a life-threatening illness or injury, what would you do: pray or go to a medical specialist? Regardless of your answer, you would do both. You should do the same with treatment.
- Addiction to chemicals is life threatening. By the time the parent learns about it, it has been going on for a significant period of time.
- An addicted child is at risk for insanity, death or suicide. You cannot let shame, guilt, or rage get in your way of getting help.
- Keeping the addiction a secret means lying to others. This consumes energy, deludes you and leads to guilt and shame.

Can you help me get over my uncertainty about treatment?

- We do not recommend "Christian" treatment centers over "non-Christian" centers. The will and desire of the addict to be abstinent is the most important factor. (We recognize there is not universal agreement on this and we do not expend energy or time debating the issue.)

- Child addicts need help with coping skills because they have been medicating themselves rather than dealing with issues.
- Treatment begins with detoxification so that the addict is in the real world and comfortable about his/her behavior. Only a sober/lucid person can be confronted.
- Our society says life should be pain-free. However, life is tough. Abstinence from drugs or alcohol is the only solution to confronting life and the reality is not easy. Treatment, then, must teach the addict how to deal with reality, to have faith in God through Christ and to live one day at a time.
- Treatment does take time, a lot of time. It can be "in your face" for a while. One father who has had three kids go through treatment says, "Every family should go through treatment, whether or not there is an addiction problem, because it is so helpful."

When do we insist on treatment for our child?
- We cannot stress too much the importance of rapid intervention and treatment.
- Treatment is a process that the parents must initiate and in which they become active participants themselves.
- You don't "send your kid off to get fixed." Parents must be involved.

Hope in Darkness

How do I have hope when things look so bleak?
- A lack of hope is something most parents experience when we discover our child is abusing drugs or alcohol. This news assaults our spiritual and emotional senses and it is difficult to keep one's spiritual balance. A parent is not a "bad Christian" or lacking in faith when this occurs.
- Colossians 1:27 has helped many parents. In this passage, Paul says, "Christ in us is the hope of glory." A number of parents have looked at this verse, thought of heaven and then worked "backwards" from the thought of heaven to the present-day circumstances, which have been bleak. They realized if they could trust God for their eternal future, then they could trust Him in the present.
- One pastor said at the funeral of his son who died of an accidental overdose of prescription drugs, "God is here, God is good and that is enough." It is easy to blame God, get angry with Him, and think He has forsaken us. We must remember God did not plan or determine these circumstances for us; He just wants to be a "very real help in our time of trouble."

- A pastor told a widow at her husband's funeral something that he later realized helped him in his child's battle with drugs. His words of advice to the widow were, "When you get home, God will be there. You may have to look for Him but He will be there." Within two or three weeks, the widow told her pastor, "It is lonely, but He is there." God is there with us parents whose kids abuse drugs and alcohol.

- The recovering addict/alcoholic learns to live one day at a time. The parents must do the same. The future can look so overwhelming. Parents who learn to walk one day at a time seem to function the best. We have known parents who have even broken up the day into thirds. If life is good until breakfast, they thank God. If it is good until lunch, they thank God, etc.

- Be encouraged by these words written by a father who discovered in 1984 that his son was an addict. The parents had some rough days, as we all do, but they kept their eyes on the future and did not give up hope. "Our family was together for a reunion recently. It gave us a time to be together without having to cook, clean, etc. We could just enjoy doing everything together. What touched us the most was seeing the fantastic change in our son, from being heavily involved in drugs and in rebellion 16 years ago, to seeing him today. He is now involved in men's ministry, praying for the sick and is really tuned into what God has in store for him. Just to sit and listen to him share without adding our two cents' worth is priceless."

- Finally, as it relates to hope, Ruth Myers' book, *31 Days of Praise* (Multnomah Press, 1994), is proving to be a great source of encouragement and hope for parents with kids who are abusing alcohol or drugs. Please take the time to mediate on this prayer found on page 94 of her book.

  "Thank You that You plan to use for good the struggles my loved ones face--including their disappointing choices, their unwise or even harmful ways of thinking and living, and their sidetracks from going Your way (as I see it--and, Lord, I know I could be wrong!).

  I praise You in advance for the part these difficult things are going to play in Your good plan for us--in eventual deliverance and growth and fruitfulness. I'm grateful that in all these things, the battle is not mine but Yours...and that the final chapter has not yet been written. How good it is that I can call on You to give me wisdom to know what to say or not say, what to do and not do...and that You live in me so that I can love with Your love, even when it's hard. Thank You that these trials force me to trust You more!

  I worship before You, my King and my God. I'm grateful that You command victories for Your people....and 'all things are Your servants.' You're a God who acts on behalf of the one who puts his hope in You. Thank You that You are at work to answer my prayers in Your good way and time.

Thank You for past victories You have won in my loved ones' lives--for progress and growth and answered prayer--and for the victories we will yet see in the future, to the glory of Your Name. I praise You that as times goes by, in new ways You will show us Your goodness in the land of the living."

Incarceration

What if jail or prison becomes a part of your child's life?

We wish this question did not have to be answered. A number of people have experienced this. It hurts. It is embarrassing. We must remember that God never gives up on our child or us. We must follow His lead.

- Some parents have said that the phone call from the police station because of their child's drug offense caused "an explosion of pain." They struggled with the question of what they had done wrong or how had they failed as parents. The parents cannot give into these negative yet normal thoughts. The only way they learned to deal with the pain was to give it to God one day at a time and to talk to friends who had been there or who could offer support.

- Other parents have struggled with whether bailing their children out of jail was enabling them. The best answer we can offer is that there is no absolutely correct answer. The issue has to be determined by whether the child is serious about sobriety and is not taking advantage of the parents' generosity. The parents' motivation is to determine whether the bail will help the child in the long run. In some cases, parents have struggled that they are rejecting their children if they do not post bail. In other cases, the children refuse to accept responsibility for their actions and accuse the parents of not loving them if they refuse to post bail. As we said, this is a tough question.

- Some parents have struggled with the fact that they are "not being Spirit filled," "not loving one another," or "not turning the other cheek" when they have refused to post bail. The enemy of our souls will attack us at every turn. The basis of the decision should not be guilt. It needs to be the long-term benefits for the child.

- As a parent, there is a lot of wasted and inconvenient time spent in court appearances, etc. The parent is responsible for his or her own attitude. Hopefully, these consequences will help the child to see the seriousness of his/her actions and cause him/her to change. Uncompromising love that does not enable on the part of the parent seems to help the addict child.

- One parent talked about the positive aspects of jail by saying, "At least I knew my child was not on the streets using and selling drugs."

- Your goal must be to maintain or rebuild a relationship with the child, even if you hate what they have done and may continue to do. This is probably not the time to "preach or teach" or to tell him/her any thing more. The pain of the consequences of jail will do that.

Glossary

[Note: Definitions for these terms are from the following sources:]

1: The National Clearinghouse for Alcohol and Drug Information
   http://www.health.org/govpubs/bkd264/dawn1316.htm

2. Glossary of Terms
   http://www.healthatoz.com/atoz/alcohol/glossary.html

3. http://www.drugabuse.gov/ResearchReports/Cocaine/Cocaine.html

4. Ton of Bricks manuscript

5. Medicinenet.com: http://www.medterms.com/script/main/art.asp?articlekey=10177&rd=1

6. Merriam-WebsterMedicalDictionary
   http://www.intelihealth.com/IH/ihtIH/WSIHW000/331/9276.html

addiction: Uncontrollable craving, seeking, and use of a substance such as a drug or alcohol. Dependence is at such a point that stopping is very difficult and causes severe physical and mental reactions. (5)

alcohol abuse/dependence: A pattern of problem drinking that results in health consequences, social problems, or both. Different from alcoholism or alcohol dependence (2).

alcoholic: a person with the chronic disease of alcoholism (2)

alcoholism: A disease that includes alcohol craving and continued drinking despite repeated alcohol-related problems, such as losing a job or getting into trouble with the law. Symptoms include craving, impaired control, physical dependence, and increased tolerance. (2)

codependency: A set of behaviors learned by family members to survive in an emotionally painful and stressful environment. These behaviors are passed on from generation to generation whether alcoholism is present or not. (2)

d.t.'s: the tremors that alcoholics get when their bodies do not have the alcohol they need (4)

denial: refusal or failure to acknowledge the truth about the substance addiction of others or ourselves (4)

dependence: A psychic and/or physical state characterized by behavior that always includes a compulsion to take the drug on a continuous or periodic basis in order to experience its effects or to avoid the discomfort of its absence (e.g., have to take, had to have, needed a fix). (1)

depressants ("downers"): medications that slow down or "depress" the activity of the brain (6)

detachment: "letting go" of the addict; trusting God in the lives of addicted loved ones (4)

detoxification (detox): The process of safely getting alcohol out of one's system. (2)

drug abuse: The non-medical use of a substance for any of the following reasons: psychic effect, dependence, or suicide attempt/gesture (1)

drug abuser: Someone who has taken a substance without proper medical supervision for psychic effect, dependence, or suicide attempt/gesture (1)

enabler: one who enables someone to continue on a path of substance abuse by providing excuses for or helping the affected individual avoid the consequences of his or her behavior (6)

hallucinogens: substances that induce hallucinations (6)

in-house or inpatient treatment: Treatment for an addiction that takes place in a controlled environment such as a hospital. The patient is checked into the hospital and remains there until treatment has ended. (2)

outpatient treatment: Treatment for an addiction that takes place without the patient being checked into a hospital or treatment center. Often, it involves several hours of therapy per day scheduled around the patient's normal daily activities. (2)

recovery: The lifelong process of controlling alcoholism or drug addiction. (2)

residential treatment: see in-house or inpatient treatment

stimulants ("uppers"): medications that speed up or "stimulate" the functions of the body (4)

tough-love: Firm but compassionate behavior toward another individual. Speaking the whole truth to another individual without overlooking his sinful behavior. Loving confrontation of improper actions with objective truth. Bringing about measured and appropriate consequences for previously agreed upon sinful behavior.

withdrawal Symptoms that occur when a person stops taking a substance upon which he or she is physiologically dependent and suffers physical symptoms, including abdominal pain, cold sweat, hyperactivity, and tremors that require treatment. (1)

Resource Directory

Services for Parents

Support Groups

Alcoholics Anonymous
Provides helpful information on dealing with alcoholism and meeting days and times.
PO Box 459
Grand Central Station
New York, NY 10163
1-800-509-2415
The telephone number of the local chapter can be found in the telephone directory.
www.alcoholics-anonymous.org

Al-Anon/Alateen
Al-Anon is a support group for those who live with the problem drinking of relative or friend. Alateen is a 12-step recovery program for teens and is part of the Al-Anon Family Groups.
1600 Corporate Landing Parkway
Virginia Beach, VA 23454-5617
1-888-4ALANON
The telephone number of the local chapter can be found in the telephone directory.
http://www.ncwsa.org

Nar-Anon
Nar-Anon provides support for family and friends of someone who abuses drugs. The telephone number of the local chapter can be found in the telephone directory. The website has numerous nuggets of information, links to additional resources, and information on co-dependency and enabling.
www.naranon.homeip.net

Overcomers Outreach

A nationwide Christian 12-step support group for individuals and families. Overcomers Outreach provides a two-way bridge between traditional 12-step support groups and people within churches of all denominations.
PO Box 2208
Oakhurst, CA 93644
1-800-310-3001
www.overcomersoutreach.org

Relief for Hurting Parents Support Groups

Based upon the book, *Relief for Hurting Parents* by Buddy Scott, these support groups exist throughout the United States. Contact them to start or attend a support group.
PO Box 804
310 Flag Lake Drive
Lake Jackson, TX
979-297-5700
www.buddyscott.com

Turning Point Ministries

Helps churches start support groups for people with addictions and eating disorders. Groups for parents and teens meet throughout North America. The website also features informative articles.
PO Box 22127
Chattanooga, TN 37422-2127
1-800-879-4770
info@turningpointministries.org
www.turningpointministries.org

You're Not Alone Conferences

Each year these conferences are hosted in various parts of the United States for ministers and others whose children are hooked on drugs or alcohol. Their website, www.notalone.org, also contains helpful answers to many of the questions parents of abusers ask themselves.
10105 East Via Linda, Suite 103
PMB 360
Scottsdale, AZ 85258
480-752-8994

Counselors/Treatment

Dr. Ray Burwick
503-579-9788
13114 SW Chimney Ridge St.
Tigard, OR 97223
rburwick@mindspring.com
http://rburwick.home.mindspring.com/

The Minirth Clinic
The Minirth Clinic P.A.
2100 North Collins Blvd., Suite 200
Richardson, TX 75080
1-888-MINIRTH (646-4784)
www.christiancounselor.com

New Life Recovery Center
Nationwide mental health clinics. Calvary's affordable, proven treatment program addresses the practical, physical, and spiritual aspects of addiction, setting the stage for long -term recovery and restored family life.
www.newlife.com

Pine Rest Mental Health Hospital
Aids parents in discerning the difference between natural growing pains in a child or teen and behavior that signals serious trouble. Pine Rest makes it easy to get professional guidance in making these judgments.
www.pinerest.org

Rapha
Rapha's Christ-centered professional counseling can help people struggling with emotional and substance abuse problems, restoring God's peace and joy to their lives
1-800-383-4673
www.raphacare.com

Zach Whaley, MA
825 West Warner Rd. Suite 7
Chandler, AZ 85225
(480) 855-0075
Fax: (480) 855-0075
www.zachwhaley.com

Terry E. Zuehlke, PhD, LP
Pathways Psychological Services, P.A.
7575 Golden Valley Road, Suite 119
Golden Valley, MN 55427
763-525-8590
Fax: 763-525-8592

Residential Treatment

Adolescent Services International
Directory designed to assist parents, providers and health care professionals in finding the best environment for the special needs of teens in crisis.
www.defiantteen.com

Boys Village
For boys 11-18 struggling with drug, alcohol and sexual problems.
P.O. Box 518,
Smithville, Ohio 44677
330-264-3232
www.boys-village.com

His Mansion Ministries
Christian residential program for young men and woman 18 and older.
PO Box 40
Hillsboro, NH 03244
603-464-5555
www.hismansion.com

National Detox Center of St. Louis, Inc.
This program provides a quick and compassionate means of detoxing as an alternative to the traditional opiate withdrawal process. The cornerstone of the program is ongoing individual and group therapy.
12303 DePaul Drive
Bridgeton, MO 63044
In St. Louis: (314) 209-7773
Outside St. Louis: (888) 480-8008
www.nationaldetox.com

Rapha
Residential treatment facilities throughout United States for addictions and eating disorders.
1-800-227-2657
www.raphacare.com

Santa Barbara Rescue Mission

The Santa Barbara Rescue Mission is a non-profit evangelical rescue and drug recovery ministry providing spiritual and physical rehabilitative care to the needy and drug dependent at no cost to the recipient. It has a year-long residential program. Steen Hudson is the director.
www.sbrm.org

Teen Challenge International

Christian drug and alcohol rehabilitation centers throughout U.S. for men and woman 18 and older. Some programs may accept teens.
3728 W. Chestnut Expressway
Springfield, MO 65802
417-862-6969
www.teenchallenge.com

Victory Outreach International

Christian drug, alcohol and gang rehabilitation program, especially for Hispanic youth.
P.O. Box 3490
San Dimas, CA 91773-4437
626-961-4910
info@victoryoutreach.org

Info and Help Lines

American Society of Addiction Medicine

Gives a list of programs as well as a discussion of approaches for various addictions.
4601 North Park Ave, Arcade Suite 101
Chevy Chase, MD 20815
301-656-3920
www.asam.org

Center for Disease Control and Prevention

1600 Clifton Road
Atlanta, GA 30333
National AIDS Hotline, 800-342-2437
National HIV/AIDS hotline (Spanish), 1-800-344-7532
www.cdc.gov

Church Growth Institute

Audiotapes sharing the *"You're Not Alone"* conference for parents who are in the ministry and are dealing with issues related to their children's substance abuse problems. The speakers are full-time ministers and parents who have faced this dilemma.

They deal with the subject in a candid, realistic way sharing the pain, wisdom, and growth that can only be attained by parents who are or have been there. In addition to these ministry parents, a Christian substance abuse counselor shares his own story and advice for dealing with an addicted loved one. These cassettes can be ordered by calling 1-800-553-4769 or by ordering them from the website: www.churchgrowth.org

Christian Recovery International
A coalition of ministries dedicated to helping the Christian community become a safe and helpful place for people recovering from addiction, abuse, or trauma. www.christianrecovery.com

Drug Free America
Their mission is to help kids and teens reject substance abuse by influencing attitudes through persuasive information. www.drugfreeamerica.org

Focus on the Family
This hotline will help connect you with specialized ministries across the country. Hotline 1-800-A-FAMILY (232-6459) www.family.org

Minnesota Prevention Resource Center
Creates materials, offers help and consultation to help others build and maintain safe drug-free communities. http://www.miph.org

Narcotics Anonymous World Services
This website contains a wealth of information in several different languages, including links to regional resources. http://www.wsoinc.com

National Center on Addiction and Substance Abuse at Colombia University (CASA)
This website provides resources and links to other sites. www.casacolumbia.org

National Center for Missing & Exploited Children
Charles B. Wang International Children's Building
699 Prince Street
Alexandria, VA 22314-3175
1-800-843-5678
www.missingkids.com

National Association for Christian Recovery
The website has a wealth of information, providing a library, referral center and interactive on-line forum.
www.nacronline.com

National Technical Center for Substance Abuses
A purpose of this website is to inform people about substance abuse treatment needs assessment and planning. The NTC is affiliated with Harvard Medical School.
www.ntc.org

National Clearinghouse for Alcohol and Drug Information
SAMHSA is the Federal agency charged with improving the quality and availability of prevention, treatment, and rehabilitative services in order to reduce illness, death, disability, and cost to society resulting from substance abuse and mental illnesses. Very informative.
http://www.health.org

National Drug Abuse Hotline
1-800-662-4357

National Families in Action
2296 Henderson Mill Road
Suite 204, Atlanta, Georgia 30345
National Families in Action is a grassroots effort to prevent drug abuse in America. The role of parent group networks in the American prevention movement.

National Institute of Drug Abuse
National Institutes of Health
6001 Executive Blvd., Room 5213
Bethesda, MD 20892
301-443-1124
www.nida.gov

National Institute on Alcohol Abuse and Alcoholism
Website for answers to questions such as how to tell if you're an alcoholic. The National Institute on Alcohol Abuse and Alcoholism (NIAAA) supports and conducts biomedical and behavioral research on the causes, consequences, treatment, and prevention of alcoholism and alcohol-related problems.
www.niaaa.nih.gov

National PTA
National PTA is the largest volunteer child advocacy organization in the United States. The site has excellent resources relating strategies for raising drug free children.
www.pta.org.

Path to Parental Health
Descriptive responses were taken from the voices of experience of parents who have a child who abuses alcohol or drugs. Recognizing that others have walked the road and have achieved some balance and faith in their lives will help those now on the journey.
http://notalone.org

Questions Parents Ask
A series of real-life thoughtful questions/answers of parents regarding drug/alcohol abuse.
http://notalone.org

Youth Crisis Hotline
1-800-448-4663

Written Resources

Growing Up Drug Free: A Parent's Guide to Prevention
U.S. Department of Education, 1998.
To order free printed copies of this guide, call the Department of Education's toll-free number:
1-877-4EDPUBS
Also, the full text of this publication is available at the U.S. Department of Education's website:
http://www.ed.gov/offices/OESE/SDFS/parents_guide

Centers for Disease Control and Prevention
A variety of publications and software pertaining to youth health issues.
www.cdc.gov/publications

R.A. "Buddy" Scott/Allon Publishing
Christian books for parents and teens.
979-297-5700
www.buddyscott.com

RPI Publishing, Inc.
RPI believes strongly in the power of the Twelve Steps and the guidance they provide to help rebuild a person's life. They offer a wide variety of books online to help readers through the process of life recovery.
www.rpipublishing.com

Self-help Sourcebook
Comprehensive online listing of support groups for alcoholics and their families.
570 Metro Place
Dublin, OH 43017
614-764-0143
www.mentalhelp.net

Straight Ahead Ministries
Books and materials designed for troubled teens and those who minister to them.
PO Box 1011
Westborough, MA 01581
508-616-9286
info@straightahead.org
www.straightahead.org

Turning Point Ministries
Materials and training conferences on Biblical approaches to life controlling problems.
PO Box 22127
Chattanooga, TN 37422-2127
1-800-879-4770
info@turningpointministries.org
www.turningpointministries.org

The Will Rogers Institute
Free booklets on the effects, composition, motives, treatment and consequences of psychoactive drugs.
785 Mamaroneck Ave.
White Plains, NY 10605
914-761-5550

Books

Dick, B. *The Good Book and the Big Book: A.A.'s Roots in the Bible*. Paradise Research Publications, Kihei, Maui.

Behnke, John. *Ninety Days, One Day at a Time*: A new beginning for people in recovery. Paulist Press, 1999.

Cline, M.D., Foster & Fay, Jim. *Parenting Your Teen with Love and Logic*. Pinon Press, 1990. Also available in compact disc at Barnes & Nobles or online at www.bn.com.

Campbell, Ross & Likes, Pat. *Your Child and Drugs*. Chariot Victor Publishing, 1989.

Cohen, Peter. *Helping Your Chemically Dependent Teen Recover*. Johnson Institute Books, Minnesota, 1991.

Graham, Ruth. *The Prodigals and Those Who Love Them*. Baker Books, April 1999. These are the powerful personal memoirs, journal and poems Billy Graham's wife shares to describe the rebellion of her son, Franklin, and her struggle to let him go.

Jeremiah, David. *A Bend in the Road: Finding God when your World Caves In*. Thomas Nelson Publishers, 2000. Can be purchased online at www.bn.com.

Jeremiah, David. *Gifts from God*: Encouragement and Hope for Today's Parents. Cox Communications Ministries International, 1999. Can be purchased online at www.bn.com.

Johnson and Murphy. *Parenting Streetwise Kids*. David C. Cook Publishing, Elgin, Illinois, 1995. A helpful workbook format.

Larson, Scott. *Parenting At Risk Youth*. Group Publishing (to be released in the fall of 2002).

Neff, Pauline. *Tough Love*. Abingdon Press, Nashville, 1982.

One Day at a Time in Al Anon. Al Anon Family Group Headquarters, Inc., New York, 1987.

Sanford, Tim. *I Have To Be Perfect*: And Other Parsonage Heresies. Llama Press, 5526 N. Academy Blvd. Suite 206, Colorado Springs, Co 80918. Describes unique challenges of a Preacher's Kid.

Scott, Buddy. *Relief for Hurting Parents*. Allon Publishing. Can be ordered from www.buddyscott.com

Spickard, M.D., Anderson. *Dying for a Drink: What You Should Know About Alcoholism*. Word Publishing, 1985. Dr. Spickard is a professor at Vanderbilt Medical School.

Waldrep, Phil. Parenting Prodigals: *Six Principles for Bringing Your Son or Daughter Back to God*. Baxter Press, 2002. Can be ordered online at www.bn.com.

White, John. Parents in Pain: *Overcoming the Hurt and Frustration of Problem Children.* InterVarsity Press, 1983. Available online at www.bn.com.

Williams, Don. *Jesus and Addiction.* Recovery Publications, San Diego, 1993.

Wilmes, David. *Parenting for Prevention.* Johnson Institute Books, Minneapolis, 1988.

Pastor Resources

American Association of Christian Counselors

AACC's intention is to equip professional, pastoral and lay caregivers with biblical, theological and psychological truth that ministers to the soul of a hurting person and helps him or her move to personal wholeness, interpersonal competence, mental stability, and spiritual maturity.
www.aacc.net

The Parsonage

The site is published by Focus on the Family and provides an array of resources for the pastor and family.
www.family.org/pastor

CareGivers Forum

The CareGivers Forum provides an annual forum for personal relationships, professional networking and shared learning opportunities. Contact person: Dale Frimodt, barnabasomaha@juno.com.
www.info@caregiversforum.org

Important Notice

We do not evaluate or rate any of the resources that appear in these pages. Listing does not, therefore, constitute an 'endorsement' or 'recommendation' of any of these resources. Neither does omission signify disapproval. The use of any of the material in these pages is entirely the responsibility of the reader. We disclaim any and all liability for any use or non-use of the materials herein. There are no warranties implied or expressed in any of the data provided herein.

CONTRIBUTORS

Pat Boris is a Pediatric Nurse Practitioner specializing in children with special health needs. Her research is on stress in parents of substance abusing adolescents. She has facilitated parenting skills groups, and support groups for parents. *Recovery Parenting* grew out of this work. Pat is married to Mike, and they have three children. She can be reached at boris005@tc.umn.edu .

Gene Bourland is the owner of an industrial cleaning company in the Twin Cities area. Gene was a long-time staff member with Campus Crusade for Christ, where he served as Director of The British Isles. He has also pastored two Evangelical Free churches. He can be reached at 612-599-5740. Email: shalom7@aol.com

Norma Bourland is the Director of Congregations Concerned for Children and has served in Christian ministry along with her husband for over 35 years. She is a conference and retreat speaker and writer. She is the mother of four adults and the joyous grandmother of three young ones. She can be reached through email: nbourland@ccc-can.org.

Alfred Ells is an ordained minister and marriage and family therapist. As founder-director of ClergyCare, Al provides ministry consultation, leadership coaching and personal counseling for ministers and ministries. Al can be reached at: ClergyCare, 1356 East McKellips Road, Suite 103, Mesa, AZ 85203. Telephone: 480-325-9350 Email: clergycare@earthlink.net.

Bill Faulkner has pastored Southern Baptist churches for 30 years. He is now the Executive Director of Missions for the Greater Orlando Baptist Association. He also speaks in leadership, church growth, and marriage conferences. **Brenda Faulkner** is Administrative Assistant for the Director of Theological Education for the Florida Baptist Convention. She is also a Bible teacher and a ladies conference speaker. She also speaks in marriage conferences with Bill. They can be contacted at Bnbfaulkner@aol.com.

Mark Halvorsen is the Producer/Host of "FrontPage" radio talk show on WWIB-FM in Chippewa Falls, Wisconsin. Mark can be reached at: 2396 Hwy. 53, Chippewa Falls, WI 54729. Telephone: 715-723-1037 Email: mhalvo@wwib.com

Bill and Margaret Hansell met while students at the University of Oregon. They were staff members with Campus Crusade for Christ for 12 years serving in California and Australia. For the past 20 years, Bill has been a Umatilla County Commissioner in Oregon. Margaret is the Court Appointed Special Advocate (CASA) director. They are active in their church and community. Their family consists of six grown children, and they have two grandchildren.

Kimball Evan Hodge IV, also known as K IV, (pronounced K4) is owner and CEO of Krytikal Mass Productions, a music production company that specializes in hip-hop and R & B. He is part owner in a studio located in Portland, Oregon, where he produces and records several national artists.

Dr. Kim and Lynda Hodge have been together in ministry and marriage for 38 years. Today they serve at First Baptist Church of Eugene, Oregon, where Kim is the Senior Pastor and Lynda is a member of the church staff. Kim has authored the book, *A Mind Renewed by God*. They can be reached at the church by telephone: 541-345-0341 or at kimlyndah@attbi.com .

Rita and Greg Iverson have been married for 28 years. They live in St. Paul, Minnesota. The Iversons have two children: Emily, who is married, and Brad, who is a senior in high school. Greg is senior pastor of Arlington Hills United Methodist Church in Maplewood, Minnesota. Presently in his 27th year of the ordained ministry, he has served United Methodist churches in Minnesota for his entire career. He is a graduate of Hamline University and Duke University (M.Div., 1975.) He did his doctoral work at Bethel Seminary.
Rita is a nurse oncologist in St. Paul specializing in women's cancers, her area of concentration since 1975. She is a graduate of Lenoir Rhyne College in Hickory, North Carolina (B.S.N., 1972.) You can reach the Iversons at: Arlington Hills United Methodist Church, 759 E. County Road B, Maplewood, Minnesota 55117. Telephone: 651-776-1547 Email: greg@arlingtonhills.org.

Jim Smoke is internationally known as a speaker, author, counselor and life coach. He has written 17 books and has conducted over 700 seminars, retreats and workshops across the United States and Canada. Jim has spoken at numerous Promise Keepers events and authored the book *How a Man Measures Success* as a result of those experiences.

In 1997, Jim was the recipient of the coveted Gold Book Award from the Evangelical Christian Publishers Association when his landmark book *Growing Through Divorce* reached the 500,000 mark in sales.

Jim is a trained Life Coach and is certified by the Institute for Life Coach Training. His many years in the field of human relationships have uniquely equipped him for life coaching. Jim's goal for all clients in life coaching is to help them articulate their dreams, desires and aspirations, help them clarify their mission, purpose and goals, and help them achieve optimum growth. The bottom line is always CHANGE. For further information contact: Jim Smoke, Life Coach, 714-657-0083. Email: jsmoke1745@aol.com

Todd Smoke is a certified Drug and Alcohol Counselor in Orange County, California. He currently works with recently released inmates of the Orange County Jail system. After 20 years of drug and alcohol abuse, and numerous years of home-lessness and incarcerations, Todd now has over four years of being clean and sober. Along with helping other alcoholics and addicts in their recovery, Todd enjoys being outdoors, spending time with his three sons camping, surfing, and enjoying the Southern California sunshine. Todd plans to continue his education in the drug and alcohol services field. He can be contacted at: tsmoke01@hotmail.com .

Noy Sparks, Jr. has served as a Southern Baptist pastor for 23 years both in Texas and Florida. He is currently enrolled in the Reformed Theological Seminary, Orlando, Florida, where he lives with his wife, Lynda, an R.N. who works for a pediatrician. The Sparks can be reached at NOYJRTSFL@aol.com.

Dr. John and Susan Vawter met while on staff of Campus Crusade for Christ, where they served for 10 years. Susan is a trained Stephen Minister and enjoys one-on-one ministry as well as serving as a docent at the Phoenix Art Museum. John has pastored churches in Minneapolis and Tempe, Arizona, as well as serving as President of Western Seminary and Phoenix Seminary. John is also author of *Uncommon Graces*, published by Navpress and nominated for The Gold Medallion Award. In 1999, the Vawters started the ministry *"You're Not Alone."* They can be reached at: 10105 East Via Linda, Suite 103, Scottsdale, AZ 85258. Telephone: 480-752-8994. Email: info@notalone.org or through the website www.Notalone.org.

Stephanie Vawter is finishing her Bachelor's Degree at the University of Phoenix and plans to get a Master's Degree in Psychology. She works as a shift manager for Starbucks. She recently celebrated five years of sobriety. She has served on the board of her Alcoholics Anonymous club. She can be reached through email at: info@notalone.org .

Zach Whaley, MA has been involved in alcohol and drug abuse prevention and treatment for 30 years. He was president of the Alcoholism Council of Colorado, served on the Colorado Governor's Advisory Committee on Drug Abuse Prevention, chaired the Colorado Summer School on Alcohol And Drug Abuse Studies, and was a trainer of drug and alcohol counselors for the Colorado Department of Health for over 10 years. He became a professional counselor in 1976 and has led church counseling ministries for 25 years. Zach currently resides in Tempe, Arizona, with his wife and two kids, and he continues to work a personal 12-step program he began in 1969. Zach is currently in private practice in Chandler, Arizona, specializing in addictions of all kinds, marriage counseling, parent coaching, ADHD, and divorce recovery. He provides intensive counseling for missionaries on leave, and is available for coaching on pastoral counseling issues and for presenting workshops on various subjects. Zach is also a family mediator and life coach. Visit his web site at www.zachwhaley.com or email him at zach@zachwhaley.com.

Dr. Terry Zuehlke is a clinical psychologist in private practice. He has a doctoral degree from the University of South Dakota and a Master of Education degree from The American University in Washington, D.C. He is the founder and director of Pathways Psychological Services, P. A. in Minneapolis, Minnesota. Dr. Neil Anderson, Terry and his wife, Julie, have co-authored the book, *Christ-Centered Therapy: The Integration of Theology and Psychology*. His practice deals primarily with spiritual conflicts using Theophostic Ministry and the Seven Steps of Freedom from Freedom in Christ Ministries. For further information contact:Terry E. Zuehlke, PhD, LP Pathways Psychological Services, P.A. 7575 Golden Valley Road, Suite 119 Golden Valley, MN 55427, 763-525-8590 Fax: 763-525-8592

Any of these contributors may also be contacted through You're Not Alone at info@notalone.org.

DATE DUE

616.863   #5934

HIT
Hit by a ton of bricks: 19
stories of hope, love and
healing.

DATE DUE	BORROWER'S NAME
FEB 2 6 '06	*Laurel van Houte*

616.863   #5934
HIT

Hit by a ton of bricks: 19 stories
of hope, love and healing.